The Psychological Dynamics
of Religious Experience

The Psychological Dynamics of Religious Experience

(It Doesn't Fall Down from Heaven)

ANDRÉ GODIN

Religious Education Press
Birmingham, Alabama

Translated from the French by Mary Turton.

Originally published as *Psychologie des expériences religieuses: La désir et la réalité* (Paris: Le Centurion, 1981).

Library of Congress Cataloging in Publication Data

Godin, André.
    The psychological dynamics of religious experience.

    Bibliography: p.
    Includes index.
    1. Experience (Religion)   2. Psychology, Religious.
I. Title.
BL53.G6313 1985   248.2   85-2354
ISBN 0-89135-039-X

Religious Education Press, Inc.
1531 Wellington Road
Birmingham, Alabama 35209
10 9 8 7 6 5 4 3 2

Religious Education Press publishes books exclusively in religious education and in areas closely related to religious education. It is committed to enhancing and professionalizing religious education through the publication of serious, significant, and scholarly works.

PUBLISHER TO THE PROFESSION

To the priest and psychotherapist
MARC ORAISON (1914-1979)
He faced trials with good humor and death with hope.

To the pastor and theologian
GEORGES CRESPY (1920-1976)
His word performed what it proclaimed: It set desire free by delving more deeply into it.

OTHER BOOKS WRITTEN OR EDITED BY ANDRÉ GODIN

Research in Religious Psychology
Child and Adult before God
From Religious Experience to Religious Attitude
From Cry to Word
Death and Presence
The Pastor as Counselor
The Psychology of Religious Vocations
Le Dieu des parents et le Dieu des enfants
Guide psychologique et pastoral pour discerner les
   troubles mentaux
La vie des groupes dans l'Église

André GODIN is a Fellow of the American Psychological Association. As a member of Division 36 (psychologists interested in religious issues) he was chosen recipient of the 1979 William James Memorial Award.

Contents

There is no more dangerous word than the word God. It covers a great many things, but not that Person who has spoken in the Bible.

M. ORAISON

The good thing about the Gospel is that it never leaves us in peace and also that it always keeps its promise: a love so strong that nothing can prevail against it. It is in no way dependent on circumstances even if it is actualized in circumstances and if that actualization subsequently varies with the movements of history.

G. CRESPY

Foreword

There has perhaps been too much mistrust of religious experience these last thirty years. In our increasingly secularized society this has probably been the case for much longer—but what about in the churches?

The tendency seems to be reversed at present. The word *experience* has regained prestige, along with its synonyms in everyday language: living intensely moments of vivid consciousness, the testimony of the *witness* of this experience in all its subjectivity. The category *God* is becoming, if not convincing, at least respectable again, especially in relation to experience, still more to experience in a group or community. In its economic, cultural, and spiritual crisis, our society is facing a resurgence of religious experiences, of interest in them and of fraudulent imitations of them. There are those who would simplify matters and even maintain that the crisis itself is sufficient cause and explanation of the religious revival. But this book does not adopt such a simplistic attitude. Let us briefly say why.

Concepts that are theologically and philosophically coherent on a speculative level are not always in touch with concrete experience.[1] They do not enable us to discern things clearly at the moment when we move from phenomena affecting the consciousness of the lived experience to a critical awareness of those phenomena. Yet such discernment is essential if a free and adult choice is to be made. A philosophical treatise on love offers no direct enlightenment to victims of "love at first sight," still less to those at the mercy of the discordant impulses of a deviant sexual-

1

ity. Observations and reflections inspired by genetic psychology that take into account social conditioning would perhaps be of more value.[2] Some operative concepts would also be necessary, concepts that are sufficiently close to the lived experiences to illuminate them in spite of the inevitable distance imposed by any kind of reflection.[3]

Far from being a hindrance to the reflections aroused by the religious experience, particularly one that claims to be experience of God, a contribution from the human sciences might be useful or even necessary in order to account for the social and psychological components, both conscious and unconscious, which make up man's longing (for the experience of God) as he moves toward a mysterious transcendence. Is that movement in the last analysis entirely subjective, even when it is collective? Or is it initiated by a Referent recognized in faith? It is *between* these two types of interpretation that most of the considerations in this book have their place. Even if it is God who supports and constitutes the experience of the absolute and of love which is peculiar to the human spirit, it is man who reflects that connection and expresses it so that it bears fruit in various forms, projects, and values. In short, neither religious experience nor experience of God fall on man from the sky.

The observations and reflections in this volume will respect the religious language used to express the "lived" quality of certain experiences which, as such, are incontestable. Then we shall embark with some rigor on an analysis of the more or less latent psychological elements which lead to the designation of these experiences as religious. Experiences of the *ego*? Of the *group*? Experiences of *God*? Of *which* God? We cannot dodge these questions. They will be raised in connection with religious situations or revivals that are fairly controversial in the Christian world today: the awakening of the religious sense in an institutional religion, sudden conversion, intense experiences of fusional joy (charismatic groups) or incitement to conflict (basic socio-political groups). It would be naive to suppose that a psy-

chologist, whether or not he is a Christian, can throw light on
certain psychological aspects of those experiences while completely disregarding his personal preferences or inclinations.
One result of his effort is rather to be aware that he is not
neutral when he presents and applies methods of psychological
analysis aimed at refining subsequent personal perceptions, starting with his own. A debatable use of these psychological approaches would not invalidate the undertaking itself.

The chapters of this book will deal with seven quite distinct
areas. For convenience and clarity they will be arranged in three
parts: functional religious experiences, affective experiences "of
God," and transforming experiences in the faith (Christian). This
methodical presentation of observations, some personal, some
supplied by other psychologists, will no doubt be helpful to all
readers but particularly to teachers and students of courses in
the psychology of religion which are appearing in the programs
of more and more institutions.

Finally a thematic glossary will redefine the strictly psychological aspect of certain concepts which have become particularly
blurred by widespread use. At the same time it will reveal the
structure of the work in broad outline. It can be referred to
during the reading.

THE PLAN OF THE WORK

1. *The experience of God is never a first experience.* It has a prehistory in human experience and, at times, in religious or atheist
education. Long before it can be said to be an experience of
God, the story of a man or woman is that of their experiences,
lived in a culture and a social environment, determined by a
family, a school, youth groups in which a first religious awakening took place. Socially and psychologically this awakening occurs first as a phenomenon of functional religion: an institutional
religion may meet psychological needs or come to the rescue in
the case of social pressures. It corresponds to functions spontane-

ously attributed to it by a certain religiosity or else gradually ceases to do so. The same is true of antireligion when it becomes organized or institutionalized.

2. *The experience of God is never immediate.* And yet immediacy is a conscious wish, both in love and in religion. Certain experiences have a particular intensity as a result of their *suddenness.* Stories of conversion will receive attention here.

3. *The intensity* of an experience, too, tends to be felt as an immediate presence. We need to reflect on moments of fulfillment, and this is even more important when dealing with certain drug-induced, group experiences.

4. *Fusional joy,* typical of experiencing God's Spirit in charismatic groups, will be considered in its psychological dynamics and in the structure of the group organizations in which it is lived.

5. *Excitement in conflict,* typical of socio-political assemblies that pray and are inspired by the Gospel, is presented as experience of a future-building God. Its importance in base communities invites us to try to discover what dynamics produce it.

6. Prepared in this way by an examination of contemporary experiences, often presented in our culture as experiences of God, *the critique of illusions* will be formulated on a different basis: we ask what experience can still be claimed as a sign and bearer of a reality beyond the ego alone, or immersed in the group?

7. *In the Christian faith,* how does spiritual experience open the door to the longing for that very special God who expresses himself in Jesus Christ? No doubt at the end of this journey some psychological components of a Christian understanding will stand out in a clearer light: vivid consciousness, an awareness and the expression of this consciousness will combine more effectively to discover, accept, and proclaim the Other and to ensure his coming such as he reveals himself in harsh reality.

Concerning religious experience, whether individual or in groups, experience of God, Christian experience, the first six chapters include no direct evaluation on the basis of Christian theology (apart from a few provisional remarks in certain conclusions). Only the seventh, analyzing as it does some cognitive elements structuring a living faith, is the work of a Christian, who for all that, still thinks as a psychologist.

If the Other, written with a capital letter, can occasionally be found in the text (see thematic glossary, part B), Love will not be found there. That capital L is used too often in a religious context to mask the *interval* in which a loving union builds its consistency and across which distinct wishes harmonize while acknowledging their differences.

Notes

1. Jean Mouroux's work, *The Christian Experience* (London and New York: Sheed and Ward, 1955), is indispensable from the speculative point of view and a classic in the field. In the same period, Henry Duméry's *Critique et religion* (Paris: Sedes, 1957), continued in his *Philosophie de la religion: essai sur la signification du christianisme* (Paris: Presses Universitaires de France, 1957), offered a criticism more concerned with fundamental categories of language (subject, grace, faith).

2. The various connections that the language of faith can maintain with speculative and scientific language have been discussed by Jean Ladrière in *L'articulation du sens* (Paris: Aubier-Cerf-Delachaux et Desclée De Brouwer, 1970). English readers with an interest in this linguistic problem are referred to the three most important works ever published on religious language vis à vis logical empiricism: R. B. Braithwaite, *An Empiricist's View of the Nature of Religious Belief* (Cambridge University Press, 1955); R. M. Hare, "Religion and Morals" in *Faith and Logic*, ed. B. Mitchell (London: Allen & Unwin, 1957), pp. 176-193; I. T. Ramsey, *Christian Discourse: Some Logical Explorations* (London: Oxford University Press, 1965). These great works have been made available to French readers by Pierre Lucier in *Empirisme logique et langage religieux* (Tournai-Paris: Desclée et Cie; Montreal: Bellarmin, 1976). Second thoughts on the matter can be found in J. L. Evans, *The Future of Philosophical Theology* (Philadelphia: Westminster Press, 1971). The sociological and psychological factors unconsciously affecting individual and group languages are completely outside the scope of logical empiricism.

3. The enrichment of certain categories of Christian thought (sin, conversion, liberation, the unity of mankind) by economic, sociological, and political analyses which make them "operative concepts for the

analysis and transformation of the world" has recently been brilliantly illustrated by Vincent Cosmao in *Changer le monde: une tâche pour l'église* (Paris: Cerf, 1979). In the same way, the Christian psychologist would hope that his analyses help Christian thought, notably in the theological and pastoral fields.

Part I

Functional Religious Experiences

"God is not known.
He is not understood.
He is used."
JAMES H. LEUBA

From Institutional to Functional Religion

The experience of God is never a first experience. It always has a long prehistory and, in most cases, a religious prehistory. Chronologically, psychologically, each boy, each girl comes to speak of God as the result of the human relationships through which he or she grows up and through what is said of God around him or her: in the family, the school, the environments of work and leisure. What is said about God and what is read about God play a part, but also religion itself has an influence on the individual.

Ever present religion

In the air the child breathes and which vibrates as he hears God discussed by people in houses or at church doors, in the streets, or in drug stores, religion or antireligion are present. They are also silent yet evident on the ground he treads: cathedrals with luminous windows or the dark ruins of burned temples, destroyed by hatred or wars of religion. They are present under the ground where not only the dead are buried in their cemeteries and necropolises but also where the traces of vanished rites are found: dolmens, caves, and rock paintings. Religion is even present in countless secular institutions, such as those that harmonize official public holidays with the calendar of religious festivals.

So religion or antireligion are present in a concrete form almost everywhere. As soon as we can walk or talk, they make their mark on human experience. Moreover, the vast majority of men are born Muslims, Buddhists, or Christians, just as they are born Arab, Thai, or Irish. This amazing submission to societies that transmit religion or antireligion is an experience in itself and is described by historians and sociologists as the experience of institutional religions. Their acceptance as well as their rejection give rise to countless struggles, disputes, persecutions, and wars of religion. The wars have frequently very little to do with the God (or gods) who were their cause or pretext. Religious experiences, perhaps, but ones in which the experience of God is often lost.

In archaeological excavations stratified layers of several temples are often found one on top of the other, as at St. Clement of Rome, where we can cross twenty centuries by going down four stories to a temple of Mithras. Similarly, according to the sociologist Henri Desroche, variations in religious beliefs and practices, which can be detected during investigations, are the result of events dating sometimes from several centuries back. Thus: "How is the religious geography of the Vendée region and its correlation with the electoral geography to be understood without reference to the traumas and excitements of the Chouan rising several centuries ago? . . . The anatomy of the land reveals the physiology of its history."[1]

Certain historians of religion, influenced perhaps by the psychology of Jung as Mircea Eliade[2] was, put forward the idea of a persistent religion corresponding to primeval mechanisms or deep psychological patternings. This would be the foundation, as it were, on which various historical religions were able to raise their temples and which survived the abandonment of such beliefs or such rites. Others claim to find in it the disguised imprint of a social order that sets its mark on savage or civilized rituals. This structure of the interhuman link is thought to remain active in the secularized counterpart of rites with no explicitly religious significance.[3]

These first remarks, taken from sciences akin to psychology, introduce the idea of strata of the religious phenomenon currently evident in their more or less rigid ancient layers and components. Scientifically, the sociologist knows nothing of the subjects as such; he simply takes them from the angle of social dynamics. As for the historian, he has only writings and monuments at his disposal; he can only make them speak by interpreting them. At first sight the psychologist seems privileged: He can listen to his subjects speaking.

But what is true of the religious field seen objectively is also true of the mental dispositions and activities of all those who speak in a religious way or about religion. As children who have grown up they have assimilated in the first place a culture provided by their family and then by their school which gave a pattern to their diffuse aspirations, their needs, and their primary wishes. One or several institutional religions formed part of that cultural heritage. Thus religious discourse, whether elementary or academic, and religious practices, whether naive or sophisticated, are always dependent on archaeology. When writing about an "archaeology of theology," Antoine Vergote accurately depicts psychology, more particularly psychoanalysis, by defining its double role: "If psychoanalysis destroys the illusion of the dominance of the imaginary and demystifies errant meanings in any religious or merely human discourses, it also lays bare the genealogical formations and profound connections which make a meaningful discourse *possible* and remain the tissue inherent in the religious relationship."[4]

Genetic psychology of religion

If religious facts and psychological conditionings are already there and are inescapable, whereas God (the gods) is not, there is room for misunderstanding or denial of God, for a search for God, but also for the mediation of human sciences. In the interval between religion and the rejection *or* experience of God (the gods) the scientific workshop of history, sociology, and psychology finds its field.

Genetic psychology of religion studies the constants and variables of religious or areligious attitudes resulting from collusions between certain formalizations of religious or areligious education and the fundamental psychic mechanisms. Thus a strong appeal is made to animism and magic, to name but two spontaneous elements in the young child, by the stories in the form of myths which normally support the transmission of religions. It will become clear in the next chapter how this kind of interference gives rise to an awakening of elementary religiosity, which has no firm future but which, as a fixation or when reinforced, is frequently detrimental to experiences of God. Psychologically, it is difficult for a functional religion to become a personal religion in which God can make himself heard. By listening as the child, and also the adult, speaks, the psychologist cannot avoid discerning the more or less primitive stratifications which give rise to their religious discourse and against which it reverberates, making it impossible for God to be heard.

A belief system or ideological atheism are late developments, adult and well-informed, which appear to be far removed from infantile religious manifestations. And yet they rest on elementary needs and psychological impulses based on trust and doubt which are, as it were, their ancient yet ever-present foundations. Research into religious psychology has established, for example, to what extent certain religious expectations are influenced by the maternal or the paternal sides when men or women give free rein to their feelings, their imaginings, and their verbal associations with the name of God.[5] In a ceaseless movement between these archaic connections and various meanings of religious symbols and discourses, religious experiences are formed whose relationships with the founder of this or that religion, be he divine or not, have become very tenuous. In bringing to light certain ambiguities of this unspoken element that is latent in the religious discourse of believers or nonbelievers, psychology can help to send them back to the very sources of the religion they accept or contest, back beyond psychically conditioned states.[6]

Without these psychological drives we have just mentioned rapidly, an institutional religion (dogmatic or theological discourse, more or less formalized liturgies) would soon be a dead letter, or rather would become the prop of a sealed letter: What would life be like in a religion that was not constantly seeking the God it proclaims? And yet history, like psychology, reveals that a religion does not necessarily die as a result; it can simply satisfy important needs of man: the security of group discipline, consolation for present miseries by incantation of an imagined afterlife, reinforcement of socialization in the crises or difficult confrontations of a secular society. For example, a social psychologist has recently measured functional aspects of a religious orthodoxy experimentally.[7] The orthodoxy of a religious language may serve quite other ends, psychologically, than those of keeping the mind open to the word of God. By thus revealing functional aspects of an institutional religion, the psychologist gives a *different* image of that religion from the one it would itself sometimes like to give. The religious discourse he receives or provokes is repeated *differently* by the psychologist. He thinks he is thus serving the cause of man's freedom, not only from possible oppression by societies or churches, but because his work constantly brings man back to the interval created all the time between religious experiences and experiences of God.

The Interval

There are people who think of God as the one who can set men free; or they think that the very idea of God is enough to create a psychological space between societies and men: a space of freedom, of hope, of love, call it what you will. In spite of the hold of the religions themselves, the experience of God in invocation or contemplation maintains that space of freedom and even deepens that undeniable psychological interval, which is often not appreciated by the nonbeliever, between religious institutions (discourse, rites, moral imperatives, traditions) and the central referent of it all: God or the gods, forms or forces, persons or powers.

It is sometimes said that religion gives life, and the role of the churches is obviously essential in transmitting religion. But, like a mother who brings into the world babies who cannot yet talk, a church can count among its members many who, in religion, have not gotten beyond cries and passive submission. Concerning God they remain mute, incapable of speech or of initiative. Without experience based on the words initiated by God through his prophets, they can neither enter into a dialogue with God nor become actively engaged in construction of a future for the world with God. From a Christian angle, the role of Mother Church might well be to lead to God the Father; in the words of St. Augustine: "We believe in the Father through the mediation of the mother's authority" (*De utilitate credendi,* XII, 26). If she fails in this role, she becomes "a stepmother rather than a mother" (Luther) since the Father, as in natural generation, can never be the object of proof.

It happens too that the religious man, particularly in the domain of mysticism, aspires to fill the interval between institutional religion and the intensity of his wish for a direct experience of God. It is not enough to assert philosophically or theologically that such an aspiration is in a way contradictory, except in a kind of pantheistic thought in which the difference and distance between man and God are abolished. It is advisable, too, to examine in detail how and when this wish for immediacy reappears today with its usual train of unadmitted illusions. This is one of the topics of this book: to emphasize that interval without which the mystical element and perhaps even the freedom of the religious man would disappear from religions.

This view is not based on an antithesis, which is probably impractical, although it has enjoyed quite a vogue: that between faith and religion. Psychologically there is always faith somewhere. Rather we would be inclined to analyze (which is not the same as to destroy) psychological aspects of religious faith, which might bring out in sharper relief certain psychological aspects of faith in God.

That a religious faith is not identical with a faith in God (whatever that god may be) is the conviction that this introduction has sought to present to the reader before we tackle in a more concrete way some of the "errant meanings" of religious discourse.

Notes

1. Henri Desroche, *L'homme et ses religions* (Paris: Cerf, 1972), pp. 90-91.

2. Mircea Eliade, "The sacred is an element in the structure of consciousness, and not a stage in the history of that consciousness," *Histoire des croyances et des idées religieuses,* vol. 1, (Paris: Payot, 1976), p. 7.

3. Ritualism as a constant game of marking and unmarking, underlining and constantly shifting the cut-off which deprives the individual and society of their origin, is the conceptual key to the gigantic effort of description and synthesis presented by Thierry Maertens in his *Ritologiques* (Paris: Aubier, five volumes so far, 1978, 1979). The functional survival and camouflage of secularized myths have been analyzed from a different angle by Mircea Eliade, notably in *Aspects du mythe* (Paris: Gallimard, 1963).

4. Antoine Vergote, *Interprétation du langage religieux* (Paris: Seuil, 1974), p. 18.

5. Some research has dealt with feelings about real parents which were effectively reflected in the evocation of God. Thus M. Hallez and A. Godin, "Parental Images and Divine Paternity" in *From Religious Experience to a Religious Attitude* (Brussels: ed. Lumen Vitae, 1964), pp. 81-114. A study of these memory-images reveals a predominance of the *maternal* in religious evocations of *men* and vice versa. Other works in varied cultural and social backgrounds have studied the components of the maternal and paternal symbols which are part of the semantic composition in the evocation of God. See also A. Vergote and collaborators "Parental images and representation of God" in *Social Compass* 19 (1972), pp. 431-444. See also *J. for the Sc. St. of Religion* 8 (1969), pp. 79-87 and A. Vergote and A. Tamayo, *The Parental Figures and the Representation of God (a Cross-Cultural Study)* (The Hague-New York-Paris: Mouton, 1981). This semantic examination of culturally conditioned paternal and maternal symbols isolates the specifically paternal components against an archaic maternal background, with no difference for the sex of the respondents but with an uneven distribution among the cultural milieus studied. In fact the memory-images and symbols, structurally reflected in the socially predominant language, complement each other and are necessary to understand the affective and religious history of

many men and women: a constant tug-of-war between the historic conditionings of their childhood and the great symbols repeated semantically in the religious discourses of the churches (Christian, as it happens). A too-perfect interlocking of these two series of conditioned religious states would abolish the interplay, indispensable to personal or collective research into the God beyond these states. Indeed it is *in* the psychological interval *between* these paternal and maternal images (historically conditioned and then symbolically coupled with a religious discourse) that the *possibility* of a specific designation of God, which escapes the structuring Oedipus law, can be inserted. This position, which has only been introduced here, will be looked at more fully in the last part of this book (Chapter 6).

6. Among the believers whom psychology and, more particularly, psychoanalysis, have led to recognize "man and his breach," to accept it as an ultimate mark of his finite nature and then to reread the Gospel with a new openness to meanings hitherto obscured, we would mention Jean-Claude and Thérèse Depreux, *Ici il n'y a point de chemin* (Paris: Privat, 1977). Among the non-Christians who, in psychoanalysis, have regained the freedom to exist emotionally only by freeing themselves from "the poisoning effect of God . . . that vindictive stopgap for social impotence and ignorance," we would mention, for its virulence, *Gottesvergiftung* and for its loving odyssey toward lost parents *Grammatik der Gefühle*, by Tilmann Moser (Frankfurt: Suhrkamp, 1978 and 1979). These two more recent works are more worthy of translation than *Lehrjahre auf der Couch* (Frankfurt: Suhrkamp, 1976).

7. Jean-Pierre Deconchy, *L'Orthodoxie religieuse: essai de logique psychosociale* (Paris: Ed. Ouvrières, 1971), supplemented by *Orthodoxie religieuse et Sciences Humaines* (Paris-The Hague-New York: Mouton, 1980; English transl., Mouton, 1985).

Religious Experiences

FUNCTIONAL BELIEFS

Let us look at some psychologically discernable effects of religious discourse.

Can God see everything?

A German psychologist, Karl Röttger,[1] reports a conversation between Gretchen, aged four, and her brother Hans, aged five and a half. The two children are playing in the living room. The little girl seems preoccupied. Suddenly she asks her brother:

GRETCHEN: Can God really see everything?

HANS: Yes, he can.

G: Can he see through the bedroom door in our house?

H: Yes of course.

G: Can he look through the outside wall and the stones?

H: Yes, he can see everywhere.

G: Can he see through the door of my dolls' closet and see the dresses there?

H: Yes, yes, yes, he can. A long silence. . . . Then Gretchen's voice firmly:

G: You know what, Hans? I think God can see best through glass, even so.

What is happening between these two children?

It is quite clear that Gretchen has heard the familiar statement: God can see everything. She has taken it literally, and that is what makes it disturbing; if God can see everything, nowhere is private. She reacts somewhat anxiously and seeks reassurance from her elder brother. Does he know that, too? And if so, what then?

But Hans is playing the adults' game. Of course he knows. He repeats the orthodox formula he has heard from the grown-ups with no explanation; God can see everything. Since it is not his problem verbal orthodoxy suffices. Gretchen must just accept it. Yes, but there is something it would be better for God not to see—over in the bedroom, the dolls' closet, especially the dresses. Are they untidy, dirty, stolen? Who will know?

So Gretchen wants to preserve a little privacy. As she is a remarkably well-balanced little girl, she finds a compromise right away and a very good compromise. She doesn't entirely reject the statement about God: He'll still be able to "see." All the same, she can't resign herself to the idea of not being able to hide certain objects in her closet or have little personal secrets. She doesn't reject the God all-seeing but she doesn't give up either. In her childish language she makes a compromise: God won't see so well when the walls are not made of glass. For the time being she can now play in peace.

Gretchen has just reinvented in her personal language what religions have always done, that is to draw a vague line, a provisional frontier between something "sacred," which is far too intrusive and something "profane."[2]

Psychological interpretations

God sees everything. God knows everything. Why are these fragments of religious discourse so embarrassing as to give rise to a certain anxiety?

To answer this question we must bear in mind a well-attested psychological mechanism: primary animism conjuring up an imaginary production of possible, indeed constant, interventionism which modifies the natural course of things. This mechanism can be infiltrated to varying degrees by guilt. We shall describe and define it.

Animism

As early as 1927 Jean Piaget tackled this disposition as a reaction assuming "immanent justice," and many researchers found it in children of different cultures and religions. It was studied by Monique Laurendeau and Adrien Pinard (1962) in the broader framework of progressive access in children to causal thought.[3] Psychologically, this is a disposition to interpret events in the world, especially unexpected or fortuitous ones, as the outcome of personalized, psycho-moral intentions. By means of this "intentionalist" reaction, a system of interpretations often systematized in the culture (lots cast, mysterious interventions from ancestors or divinities, intentions of providence) can integrate a host of strange, usually tiresome or catastrophic incidents into human thought or even control. These intentions are often directed toward the maintenance or restoration of a moral order by punishing the guilty.

On the basis of observations in very diverse cultural environments it must be stressed that guilt, real or supposed, introduces into the animistic reaction a depressive type of anxiety which emphasizes punitive interpretations.[4] In spite of certain religious statements to the contrary—for example the Christian ones, "God is love," "God protects," "God forgives"—the fundamental psychism always reacts more strongly in terms of a God who sees evil rather than good. Whatever the age of the man who feels guilty, the unease he feels is accompanied by an uncontrollable tendency in the unconscious (although each may hide it even from himself by conscious efforts) to *feel* that his fault is known (aspect attributable to guilt) and to *interpret* unfortunate events as provoked by supposed punitive intentions (aspect attributable to primordial animism), henceforth assumed to be punitive.

Interventionist imaginings

The anxiety aroused in Gretchen by the phrase "God can see everything," based on a more or less guilt-ridden animism, includes an imaginary proliferation of possible divine interventions. We can sense it in the drift of her conversation with brother Hans: "the dolls' closet" . . . "the dresses there." No problem if God just knew, "saw," but remained passive, without hands, or "with his arms bound" (as Peguy wrote with such insight about the heavenly Father at the death of the Son), in short, if God did not *intervene.* This conception of God which many religions do not adopt (and what about certain aspects of the Judeo-Christian teaching?) could not possibly come spontaneously to the child. At her age Gretchen can only *imagine* God in line with the images of her father and mother. Now, what does any father (according to the flesh) worthy of the name do? He intervenes to restore order, to force the negligent or disobedient child to do what it does not want to, perhaps not to do what it wants to, and finally to want to do what its parents say is good. As for the mother, she intervenes in countless ways, even in cultures where the punishing authority rests rather with the father. Noninterventionist parents would be weak and, moreover, incapable of fulfilling their role as educators of their young children.

In short, if God can see everything and, in addition, is said to be all-powerful, how could he not intervene? Wouldn't it be scandalous of him not to intervene if his all-powerfulness is imagined on the level of interventions aimed at modifying or restoring order?

Anthropomorphism you will say: The child can only make a representation of God using characteristics from human beings, notably its parents. So be it, as long as we bear in mind the underlying intentionalist-animistic mechanism which is still active and probably essential if the symbolic functions of the helpful God, the punitive God are still to mean something affectively in religious life. As for its share of intentionist imaginings, anthropomorphism does not consist in representing God (or the gods) as being a man, but in representing him on the basis of the *wish that God be thus,* in this instance still capable of intervening, possibly to punish. Now, who could have the wish or the need for an interventionist God, when all the current evidence indicates the nonintervention of God in the world, even when things are going badly?

So who has an interest in an all-seeing, all-knowing God? For

Gretchen's anxiety justifies this last reflection: *who* calls upon a God-who-sees, possibly a God-who-intervenes? Not Gretchen, apparently, since we found her very much of two minds on this point.

Without much fear of mistake, we can suggest that it is the parents, the authorities who need one and who have probably talked like that. Such a God, protected by his invisibility, is a useful reinforcement of their authority when it falters. In spite of the efforts of an updated catechesis (not so very different, and certainly not everywhere),[5] the great mass of parents, Christians though they may be, continue to use God in this way. Half bogeyman and half Santa Claus; these roles, which are hardly appropriate to the God of the Gospels, along with the tribe of devils and guardian angels, help to transmit elements of what we must call a folklore Christianity, considered as marginal by the official and academic catechesis but rarely denounced, so closely is it linked to the most elementary religious faith.

In many ancient societies religious myths fulfilled this function of supporting the existing social power. On this point the resistance to a specific character for the Christian God (which we shall save for the last chapter of this book) is and will continue to be very strong. From a psychological point of view, man thus appears to be spontaneously religious but is far from being spontaneously Christian. No catechesis will be able to change this initial condition in religious education.

God knows the pure in heart

It is not only parents or the authorities who make use of religious teaching, a fragment of which we have just been examining for its functional force. As he grows, the child too can find succor in it and security during the awakening of his personal moral conscience.

At the family table, Peter, aged eight, is angry: his father has treated and punished him unjustly. He didn't do what he is accused of, or at least not on purpose. So he behaves intolerably, protesting by kicking the table. In the end he is sent up to his room and shut in. He stamps and shouts. Suddenly he stops. After a heavy silence he proclaims loudly: "I am telling you: God, yes God, *knows* I didn't do it (or didn't do it on purpose)!"

So what they teach at school is useful after all. But for what?

Religious experience?

Has Peter just had an experience of God? No. Was that perhaps his first religious experience? Psychologically, we can say that is so and, to be more precise, in the following sense: In the injustice done to him, Peter has just experienced a need, even a wish, for someone who knows everything and can be a witness for his defense. He calls the witness against his father. His imagination leads him quite naturally to make use of this God that he hears spoken of, often in incomprehensible and academic terms. The omniscience of God has just acquired a new sense for him. What was hollow and academic begins to have meaning thanks to his affective state with regard to his father.

If Peter is consoled, calms down, returns to the family circle more serene, his God will have "functioned" well. Perhaps he will still be available to fulfill the same function when the boy grows up, at least for a time.

This utilitarian dimension of the religious discourse, centered on animism, forms a religious point of departure, at least for Peter in the situation described. But how many adults find it difficult to go beyond this functional point of departure and continue to experience God affectively or sentimentally in this way? How many decide one day to reject him, either because they have less and less need of him or because they are disappointed with a witness elsewhere who knows everything but is always passive and apparently absent? It is sometimes said that the silence of God is a scandal. It is true that people are not often listening when he speaks. In all this, they want to find him where their wish expects him, not elsewhere. Moreover, for many adults the notion of divine Providence comes along conveniently to fill the void opened by the animist reaction: Does God intervene here and there, punctually? Or always? Or never?

Animism, chance, and Providence

The incredible success of the religious theme of divine Providence certainly raises a psychological question. First, because this notion is a late philosophical elaboration of ill-assorted scriptural writings.[6] Then because, on the devotional level, it is often used as a belief which facilitates resignation to situations that cannot be avoided. This has often made atheists laugh: Has not divine Providence made rivers flow through the center of towns (Voltaire)? But Paul Claudel did not want to laugh when he wrote: "Who is better able than the priest to interest the classes of society in each other? Classes which Providence made different only so that they should be necessary. (*Figaro litteraire,* 4 April and *La Quinzaine,* 15 April 1954). Moreover, divine Providence has had to be harmonized, in apologetics, with the presence of evil in all its forms, particularly when man is in no way responsible for it. For people have wanted to "justify God for the scandal of evil," as can be seen in the excellent philosophical and apologetic anthology that Jean-Pierre Jossua published in 1979.[7] This is often a ruinous undertaking and often, by its nature, shifts the scandal toward the images of God on the basis of which such justifications had to be invented.

The psychological success of Providence, a divine attribute usually accompanied by two others, Omniscience and All-Powerfulness, can readily be explained, however. It generalizes the animist reaction attributing intentions (sometimes punitive, sometimes protective or benevolent) to certain inexplicable or fortuitous happenings. The notion of Providence comes along to block the category of *chance;* but this is a category necessary to adult thought, faced with happenings that are the product neither of blind determinisms (data that are known or knowable through science) nor of intentional decisions (free or not). Let us look at an example.

> A family, father, mother, and two children, decides to leave the small town where they have been spending their holidays on a Sunday at 4 P.M. They have decided to return along the left bank of a river. At a spot on the road, overhung by picturesque rocks, a boulder, undermined by recent rains, hurtles down on top of the car. Father and one child are killed, the second child is severely paralyzed. A year later the mother seeks out a priest and tells him of her sufferings but also of her doubts: "I used to have faith. All our family life was so obviously guided by Providence. But not now. If God is good, as people say, how could he allow this to happen?"

To account for the course of events in the world we are obliged to allow for the involvement of both the necessity of determinism (the unnoticed erosion of the rock) and the free decision to follow a chosen route. We also must allow for the possibility of seeing either two series of causalities, or one predetermined series and another freely chosen one *intersect fortuitously.* To generalize the explanation by a system of divine intentions (even if, according to a refinement of the learned discourse, they are permissive) is to suppress psychologically the notion of *chance,* a category necessarily open to anguish or anxiety since it produces effects outside any control. Functioning in this manner, the notion of divine Providence conceals not only inevitable events, by dispensing with the need to look for a meaning other than that of resigned submission, but, by involving God (the gods, ancestors, sorcerers) in situations which have nothing to do with them it reduces the anxiety without thereby stimulating the wish to change the situation by appropriate means: social mediations in the case of Claudel (we have seen that he attributed them primarily to priests), an increased check on dangerous sites in the case of the accident described above.

Whereas human anguish before uncontrollable events and hazards has led, especially in the material order, to an appreciable mastery of the conditions of life (health, production and circula-tion of good, forecasting of natural cataclysms) on the collective scale, recourse to religious language by way of explanation has obvious advantages at the level of individual anxiety: It consoles and makes even the intolerable, like death, bearable. The wish for security and control by thought alone finds satisfaction in it. But functioning in this way religious discourse also prevents the achievement of complete maturity and, by the same token, makes it impossible to discover the word that God might at some stage pronounce to express his wish for the world.

Even though it is open to another theological (or learned elaboration, as are most of the philosophical attributes of God according to L. Malevez (quoted in note 6), most of the time the function of the word *Providence* is only that of replacing the notions of chance (more anxiety producing) or destiny (more fatalistic). So psychological animism sustains a religious system of thought or interpretation which faith undertakes to ontologize as a center of external control parallel to but not superimposable on the notions of chance or fate in profane discourse. And this is how a psychologist has proposed to approach the study of it: "Religious space" he suggests, on the occasion of a catalogue of research already carried out, "is, as it were, torn between two poles. On the one hand the idea of an *external control* . . . exer-cized on the environment (but) also on man by beings or forces, either beneficent or maleficent, which cannot be located empiri-cally . . . allows man to forget functionally that it is he who has manufactured these gods who dominate him. On the other hand, the religious attitude tends to attract the external control element into the sphere of *internal control,* a sphere of mysticism, contemplation, models of action and social rituals with or with-out the possibility of retribution in the afterlife. It could even be said, without exhausting the theoretical problems thus raised, that religious attitudes and behavior take shape in a sort of subtle blend of these two formal types of belief, in a sort of dialectical tension between two focal points which find their reality in just this system of tension."[8]

Sociologically it may be thought that the social groups which are most subject to the vagaries and instabilities of existence will be the ones in which a hidden god or allied notions such as that of providence function most actively: He, at least, controls the world.

At the end of some interesting research into the conditions in which a quality of sacredness appears, this is how two sociologists present the question:

> A social group characterized by insecurity of employment, and so instability of income, would have a tendency to view life as a game of chance, everything in its life being the result not of choice but of factors beyond its control. It would then be likely to hold a hidden God, personal or impersonal powers, responsible for the situation and would attempt to conciliate them through some indirect mastery. . . . Weak or unstable socio-economic conditions tend to construct a sacral view of the world, which can be mastered either by intermediaries capable of bringing immediate help or through dreams. . . . On the other hand, those whose economic security is sufficient tend to develop a view of the world which centers on mastery through action. In that case it is not so much the world as such that is sacralized but rather the order manifest in it and the need to conform to technical and moral rules to obtain mastery of it. However, economic security may equally develop a view of the world essentially as a game. But unlike the previous case there is no confusion between game and reality. Social life and religious life can be lived according to two quite separate codes; they are lived not only in the serious mode but also in the nonserious mode of the gratuitous and useless. . . . In such groups a critical attitude develops in relation to the symbolic, stated explicitly. What then becomes symbolic and legitimately sacred is a "personal" construction of significant relationships, independently of explicit social guarantees (Jean Remy and Emile Servais).[9]

Thus the theme of Providence stands out in striking relief. Elaborated philosophically and subdivided into "ordinary providence" (divine government through the stable laws of the world) and "extraordinary providence" (prompt interventions by the all-powerful divinity to modify situations, occasionally, in favor of the divine plan), it can function affectively either by reducing anxiety in the face of the inevitable occurrences of chance or by stimulating hopes of repeated divine interventions. For on the basis of spontaneous animism it is difficult to be consoled for certain noninterventions by God, when, after all, he has been declared all-powerful. In fact what is the use of believing in him? What is the use of invoking him? We are now faced with functional aspects of the rites and prayers for obtaining favors.

RITUALISM AND FUNCTIONAL PRAYERS

According to the psychoanalyst T. Reik, man's evolution toward his religious maturity presents three mutations of the wish: "a) My will be done; b) My will be done with the help of God; c) Thy will be done."[10] So they are parallel or homologous with mutations in the affective life of the young child in the bosom of his family relationships. The examples and reflections that will be presented are located on the level of the second mutation in which functional religiosity is able to latch on to the actual or expected fulfillment of wishes by modifying interventions originating with the god invoked.

The birth of an idol

Here is a paragraph taken from the memories of childhood in an autobiography published by T. Flournoy under the title *A modern mystic: Mlle Vé*.[11] From a psychological point of view it merits careful reading:

One of my earliest memories relates to my mother. She was very ill and had been in bed for weeks. A nurse had told me that there was no doubt she would die in a few days. I must have been four or five years old. *My most precious possession* was a little brown wooden horse, covered with "real hair," as I used to say, and with a saddle and bridle that I could take off and put on again. The horse had as its stable a little ladder of waxed wood in the corridor. In bed, I refused energetically to say my evening prayer because Mummy was not there to listen. But *I began praying to the horse, kneeling in front of the ladder* and reciting the few phrases of our evening prayer in German very quickly and without understanding them at all. *I was sure* that my mother's recovery depended on my faithfulness in praying thus. As the recovery was delayed, a curious thought grew in my mind: that *I had to give up my horse* so that my mother could recover. It was not accomplished in one go; it cost me agonies! I began by throwing the bridle and saddle on the fire, thinking that "when he is very ugly I shall be able to keep him after all." I don't remember the order of events exactly, but I know that, in great despair, I finally smashed my horse and that, seeing my mother on her feet in a few days later, *I was convinced for a long time* that in some mysterious way my sacrifice had cured her.

A few words, printed above in italics, emphasize the psychological elements that give this episode its amazing richness. Reading or listening to the text, one may well find oneself smiling, but never laughing; it makes plain reactions that each one of us recognizes, confusedly at least, as profoundly human. We will itemize some of them.

Isolated from her mother by an illness said to be mortal, the little girl feels a deep anguish. Between four and five years old, her prayers were just a ritual memorized recitation ("without understanding them at all"), and their value for her came from saying them each evening in the presence of her mother who listened.

If the mother isn't there, what can she do? Invent a presence in an object ("my most precious possession") which is both symbolic through its great value and is also a game as will be seen in the continuation of the story: the child will be able to exercise her mastery of the little horse, first a cult object (idol), then an object to be destroyed (insofar as it resists her wish) as a possession to be sacrificed.

In her mother's absence, the child takes an important step toward her human and perhaps religious maturity. From a ritual formula learned by heart and recited in her mother's presence (but not addressed to her mother) the child moves on to a request (still implicit under the routinely recited text) directed to the idol ("I began to pray to the horse"). Of course she doesn't ask the horse for anything directly and yet she is certain ("I was sure") that if she keeps it up for long enough ("my faithfulness in praying thus") her wish will be fulfilled. On the ancient base of the all-powerfulness of the wish, a decisive test in her maturating will be played out.

For the reality of her mother's illness resists her wish, breaches the affective illusion of all-powerfulness. A dull anger is then turned against this "precious possession," this horse placed in the position of an idol. And so "a curious thought" grows: the destruction of the object, which, after all, is only a "possession" even if it is "the most precious possession." This time the wish involves the child herself; it distances her from a prayer which may be magic, but also from the object as a symbolic prop. It is going to be a question of real sacrifice at the level of play, a sacrifice, however, that the child will connect "mysteriously" with her mother's recovery. For a long time, but not for ever; when she is writing her story, Madame Vé has given up believing in the magical aspect (including a causality) of this granting of what she then wished, one of the most essential wishes of a child: that her mother should live. And, if necessary, that the idol should perish!

Religious experience?

Has the Vé child just had an experience of God? No. In her evening prayer and then in her conduct toward the idol, has she had a religious experience? Psychologically, we can say that is so and, to be more exact, in the following sense: The child has just confronted the all-powerfulness of her wish with the resistance of reality by involving the mediation of prayer. From an initial ritual position, accompanied by the production of an idol-object, she has proceeded to a sacrificial destruction with an interposed symbolic object.

If she was able "for a long time" to interpret her mother's recovery as an effect of her "sacrifice," that would be the result of a magical mode of thought which more often than not is the spontaneous accompaniment of the rites offered by all the religions of the world as components of their cultural heritage (in close connection with beliefs and mythical tales). But this magical aspect is not affirmed in the episode analyzed.[12] By contrast, considerable light is thrown on the functional aspect of her religious conduct: There is a wish, a prayer, then a sacrificial act, which is intended to gratify it, and finally there is a provisionally triumphant interpretation when faced with the result she had hoped for, expected, and demanded. Even if they had not been gratified, these items of religious conduct would still have "functioned" by reducing her initial anxiety.

Functional ritualism

Whereas the Vé child was using her idol-object for private ends in the absence of a sick mother, religions offer so many idol-objects to children and adults alike that they hardly need search, still less invent, in order to find in them something on to which to support their religious needs, answer their cries for help, and sustain their claims to modify reality by symbolic means: amulets, talismans, medals, candles or scapulars; candles and pilgrimages; relics, phials of blood, images mysteriously imprinted on shrouds, sanctuaries with miraculous inscriptions; tatooings, sacred mutilations. All these symbols (objects, rites, painful behavior) could serve as mediations on the road to an encounter with God or the gods: In this sense the whole universe would be a store of sacramentalizable objects and bodily activity would provide an inexhaustible source of appeals to a more or less personalized Other. But these symbols can also serve to promote, soothe, or defer men's needs by maintaining them religiously at the second stage of the mutation of the wish: "My will be done with the help of. . . ." So the object of the wish remains a marvelous operation and not that "elsewhere" whence comes help, just as the child wishes for milk or the magical breast before it can recognize its mother as a person and express its wish in any way other than initially undifferentiated cries.

The magical mentality

The functional aspect of the rites in a religion is the result of a psychological movement that latches on to them to meet individual or social needs. But certain features of the magical mentality may step in and prevent these rites or sacred objects from becoming symbolic props for a possible encounter with God (or the gods).

The magical mentality is seen in both children and adults when a causal relationship is stated or supposed between an object or mode of behavior, looked at from a material point of view, and various results obtained on a higher plane (moral or spiritual) without an adequate effort having been made on that plane. Its influence is seen in many nonreligious sectors of our culture. Take advertising as an example.

When an advertising campaign offers children a doll with the exhortation to "Be Michael Jackson," it might be thought at first sight that it is inviting them to grow up identifying themselves with a famous adult. Nothing of the sort. They remain totally ignorant of the story, the efforts, and the conditions of the famous adult's success. What the advertisement is saying amounts to this: As soon as you have bought this toy, that's it: "You are Michael Jackson." You are Jackson in your play to such an extent that there is no need for you to actually become him. And, in play, this is no disadvantage.

Adults too can be taken in by advertisements offering them "status" if they buy a luxury car, "joy" by buying oranges, "charm" with a soap or "the warm intimacy of the family home" by a coal fire. Advertisers in their training learn this manner (sometimes called "symbolic") of presenting the material object in terms of captivating motivations which stimulate the imagination. Social psychologists have been able to demonstrate that, in our consumer society, things sell better if they are presented in this way.

In religious manifestations, currently known as "popular," this hope of gaining material or spiritual favors through the proper use of some sacred object has been strongly felt. According to H. Aubin, these rites may lead to a summons rather than an invocation."[13]

Even sacramental practice in Christianity can easily be subverted by these features of the magical mentality: 1) *Automatic* causal relationship between the material sign (confession without repentance) and the spiritual effect (psychological well-being to some extent confused with divine forgiveness); 2) Causal relationship between a sacrament received (the eucharist, for example) and a *miraculous* physical result (protection in an accident that was fatal for those who had not taken communion). In more general terms it will be said that this is a confusion between the sign and what is signified. Very careful research has shown on the one hand the difficulty, fairly general in young children (8-12 years), of understanding sacramental action otherwise than on the basis of magical interpretations, and on the other the very slow progression by which boys and girls succeed in understanding symbolic mediation of the sacramental signs.[14] And yet it is often only a question of a more and more general use of the language of Christian catechesis at the age of about 14-16 years. For it seems that the features of the magical mentality are always liable to reappear in force in certain situations, particularly when there is individual or collective anxiety (wars, cosmic catastrophes like floods or earthquakes).

Rites always persist much longer than beliefs. This sociologically well-documented observation results, it seems, from a easy regression from purely functional prayer ("My will be done with the help of God") to a prayer imbued with the magical mentality ("My will be done") every time the request couples the wish with the causality of an object or some form of ritualized behavior.[15]

Functional prayers

Nobody will deny that many prayers, whether private or collective, have a functional aspect as "requests for favors." It is probably essential to any religion that this should be so. The request for any kind of success (in exams, employment, marriage) or protection from harm, illness, premature or even inevitable death, is part of the language of believers who place God (or the gods) in the midst of the vicissitudes of their daily lives or make him their last resort in adversity. These petitions ("with the help of God") allow the too often implicit phrase ("if it be his will") to become blurred or to disappear; so much is certain although not always easy to discern psychologically. It has been proved that belief in the efficacy of these prayers tends to lose ground rapidly in young people educated in a technical and urban culture.[16] On the other hand, it is generally observable in nontechnical rural cultures that nongratification in no way deters people from these "requests for favors" (in the sense of a protection against or in defiance of natural laws). Perseverance in these prayers to obtain "favors," despite even repeated experience of their nongratification (in the long run these prayers are bound to come up against the ineluctable fact of death) probably shows that believers praying in this way are inspired by a functional aim, largely independent of gratification. To give expression to the sum total of one's wishes, the humblest or the most sublime, is it not just that opportunity that is opened up by prayer? Is not any situation, even the most dramatic (the death of a mother for a child, for example, or indeed at any age), already being transformed when we begin to see it through this window opened up by religious supplication? Certainly, this is true so long as the prayer does not divert us from using all possible means of delaying that death (a diversion encouraged by the presence of objects or ritual behavior flattering to the magical mentality) and so long as possible nongratification and confrontation with hard reality do not lead to revolt and radical skepticism about the religious sense of these prayers. Psychologically, nongratification is a test of the attitude normally claimed by the believer: "Thy will be done," an attitude which is obviously not merely a question of words. The ordeal of unchanged reality helps to reveal the underlying attitude.

Any prayer that asks a favor involving a modification of reality would thus have a functional significance: First, it would transform the praying subject, however slightly. He would thus be preparing himself, in the absence of any magical distortion or consequent revolt, to accept the reality, whatever it might be (recovery *or* death, to take the extreme case).

And yet this purely psychological apprenticeship to a perception of the events of nature and history in a religious perspective would often be merely an apprenticeship to resignation. Even if it gives a predisposition to recognize the "divine will" as identified with ineluctable reality, this functional benefit does not lead directly to an experience of God (or the gods). It is not, as such, accompanied by any enlightenment as to the divinity itself or its own plan for a transformation of the world, at least if it has one that differs from our wishes.

Once again, any move toward the discovery and knowledge of our personal limits can be concealed for a long time by this functional aspect of such prayers. Yet this movement is only severely checked if the magical mentality is coupled with functional expectation, as we have seen.

Ritualism and functional prayers, centered on the fulfillment of wishes, can be psychologically transforming, even if that transformation does not proceed from a knowledge of or love for the wishes of a specific god. So Reik's third stage, "Thy will be done," is delayed indefinitely.

VARIOUS FUNCTIONS OF MYTHICAL AND INSTITUTIONAL LANGUAGE

In addition to the functional aspect of beliefs, based on a fundamental animistic reaction, and of certain prayers, especially ritualized ones, the transmission of religions by a mythical language and their institutional organization favor, psychologically, various personal or collective functions. They can come into play even in spite of an official teaching that points in the opposite direction. Psychologists, sociologists, and historians of religion have dealt with these functional aspects, often without sufficient awareness of the sometimes obvious distance which separates them from a consciousness or internalization of God (or the gods) with whom they nevertheless nominally claim kinship. Let us look at some examples.

Imaginary companions

Various imaginary companions have often been presented by psychologists, primarily as a means of reducing the fears and anxieties peculiar to children, but also as a preparation for real encounters expected in the future, particularly in adolescence.[17]

> One day when I was asking a little boy of six whom he had been playing with during his afternoon break, the only answer I got was: "You know, I played with the other one!" I persisted: "But what's he called, this other one?" "He hasn't got a name," the child said. "So it's nobody," I said. "No, it's not nobody." "Well, who is he like, if he's not nobody?" A moment's silence and then this reply which could only come from the mind of a child: "It's someone I make up."[18]

There, if nothing else, is food for thought or for dreams. The child has not made this imaginary companion up out of nothing. To be more precise, the very young child probably plays with another who is like a part of himself and fits in very well functionally with his own needs. But in a few years stories of grownups will come along to enrich or impoverish this make-believe. On the whole it will enrich, because even terribly poor, possibly sadistic and monstrous characters from cartoon strips help the child, and later the adolescent, to progress by showing him "others" who are not at all like himself and do not even reflect his own needs. In any case, he will select from among them.

Any child brought up in a religion hears tales in the form of myths in which prestigious characters act in situations which may correspond to stages in his life or with certain of his moods: Isaac and the danger from his father; Moses and the wandering in the desert; Samuel and the voice heard in his sleep; the adolescent Jesus listened to by older people (and in the Temple, too: wonderful!); the man Jesus, a miraculous healer, in a situation of conflict with the multitudes. From the Virgin, visited by the angel, to Bernadette, visited by the Virgin, or from Judith to Joan of Arc, there are plenty of feminine figures in the Judeo-Christian tradition to accompany girls in their imagination, if perhaps they identify less easily with masculine models! In short, depending on cultural or social climates or periods, all the saints in paradise, of both sexes, are capable of performing this function of the imaginary companions who, starting from models-in-a-situation, play socially successful and religiously structured *roles*. Bringing together complex situations from our own day and these great biblical images may be illuminating and is certainly ennobling; it is an important act of religious devotion. It has not escaped the attention of the psychologists, notably at Stockholm and Uppsala, under the inspiration of the psychologist and historian Hjalmar Sundén.[19]

From the psychological point of view, this matter of imaginary companions immediately raises several questions: Do these stylized characters, illuminating or metamorphosing socially problematic situations, allow the subject entertaining them to get outside himself, if only by an invitation to become other? Are they not the object of imaginary distortions which make each person close up, while appearing to be opening out to another?

When young Jim, age six, attracts the attention of his therapist, Hanna Colm,[20] by lying down in a little tub of sand and saying: "Look Miss, I'm tiny like the baby Jesus when he was born," he is assigning himself a role in which his wish to be all-powerful makes the adult come and bow down before him as he had seen done before the crib one Christmas day. He is quite clearly using his imaginary associate to gain recognition of himself.

When Edmond, aged nine, after hearing the story of Isaac and Abraham, draws a child in the clothes of his brother, age five, on the altar, he is showing that all he has retained of the tale (which is reassuring since it rules out human sacrifice) is the threat of death from the father. The death is neatly avoided, however, since he bestows the role of victim on his little brother.[21] In imagination, he is getting rid of his brother rather than suffering the anguish, born of a misunderstanding, of being Isaac.

When Robert, having entered the seminary at twenty, is writing the story of his vocation, he mentions that at eighteen he read the life of Jean-Marie Vianney and prayed assiduously to the Blessed Curé of Ars. Robert was accepted at the seminary although he had still not passed his high-school exams. After six months, he complained to the superior of the seminary because he had to attend so many "lectures and discussions," as if "all that stuff" was really necessary simply to proclaim the word of God. He decided to leave the seminary at the end of the first year, but he added that the Curé of Ars had been ordained priest without all that studying. His life plan had been blocked as it unfolded by this associate who was more imaginary than real. Robert remained true to himself, but left the seminary.

When the blood of San Gennaro in the cathedral at Naples does not liquefy (3-10 May 1976), Concetta Psicopo declares to a journalist: "St. Gennaro is annoyed. . . . He doesn't like the way things are going. . . . I am telling you, the world is evil. You'll see: the miracle won't happen this year."[22] What she says is identified in her imagination with the intentions of the saint, and it leads her from herself to herself and not from the other (the inertia of the relic which is difficult to interpret) to her. An object, especially one that, against all expectations, is inert, is used to support projective meanings that are indefinitely malleable and often cause conflict.

These few imaginary uses of religious figures have been quoted because in each case the context shows that there was no genuine symbolism of a transition from self to the other or the other to self as will be described in chapter 6. The imaginary companion is respectively an associate instrumental in self-expression, a disturbing hero to identify with who arouses defenses, a fixation preventing the person from evolving in response to the demands of reality, and, lastly, an egocentric assurance against a fact that is difficult to interpret.

Let us add that the function of mythical figures or tales in the imagination is much more varied than the securing or evading of what is real, too often held to be negative functions. The reforming, stimulating, or creative power of myths, especially of a messianic type, has hardly been studied psychologically, even though sociologists (Henri Desroche) or historians of religion have often mentioned it. The amazing epic of people in makeshift craft hopping from island to often very distant island in order to populate the Pacific archipelagoes may be understood in these terms: "Launched on a grandiose nautical adventure, the Polynesians endeavor to deny its novelty, the unprecedented and dangerous nature of the adventure." They live it as "a rerun of the voyage undertaken by some mythical hero in times past in order to show men the way by setting an example. Now, to live a personal adventure as the rerun of a mythical saga amounts to dodging the present" (Mircea Eliade),[23] or, more exactly perhaps, to toning down present distress which might hamper the spirit of adventure. In contrast to this retrospective myth, it is forward-looking myths that underlie politically transforming commitments based on messianic promises or eschatological expectations.[24] In any case, whether they bring security, creativity, or stimulation, these tales are functional insofar as they gratify or reinforce human wishes although revealing nothing which is relative to God (or gods) in the sense of a specific wish. Such a wish, as we shall see further on, necessarily introduces a process of symbolization, based on signs or words, which goes beyond the imaginary because it transforms or deepens human wishes.

Psychological research is too often limited to children and students and hardly gives us a clue as to what becomes of imaginary companions in adults. Statistically, the tendency to attribute to God qualities of friendship, comradeship, and trust reaches its height between the ages of fourteen and sixteen (Deconchy); it then seems to decline, especially in boys, at least in a French student population which still claimed to be Christian (Babin).[25]

Functional eschatology

At the present day, a substantial percentage of believers (up to 30 percent) no longer adhere to a group of beliefs that are part of traditional Christian teaching; this is the group of so-called "last things": paradise, hell, and purgatory (limbo having practically disappeared from the catechesis), elaborate theological designations which a less academic population associates with the more commonplace words: survival, immortality, heaven, the afterlife.

For thirty years now results of sociological surveys have been showing this rupture in the wholeness of the faith. Certain commentators interpreted this situation as reflecting a search for meaning in connection with *each* belief or dogma; this has become a central preoccupation for a number of Christian writers following the so-called "modernist" crisis, but in fact can be seen statistically in the population generally. Catholic commentators stress that the edifice of beliefs is less shaken among Catholics than among Protestants.

Comparative statistics for belief in the afterlife have been provided by Pierre Delooz for more than ten countries over a twenty-year period. He shows a rapid divergence between religious beliefs in general and that group of Christian dogmas under the subhead "last things," which is quickly becoming a matter of opinion. In a period of twenty years (1947-1968), belief in God had dropped slightly (or risen slightly: from 66 percent to 73 percent in France), but belief in life after death had dropped everywhere, and sharply, (from 58 percent to 35 percent for French people). It is perhaps normal that the statement "God exists" should receive more support than the statement "Jesus Christ is God." But it is surprising to discover that the assertion "Jesus Christ has risen" should receive 81 percent positive responses (in 1970, in a sample of the population of Rome that was clearly very believing), whereas the assertion "There is something after death" receives only 60 percent and "Hell exists" only 54 percent. The contrast is greatest in the age group thirty-six to forty: 83 percent believe in the resurrection of Christ; only 52 percent in personal survival.

Some years later in France, a survey showed that 39 percent of *French people* asserted that "Christ is God and is alive today," whereas only 49 percent of *practicing Catholics* (14 percent of the French population) thought that there was "a new life after death" (S.O.F.R.E.S., 1973 and 1975).[26]

So it looks as though, for a third of believers in several countries and for half the practicing Catholics in France the resurrection of Christ has a meaning in present-day life, even when separated from belief in a personal resurrection. This situation has been made clear in two analyses, one linguistic and the other psychological.

a) By hierarchical analysis of statements made about the afterlife (1524 Frenchmen, aged from eighteen to thirty-four, in 1961), A. Martins shows that the most fragile connotations and those most often abandoned are the following: *reunion with those we love* or *influence of the present life on a future life* (and also *preparation for a future life*). They obviously have a strong imaginative and ethical flavor.[27]

b) During a summer training session for catechists and social workers in Paris in July 1969, ten participants, who the previous day had replied in a sociological type of questionnaire that they believed in the resurrection of Jesus Christ and not in their own resurrection, were chosen for private interview. These interviews, some passages of which have been published with commentaries by theologians, show uncertainty in the imaginary dimension ("I can't imagine that we shall be reunited later, my wife and I, for example"), on the possibility of final retribution ("this incentive to make us do good . . . which I think was in the mind of my parents and of many priests"), and on the prospect of an easy death ("or at least one free from danger, so long as one has behaved well or made a last-minute confession"); these matters were much emphasized in former days, especially in sermons.[28] They appear now to be a reason for rejection.

Why do these functional aspects appear to "function" less and less in connection with belief in a personal resurrection? To this question there is no simple answer. Psychologically, we may suspect that these functions no longer correspond to needs or, more precisely, that the needs can be satisfied in other ways. It is well known among historians[29] that death has been recently tamed, even in nonreligious human thinking. The thought of it and its simple acceptance have become relatively more common; people are using secular means to familiarize themselves with this intrinsic limitation of the human condition.[30] The churches' teaching on the mystery of the resurrection, too often linked with ethical connotations, seems to be seeking less functional meanings, in line with a "quite other" presence of the risen Christ (as will be suggested in the last chapter of this book).[31]

As to the idea that religious belief in an afterlife is "consoling" or "soothing," we may even wonder whether psychologically this promise was ever kept. Results of varied and extensive surveys indicate that neither beliefs nor religious practices go hand in hand with a decrease in the fear of death or in anxiety at its mention or, indeed, at the approach of death. Statistically, the distribution is practically the same between anxious or nonanxious believers and anxious or nonanxious nonbelievers; it looks as if an anxious personality found new reasons for anxiety in belief (the theme of judgment, for example) or in nonbelief (sometimes perceived as a lack of or a revolt against faith), whereas a personality with little predisposition to worry finds new reasons for not fearing death in his belief or in his nonbelief.[32]

It has been written that fear created the gods and death created religions. The philosopher sometimes joins hands with the man in the street, affirming that "religion resolves the problem of death. . . . It removes the insignificance of man's finite nature and puts him back in a situation of hope."[33] The psychologist, as we have seen, approaches such general affirmations with great reserve. He sometimes confirms that functional fall-out from forceful sermons catches up with certain believers in their imaginary world, by underlining the continuity of life in an afterlife (and so gratifying their wish to avoid death); but he also establishes the progressive insignificance of orthodox teaching, inspired too much by functional aims which neglect the personal presence of an otherwise absent Christ. The scriptures no longer invite us to seek him by looking heavenward, or by turning in on ourselves, rather we are urged to go out and proclaim him, finding him again in the poor and humble and *so* to transform the world. An acceptable invitation, certainly, but psychologically *dysfunctional*: It does not respond to the wish to avoid death or to the image of the divinity which man spontaneously needs.

Functional orthodoxy

The notion of orthodoxy has not been much studied until recently. The word, although much used, is rarely defined. In casual use we find that for some (40 percent) "orthodox thought" is "accurate or true thought" and for others (46 percent) it is "conformist thought," that is to say, thought that harmonizes with a doctrinal or ideological whole proposed by an institution (church, movement, party, scientific or commercial organization, etc.).[34] As always in such cases some responses are unclassifiable, notably those which combine the two categories being used. In the Petit Larousse dictionary we read: "Orthodox: conforming to the religious opinion held to be true." Theologically, the word does not appear in five of the most frequently consulted, classic dictionaries of theology. In more recent and modest dictionaries we find orthodoxy defined sometimes as:

"straightforward opinion: word applied traditionally in the church to the profession of authentic faith, as taught by the church,"[35] sometimes as "quality of theological thought that conforms to revealed teaching."[36] The first definition suggests a movement of faith that surpasses declared beliefs; the second, more restrained in this respect (mentioning "thought" and "teaching"), is more ecumenically open.

Is the aim of orthodoxy truth by means of social conformity? Or the reverse? And how does this delicate connection between the end and the means function concretely?

In social psychology some experimental work has been carried out in natural environments by ingenious devices based on rigorous axiomatization. The partially published work of J. P. Deconchy[37] draws attention to the functional aspects of orthodoxy (religious, as it happens), looked at from the point of view of how it regulates itself.

We do not intend to describe here the method used or the observations which give these orthodox regulations a more precise psycho-epistemological status;[38] it is enough for the general purpose of this book to mention some psycho-sociological conclusions which theology can no longer overlook.

The vocabulary of an orthodox religious discourse (about God, for example) is poor, using few semantic roots, not because it is almost impossible to speak of God "the ineffable" or as the result of a specific "revealed" teaching, but because the teaching is programed by and, above all, testifies to membership in the group-church. This can be observed when the vocabulary becomes even poorer if some slight anxiety is induced, suggesting that the symbols or social coherence of the group might be threatened from the outside. Even if this is not its only "function," an orthodox vocabulary meets the needs of the group as such, needs for integrity and possibly defensive cohesion, which lead it to shut itself inside a pre-established verbal enclosure. The set of significant words which symbolically would have a much more extensive vocabulary at its disposal when speaking of God or heaven than when speaking of more circumscribed realities such as the father or the house, finds its informative richness or its creative capacity (the mystics give us some idea of this vocabulary) impoverished by its socio-regulatory aim. However, the explosive effects of messianic cries and hopes continue to cause active conflict in live religions. The constraining import of this first lexical observation will be further reinforced when the results of parallel research (currently planned) on the regulation of orthodoxy in nonreligious groups (Marxist, for example) are available.

The plasticity or rigidity of orthodox opinions is modified by the action of various programing centers: the (supposed) intervention of a theologically qualified authority, or, again, the results of a (supposed) survey expressing the consensus of other groups held to be orthodox. This action does not make itself felt consistently. Thus, the intervention of a programing center is much *less* effective if it recommends adopting *more liberal* attitudes than the initial one spontaneously adopted. It will be much *more* effective if it recommends *abandoning* a proposition initially accepted than if it urges the acceptance of a proposition initially rejected. In all this, the content of the information is less important than the psycho-social control and, in more general terms, the tenuousness of the information is compensated by the vigor of the regulation. Regulation, which benefits the cohesion of the group, is more important than the meaning of the words it conveys and protects.

The relationship to the biblical corpus, usually asserted for propositions adopted, and very firmly held, by the respondents, is not really effective for rejected propositions, even if they are thought to have a foundation in the Bible. In these cases, programing influences outside the Bible, psycho-social ones, for example, are more effective. This lends support to a theological view which holds that tradition carries more weight than the Bible. Orthodox subjects use the biblical source *less* to *prospect* for possible, even new, information than to *protect* acquired information, already regulated by the group-church.

Strong or reinforced social cohesion, (in a school group, for example) leads to a strengthening of the orthodox status of certain doxemes (small units of information with a potential

for integration into the orthodox corpus), even when they diverge from the traditional vocabulary; on the other hand,
these doxemes remain relatively weak in another class where
cohesion is weak (although it is at the same level in the same
Catholic institution). This is a somewhat disturbing observation for catechists: Through assured psycho-social cohesion in
the group, rather *indifferent* doxemes are likely to "get by" and
even to be considered as conditions for membership in the
group. But what would the information be in a case like that?
Such doxemes seem flat, almost meaningless, *except* in their
connection with group membership. The catechist, no doubt,
will be reluctant to see religious statements thus reduced to
the level of slogans. Moreover it must be acknowledged that
certain religious statements function *additionally* in this way
and that they even tend to function *mainly* like this in sub-
groups (of young people, in this case) with strong social cohesion, where their informational value is no longer drawn from
the biblical corpus in which they have their origin and might
also find the source of a creative renewal.

By following step by step the conclusions of these four main
pieces of research by J. P. Deconchy, the Christian reader may
feel two types of reactions: either he will see in these regulations
thus spelled out a guarantee of fidelity to the object around
which the church groups are gathered in the faith, preferring
prudent silence to incautious speech; or else he will see a threat
of robotization for a messianic prophetism which is careful to
respect and assume the creative potentialities of thought and
human hopes. "Conflict is almost always resolved to the advantage of orthodoxy, but is constantly being renewed" (J. P. Deconchy, *o.c.*, p. 222).
Absorbed in its function of maintaining the cohesion of the
group-church, an orthodoxy would become functional to the
point of no longer stimulating the work and tension appropriate
to the interval that separates lexical attainments from their symbolization; this work and tension must be constantly renewed if
they are to signify and uphold the personal relationship of each

member and of the group to the personal message of a prestigious founder (prophet or God).

In any case, any social group exercises some control over the system of symbols (creation, preservation, dispersal whereby its members can communicate on the basis of a common identity, which, in variable ways, is actually foundational. According to Jurgen Ruesch[39] the *protection* afforded *the symbols* by the institutional apparatus stems from the fact that subjects *outside* the group tend to *use* these symbols, at the risk of giving them a new *meaning*. This would be the case in our own day if Marxist and nonbelieving subjects endeavored to introduce certain Christian symbols into the original Marxist corpus by way of cultural enrichment. Or vice versa, if Christians, unconcerned with distortions in the Marxist teaching, took over certain classic concepts (class warfare, for example) to enrich their own efforts to construct a better world. Ruesch's point of view is relevant as a sociologist who is on the frontier between the teachings of two different ideologies. For his part, J. P. Deconchy leans to the view that "this control of the symbolic material is aimed first and foremost at keeping *within* the group *those* who are already there."[40] Although he does not disregard regulation applied to persons, the social psychologist is more sensitive to the mechanism of messianic protestation, which, arising *within* the group, should be studied, not only on the basis of an "oscillatory" model and in relation to orthodox regulation, but by raising the question of an "extra-ideological breaking point," a claim which is obvious in religious discourse.[41]

Even if the movement of faith which finds support in "orthodox" groups and beliefs goes beyond this functional aspect of the existing religious institution, it is no doubt important to discover how this function operates and the considerable *divergence* which separates it from the moment when the truly prophetic function comes into play. The orthodox cohesion of a speaking group constitutes neither a peculiarity nor a guarantee of the "Word of God," even if it is probably a necessary function of it.

Accepting that one's religious language be regulated is not necessarily to understand what the words mean.

Religion in the service of man's needs

The abundant variety of religious discourses, rites, myths, and themes, as well as the disconcerting diversity of profane conduct or commitments entered into in the name of religion, make the hypothesis of one underlying and unifying *religious need* a rather vain one. Wherever some thinker, more philosopher than psychologist, has introduced this hypothesis as a principle of intelligibility, it has proved of little use to psychological or sociological research.

Besides, what religious need could there be in theism, other than a need of God? In the strict sense of a "state of internal tension requiring satisfaction in an object and specific action," psychology is incapable of establishing that man has such a need of God. On the contrary, everything indicates that man can remain areligious, move from religion to atheism without hampering or even modifying the functioning of his psychism. A man without God is not mentally ill. Moreover, in these very general terms, what God are we talking about?

On the other hand, we find that when man is mentally ill he frequently makes use of ideas or practices borrowed from institutional religions, almost always as fragments isolated from their context. Thus, at the end of a rigorous piece of research in a Chicago hospital, a team of Christian psychiatrists was able to formulate a correct diagnosis of the mental disturbances of forty-six patients (out of fifty studied) by using nothing but their religious interests and ideas which had been collected by a psychologist in a forty-five-minute interview.[42] This shows clearly the functional relationship that can be established between elements of the teaching or practices of a religion and certain, often barely conscious, psychic motivations in the case of mentally disturbed persons. Futhermore, the choice and use made by certain neurotic and prepsychotic persons in the whole of the data presented institutionally by a religion can have obvious, at least partial, therapeutic effects. This functional aspect of religion has just been amply illustrated and commented on with insight (notably in the case of Therese Neumann) by Antoine Vergote, from whom we are borrowing these conclusions: "Religious visions, distorted as the disease lays hold of them, not only . . . corroborate the disease, but, in so doing, create the symbolic site on which a partial cure can be effected. . . . We believe that popular religion is a fertile humus on which such experiences can blossom. . . . The examples analyzed derive from religious desire and belong to hysteria. Other types of vision with a prophetic aim are more suggestive of paranoid personalities." In more general terms he also writes: "If we consider all the elements that go to make up religious desire, we can understand that its very varied forms . . . come together in the common tendency to make the fundamental lack null and void by clinging to the divine being and experiencing in that bond the confirmation and expansion of its own being. . . . So it is in the nature of things that in the religious vector the frontier between the normal and the pathological should be particularly mobile" (A. Vergote).[43]

Some functions performed by religions

Abandoning the unitary, pseudo-explanatory idea of a religious need, psychologists and sociologists of religion have turned toward the study of the motivations, whether conscious or unconscious, of religion in terms of the four "dimensions" accessible to observation: beliefs, rites, experiences, and conduct derived from religion.[44] The majority of psychological studies of religions and their crises agree in designating certain motivations that can be pinpointed in individuals or religious groups. Here are the main ones:

— Soothing of anxieties or frustrations inherent in the human condition: distress in dangers or wretchedness, guilt, revolt against injustices and death; these are met by the functions of God-providence, God-consolation, God-relief, and God-retribution in the afterlife.

— Support granted to the organization of societies (the origins of power) and to morality. It happens, especially in so-called primitive societies, that religion exhausts itself, so to speak, in this function of support and legitimation of the civil power. Bergson (in "The Two Sources of Morality and Religion") had already brilliantly described the social functions of what he called "closed" religion, distinguishing it from the "open" religion of the mystics, saints, and prophets. Summing up these sociological findings and analyses, Vincent Cosmão has designated one function of Christianity, currently in crisis, as "the civil religion of the West."[45] He hopes it will disappear.

— Response to intellectual curiosity: giving an ultimate meaning to existence, attenuation of uncertainties arising from facts that are absurd or attributable to chance, new categories of religious semantics, making it possible to speak of the afterlife, for example, in terms of hell-purgatory-heaven and formerly of limbo (ideologically useless today). In numerous Greek tragedies, the implacable cruelty of the situations in which everyone nevertheless does his duty (Creon just as much as Antigone) is attenuated by the gods. This function of attenuating a blind or absurd necessity means that we can no longer believe in a moral order protected and restored by the gods.

— New or strengthened satisfactions of the need to belong to groups in which a certain warm unanimity triumphs over divergences. This functional aspect is regaining favor today, as we shall see in chapter 4 (part II).

Most of these various functions performed by religions[46] are at present in crisis or being questioned in our culture and in connection with Christianity. But they can also be embarrassing to representatives of other religions such as Buddhism, Islam, Hinduism.[47] They prove neither the truth nor the falseness (illusion) of a religion or of a particular aspect of a religion, as we shall have to consider in detail in chapter 6 (part III). At the very most, the study of these functions indicates their psychological truth, the role they play for the individual, the place they fill in a particular society, group, or period. For a quarter of a century psychologists and sociologists have been joining forces with historians[48] to reveal these functional roles, at times more extensive or pregnant than the moral exhortations or the intentions proclaimed by responsible people in the churches. If the latter know what they want to say or do, they never know whether they are doing or saying only what they want to. They always say or do more than they want to. The excess or the divergence is only appreciable at a distance from which certain discordances in their speech or action are perceptible. The exercise of power in the Christian churches is currently meeting critical opposition which can be explained in this way: It devotes too much energy to maintaining unity in conformity with the letter while proclaiming the Spirit which ensures union in diversity (cultural diversity, for example). Though functional in the short term, this rigidly imposed unity (while satisfying the religious wishes of certain people) becomes disastrous in the long term because its dissonances are soon flagrant in relation to the evolution of cultures and also in relation to the evangelical exercise of the authority which takes advantage of it.

CONCLUSION: FUNCTIONAL RELIGION

This first part has dealt with religion and religious experiences. It has described situations and reactions in which religious discourse, belief, prayer, imagination, the organization of religious language clearly functioned in the service of human wishes or needs, individual or collective. From this point of view, religion appears to be dedicated to filling voids, calming fears, gratifying wishes, and reinforcing beliefs while at the same time tightening the membership of the group by strengthening its cohesion.

A religion will be said to be *functional* insofar as its beliefs, rites, myths, language, or organization respond to culturally conditioned, conscious or unconscious attitudes. These mentally and culturally conditioned dispositions as a whole constitute religiosity, spontaneous manifestations of which are the result of dynamic couplings of these dispositions to the institutional structures of one or more established religions. Religiosity, thus understood, is the proper subject of scientific psychology of religion and can be analyzed by operational concepts designating coupling mechanism, some of which have been described in this first part: animist intentionality, magical intentions, imaginary (nonsymbolized) projections, orthodox regulations. Finally, we have used the expression *functional religious experiences* for conscious encounters between this religiosity and the existing religion.

Looked at this way, religion comes into play as a regulatory function of a religiosity which is irrational in itself, and for which the said religion supplies beliefs and rites. Sacral elements, more or less diffused in cosmic realities, as well as vaguely threatening or protective intentionalities on the affective plane find a religious language (usually in a mythical vein) so that they can be talked about; but above all they find ritual conduct which ensures a certain control over the irrational element which is out of reach. Many religions, but not all, introduce God (or the gods) as ultimate referent(s) or supreme guarantor(s) of this regulatory function. They are psychologically functional, or become so, when they place God in the position of gratifying wishes, meeting needs, giving meaning to what would otherwise be absurd, making relative commitments absolute, appearing to dodge the mortal condition, cementing societies that would crumble otherwise, and, finally, making religious institutions or groups function in isolation, or near isolation. Certainly such a God is superior to man in that he has powers that men have not. Even if the relationship with such a God can culminate in a feeling of adoration or gratitude, it stays on an axis of dominance-submission which has difficulty in accommodating love. Starting from a concept of divinity elaborated by man on the basis of his wishes, the practice of functional religion remains enslaving and does not provide a symbolic order which would allow man to meet God in his difference, if indeed that difference can be recognized in reality. This radical difficulty, the basis of the Freudian criticism of illusions, has so great a cultural impact at present that all manifestations of functional religion are threatened and become, rightly or wrongly, widespread causes of disbelief. It will claim our attention at the beginning of the third part (chapter 6). But here it must be added that all religion is partially functional. A religion that was in no way functional or tended to become totally dysfunctional, would not exist or would soon cease to exist.

When that happens, how can God, in his specificity or his proper wish concerning the world, make himself heard? Such perhaps is the question that the reader may have asked several times in the course of this first part; and now it is spelled out. We must give it proper emphasis; a religious faith in which, psychologically, there was no place for a search after God (the gods), no passionate or tranquil wish to know him, understand him, introduce him into private or public life, whatever awkward or dysfunctional aspect there might be to this divine penetration, such a "religion" would be a mere diversion, psychologically suspect and sterile from a Christian viewpoint. Worse still, it would quickly and rightly be suspected of settling men and societies in their most entrenched imaginary nook around a tree with fruits of death: egocentricity confirmed, nationalism or groupism strengthened, implacable intolerance divinely justified.

But are there any men today who, on the basis of their experience, have claimed to speak with God? Are there any groups, in particular Christian groups, that offer experiences of God? The second part of this book will approach this question psychologically in four chapters: sudden experience (conversion), intense experience (with or without drugs), uniting experience (charismatic), and experience of conflict (socio-political). Does God speak other than on the basis of subjective or collective wishes? That will be the fundamental question that will lead us to reexamine experiences often already described and perhaps to free the very notion of experience of its ambiguity.

Notes

1. Karl Röttger, quoted by L. Barbey, "La notion de Dieu chez l'enfant," in *Lumen Vitae* (1947), 2, p. 123.

2. A philosopher will certainly prefer to write "God knows everything." In any case, the child will imagine "know" when he says "see." The difficulty remains, however, in both cases. We do not need reminding of the theological deadlocks that obstructed theologies of prevenient grace and predetermining divine decrees in the late Middle Ages when Christian thinkers were concerned with looking analytically at the conditions of a theism rather than at evangelical situations. Gretchen's compromise about "seeing" is neither better nor worse than those of the theologians about infinite "knowing" and "willing." In short, they have the same function: to allow man to live freely, even though God (the philosophical infinite) exists. The dialectic of the sacred and the profane, as detected by Mircea Eliade in various religions, responds to the same preoccupation. There is nothing specifically Christian about it.

3. Monique Laurendeau and Adrien Pinard, *La pensée causale chez l'enfant* (Paris: Pr. Univ. de France, 1962). The trail blazed by Jean Piaget (*The Moral Judgment of the Child*, London: Routledge and Kegan Paul, 1932) has been followed by many researchers in numerous children, adolescents, and adults of varied religion and culture, notably in the United States and Africa. A good statement of these researches and its results has been given by Bernadette Van Roey, "Immanent Justice and Divine Protection," in *Lumen Vitae* 14 (1959), 1, pp. 129-148. The interpretation of a punitive reaction to explain fortuitous events corresponding to natural casualities declines steadily with age in the various groups studied. However it persists in a fair number of adults in cultures where a religious teaching accepts notions such as dies cast ("ndoki") in certain African groups. The considerable role played by these animist and intentionalist interpretations in Christian populations in Europe has been strikingly described by Jean Delumeau in his *Histoire de la peur en Occident*, XIV-XVIIII centuries (Paris: Fayard, 1978).

4. This is true even in Christian children, oriented pedagogically toward divine interventionism of the protective type ("providentialism"), as the research of B. Van Roey, already mentioned in the previous note, has shown. The anxiety of guilt seems to be related to the educational behavior which adults feel obliged to adopt toward their young children: severe parents go with cruel divinities—indulgent parents with divinities that are benevolent or easily placated with offerings. These correlations are quite well established by comparative studies in cultural anthropology. Thus: M. E. Spiro and R. G. D'Andrade, "A cross-cultur-

al study of some supernatural beliefs," in *Amer. Anthropologist* 60, (3) (June, 1958), pp. 456-66, or W. E. Lambert, L. M. Triandis and M. Wolf, Some correlates of beliefs in the malevolence and benevolence of supernatural beings: a cross-societal study," in *J. of Abnormal and Social Psychology* 58, (2) (March, 1959), pp. 161-9. *Les maladies mentales et thérapies traditionnelles en Afrique Noire* (Mental illnesses and traditional therapies in Black Africa) have recently been studied by Francois Laplantine (Paris: Delarge, 1976) in the framework of "socio-cultural matrices of the collective imagination." Punitive intentions play a preponderant role in the grasping and affective mastery of oppressive events. The therapeutic effectiveness of these beliefs is dependent on the broad social consensus vested in them. For a more theoretical overall view, the reader is referred to F. Laplantine, *Les trois voies de l'imaginaire* (Paris: Ed. Universitaires, 1974).

5. The way parents and their moralizing attitudes curb religious awakening in young children has been described and then discussed with them in three conference-debates: A. Godin, *Le Dieu des parents et le Dieu des enfants* (Paris-Tournai: Casterman, 3rd edition, 1966). Since the first edition of these observations and reflections the author had assumed that most would now be out-of-date. Alas! The moralizing catechesis is still there well backed up with images (cf. *La nouvelle miche de pain*, Paris, Tequi, 1975) and cartoon strips, which, based on both the Old and New Testament, reinforce mental images of an interventionist and punitive God. Is it essential to the collective memory of Christianity to be present in imagination at the Flood or the destruction of Sodom and Gomorrha? Are not these episodes, with their mythical style, retold in the gospel with a very different purpose, foreign to punitive divine interventionism? In this connection, see the severe but sensible reflections in "Vivre et croire avec les enfants," *La Lettre* (May-July, 1979), pp. 248-250.

6. The classic "divine attributes" (omniscience, all-powerfulness, providence, etc.) must undergo a profound reshaping if they are to move from a philosophical, theist character to the evangelical and Christian one. The necessity for this mutation of meanings and a good outline of it were presented by Leopold Malevez, "Nouveau Testament et théologie fonctionnelle," in *Recherches de Sciences Religieuses,* vol. 48 (1) (1960), pp. 258-90.

7. J. P. Jossua, *Discours chrétien et scandale du mal* (Paris: Chalet, 1979).

8. J. P. Deconchy, "La théorie du "locus of control" et l'étude des attitudes et des comportements religieux," in *Archives de Sciences Sociales des Religions,* no. 46 (1) (1978), pp. 155-56. The wish to introduce order where events are due to chance has been studied among children (8-12 years old) by Jean-Denis Souyris, "Etude génétique d'une attitude anti-

hasard," interprétée comme "moyen mythique d'appréhender les choses comme intelligibles" (*Psychologie française* 14, 1969), pp. 279-287. Several American studies found some evidence showing that causal explanations of natural phenomena persist longer among children when they receive a religious education, for instance the study made by Melvin Ezer, "The effect of religion upon children's responses to questions involving physical causalities" (1962), reproduced in the anthology published by B. Beit-Hallahmi, *Research in Religious Behavior: Selected Readings* (Monterey: Brooks-Cole, 1973), pp. 60-79.

9. J. Remy and E. Servais, "Fonctions de l'occulte et du mystérieux dans la société contemporaine-II: Les conditions de l'apparition de la sacralité," in *Concilium* 81 (January, 1973), pp. 73-74.

10. Theodor Reik, "From Spell to Prayer," in *Psychoanalysis* 3 (4) (1955), pp. 3-26. The parallelism or homology of these mutations with the evolution of the relationship between a child and his mother has been well described by Jacques M. Pohier, "Religious Mentality and Infantile Mentality: Some Forms of Prayer in Child Psychology," in *Child and Adult Before God*, (Brussels: Lumen Vitae, 1961), pp. 21-44.

11. T. Flournoy, *Une mystique moderne: Mlle Vé, Archives de Psychologie* XV (57/58), special issue of 224 pages (Geneva: Kundig, 1915).

12. There might be evidence of the magical mentality if Madame Vé's autobiography revealed a propensity to repeat sacrificial or ritual conduct *in order to* obtain divine interventions.

13. H. Aubin, *L'homme et la magie* (Paris: Desclée De Brouwer, 1952), p. 227.

14. A. Godin and Sister Marthe, "Magic Mentality and Sacramental Life," in *Lumen Vitae* 15 (1960), 2, pp. 277-296. Bear in mind, however, the critical reflections of J. P. Deconchy, "Dans quelle mesure peut-on parler de magie chez l'enfant?" in *Mélanges de Science Religieuse* 23 (3-4) (1966), pp. 217-36. Access to the symbolism of sacramental signs and the priestly role is described in different ways and very methodically for girls and boys by Anne Dumoulin and Jean-Marie Jaspard, *Les médiations religieuses dans l'univers de l'enfant* (Brussels: Lumen Vitae, 1971). Partial publication in English, *Lumen Vitae* 26 (1971), 2, pp. 237-262 (Jaspard), pp. 316-332 (Dumoulin).

15. This regression or fixation can be induced not only by certain religious preaching, but also by inscriptions and church furniture suggesting an automatic causality in the obtaining of "favors." For example the prie-dieu recently withdrawn from a Marian sanctuary, where the kneeling worshiper could see two slits surrounded by copper, one for the pink slip on which was written the "favor requested," the other for the white envelope to receive the money.

16. The diversity of methods and of the populations questioned is

particularly convincing in L. B. Brown, "Some Attitudes Underlying Petitionary Prayer," in *From Cry to Word* (Brussels: Lumen Vitae, 1968), pp. 65-84. In order to discriminate "between superstition and prayer of request," a deep philosophical and psychological essay has been presented by D. Z. Phillips, *The Concept of Prayer* (London: Routledge and Kegan Paul, 1965), Chapter 6.

17. The classic work is still Juliette Boutonier, *L'angoisse* (Pr. Univ. de France, 1949). A complementary work is Philippe Malrieu, *La construction de l'imaginaire* (Brussels: Dessart, 1967).

18. Quoted from Claire Kebers, "L'enfant et l'Autre. . .", in *Santé mentale* 2 (1979), p. 41.

19. Hjalmar Sundén, *Die Religion und die Rollen* (Berlin: Topelmann, 1966), and *Den Heliga Birgitta* (Stockholm: Wahlstrom, 1973), a book already sketched out in a German article, "Die Persönlichkeit der heiligen Birgitta," *Archiv für Religionspsychologie*, Band 10 (1971), pp. 249-63.

20. Hanna Colm, "Religious symbolism in child analysis," in *Psychoanalysis* 2 (1) (1957), pp. 39-56.

21. A. Godin, "Isaac at the Stake: a Psychological Enquiry into the Manner of Presenting a Biblical Episode to Children," in *Lumen Vitae* 10 (1955), pp. 65-92.

22. An extract from observations collected and analyzed in A. Godin: "L'inertie d'un objet merveilleux: absence de miracle et construction de significations," in *Ricerche di storia sociale e religiosa*, vol. 14 (July-December 1978), pp. 289-302.

23. Mircea Eliade, *Mythes, rêves et mystères* (Paris: N.R.F., 1957), p. 31.

24. For a study of this messianic dimension in myths, the work of Henri Desroche makes a good starting point, notably his *Sociologie de l'espérance* (Paris: Calmann-Levy, 1973). The development of the myth on which the "Cargo Cults" throughout the colonized islands of the West Pacific are based is still being used as a laboratory to observe the effects on very primitive and colonized animist populations when a myth appears (1857-1867) that offers a liberating religious space. But what kind of liberation? The myths of the Cargo and their variants, which can be located geographically, have been the subject of a preliminary work by Peter Worsley and Jean Guiard, "La répartition des mouvements millénaristes en Mélanésie," in *Archives de Sociologie des Religions* 5 (January 1958), pp. 38-46.

25. J. P. Deconchy, *Structure génétique de l'idée de Dieu* (Brussels: Lumen Vitae, 1966), pp. 205-213. Pierre Babin, *Dieu et l'adolescent* (Lyons and Paris: ed. du Chalet), 1963, pp. 219-223.

26. Sources of the statistics mentioned: Pierre Delooz, "Who Believes in the Hereafter?" (National and International Surveys), in *Death and Presence* (Brussels: Lumen Vitae, 1972), pp. 17-38. The S.O.F.R.E.S.

survey, 1973 (September) is the subject of comments by J. Potel in *Le Pèlerin*, no. 4744, (28. October 1973), pp. 43-49. The S.O.F.R.E.S. survey 1975 (July) is compared with previous surveys since 1952 in *La Croix*, no. 29/30 (June, 1975).

27. A. Martins, "L'analyse hiérarchique des attitudes religieuses," *Archives de Sociologie des Religions* 11 (1961), pp. 71-91. The tables and commentaries also appear in *Death and Presence* (1972), opus citatum, pp. 63-68.

28. Texts from "Documents and Commentaries," in *Death and Presence* (1972), opus citatum, pp. 69-84.

29. Philippe Ariès, *L'homme devant la mort* (Paris: Seuil, 1977). And for the evocation of funeral rites, Jean-Thierry Maertens, *Le jeu du mort* (Paris: Aubier, 1979).

30. For Ariès (see above), medical opinion is changed concerning a death objectified by disease and aging: There is a new dividing line, this time between the useful (those who produce), and the useless (those who no longer do so). But in a secularized country like Sweden study has shown cemetery visits to be an occasion of serene meditation on death (see, in the volume of *Death and Presence* already quoted, Berndt Gustafsson's research: "The cemetery, as a place of meditation," pp. 85-96). But the great human theme of revolt against death is singularly deflated there behind a socially conventional serenity.

31. While these documentary paragraphs on the state of beliefs in the afterlife were being written, the Roman Congregation for the Doctrine of the Faith sent to the bishops of the episcopal conferences a reminder, on seven points, of the faith of the church concerning "last ends," what lies beyond death and eternal life. The statements are brief and dogmatic in tone. Hell is "a penalty always awaiting the sinner deprived of the sight of God; it reverberates through his whole being" (this Letter occupies four columns of *La Documentation Catholique*, no. 1769, 5 August 1979, pp. 708-710). A paragraph records the "danger of imaginative and arbitrary visions whose excesses play a large part in the difficulties often encountered by the Christian faith." It goes on to say that "the images used in the Scriptures are worthy of respect" but "their profound meaning must be grasped and the risk of diminishing them avoided." This disengagement of the meaning from the husk of the images is delicate work; it is pastoral work for which the contribution of the theologians is essential. The latter are nowhere praised but are reminded that among "their grave duties" is that of "not boldly spreading their research initiatives among the faithful." Furthermore, the crisis in belief and the generalization of doubts about life beyond the grave are presented in the introduction to this *Letter* as "the unwanted repercussion of theological controversies circulated widely in public"; all this, according

to comparative statistics of beliefs, is historically an obvious untruth. It is the lack of meanings found by contemporary man in certain dogmatic pronouncements (a study largely frozen since the modernist crisis and until Vatican II) that has led, since 1950, to the progressive collapse of adherence to certain "truths" about life beyond the grave. The variety of social dynamisms implied in these breaks in belief and these rifts in the fabric of the late Christianity is analyzed from various angles in the works of Emile Poulat, notably the most recent *Une Eglise ébranlée: de Pie XII à Jean-Paul II* (Paris-Tournai: Casterman, 1980).

32. David Lester, "Religious Behaviors and Attitudes Toward Death" (Critical Analysis of American Researches), in *Death and Presence* (opus citatum, 1972), pp. 107-127.

33. D. Becker, *The Denial of Death* (New York: The Free Press, 1973), p. 204.

34. Further details of a survey, admittedly brief, in A. Godin," Orthodoxie religieuse et psychologie sociale," in *Nouvelle Revue Théologique* 94 (6 June 1972), p. 621.

35. L. Bouyer, *Dictionnaire théologique* (Paris-Tournai: Desclee et Cie, 1963).

36. De La Brosse, Henry and Rouillard, *Dictionnaire de la foi chrétienne* (Paris: Cerf, 1968).

37. J. P. Deconchy, "Milton Rokeach et la notion de dogmatisme," in *Archives de Sociologie des religions* 30 (1970), pp. 3-32; *L'orthodoxie religieuse: Essai de logique psycho-sociale* (Paris: Editions Ouvrières, 1971); "Expérimentation et processus d'influence idéologique," in *Psychologie Française* 21, 4 (1976), pp. 281-86; "La psychologie sociale expérimentale et les comportements religieux," in *The Annual Review of the Social Sciences of Religion* 1 (1977), pp. 103-132; *Orthodoxie religieuse et sciences humaines* (La Haye-Paris: Mouton, 1980).

38. For a more detailed account and critical discussions the reader is referred to the article already quoted in the *Nouvelle Revue Théologique* (June, 1972), pp. 620-37.

39. Jurgen Ruesch, "The Social Control of Symbolic Systems" in *J. Commun.* 17 (4) (1967), pp. 276-301, quoted by J. P. Deconchy, *L'orthodoxie* (see above), p. 37.

40. J. P. Deconchy, *L'orthodoxie* . . . (see above), p. 37, note 3.

41. This is J. P. Deconchy's final conclusion on page 346 of the work, the broad outlines of which have been reviewed in the preceding account.

42. E. Draper and associates, "On the Diagnostic Value of Religious Ideation," in *Arch. of General Psychiatry* 13 (September 1965), pp. 202-207.

43. Antoine Vergote, *Dette et désir* (Paris: Seuil, 1978), p. 262 and p. 179.

44. This pluridimensional theory, with some variations, found expression and numerous applications on the basis of Charles Y. Glock and Rodney Stark, *Religion and Society in Tension* (Chicago: Rand McNally, 1965).

45. Vincent Cosmão, *Changer le monde: une tâche pour l'Eglise* (Paris: Cerf, 1979).

46. A Vergote has commented on several of these motivations giving a functional scope to religion in his classic work *The Religious Man* (Dublin: Gill and Macmillan, 1969), chapter 2. The functional relationship between myths and rites is tackled by Michel Meslin, *Pour une science des religions* (Paris: Seuil, 1973), pp. 223-34. In the United States, the psychologically functional aspects of religion have been studied from different viewpoints and presented in many classic volumes and textbooks: G. W. Allport, *the Individual and His Religion* (London: Constable, 1951); C. D. Batson and W. L. Ventis, *Religious Experience* (New York: Oxford U. Press, 1982); W. Pruyser, *A Dynamic Psychology of Religion* (New York: Harper & Row, 1968); M. P. Strommen, ed., *Research on Religious Development* (New York; Hawthorn Books, 1971); O. Strunk, *Religion: A Psychological Interpretation* (New York: Abingdon Press, 1968). In England, the behavioral and social aspects are underlined in general textbooks by M. Argyle, *Religious Behaviour* (London: Routledge and Kegan Paul, 1958) and *Psychology and Social Problems* (London: Methuen, 1964); also by G. E. W. Scobie, *Psychology of Religion* (London and Sydney: Batsford, 1975). The Freudian critical problem, arising when a religion is mostly functional as a response to spontaneous or social wishes, was rarely tackled seriously until recent years. This is probably due to a Jungian all-invading influence well represented by E. Fromm, *Psychoanalysis and Religion* (New Haven: Yale U. Press, 1952).

47. "Buddhist dimension, social dimension, animist dimension," these are the three fields of force presented by the person responsible for the Bureau of Buddhist studies at Vientiane (Laos), Marcel Zago, in "Christian Message in a Buddhist Environment," *Lumen Vitae* 2 (1974), pp. 235-265. Mohammed, like Jesus, had to fight against magical manifestations of the established religion.

48. Jean Delumeau, for example, in *Le catholicisme va-t-il mourir?* (Paris: Fayard, 1977).

II

Experiences of God?

The metaphysical event of transcendence—welcome extended to Another, hospitality, wish, language—does not find its achievement as love. But transcendence of discourse is linked with love. . . . Relations between beings do not represent their entirety. The speaker is always outside.

Emmanuel Levinas

Introduction

Encounters and Experiences

A good many of our contemporaries are no longer able to find God through the usual institutional mediations. They often prefer to trust in their "experiences" or listen to witnesses who have "met God" speak of their own experiences. This attitude certainly carries the seeds of possible revivals: religion and faith have frequently withered through concentrating on dogmas or rites divorced from any affective experience. It also involves risks: religious sentiment and the very notion of experience are not lacking in ambiguity. Religious emotion can easily be confused with artistic feeling, love, generous impulses with the mark of the absolute, the feeling of oneness with the universe, intense awareness of the life of a group. The years pass and we wonder whether we had ever, in fact, encountered something other than ourselves.

Have you met God?

This question may seem odd to you and your answer would probably be "no." But there are people who answer "yes." How can that be? Is it a meeting in the real sense or just a way of speaking, a metaphor? What can people who speak or write like that really mean?

Encounters and encounter

The experience of God is never immediate. We do not meet God in the same way as we meet a neighbor in the street. Moreover, simple encounters with neighbors in the street, when we might possibly say "hello" or jostle each other in the same door-way, are not "meetings" in the real sense of the word: Although they really happen, these encounters are not felt to be an experience of personal relations, of friendship between neighbors, for example. They may be fleeting perceptions of an ambiguous look or gesture, a collision of bodies in a too-narrow doorway, transient impressions, maybe pleasant, maybe unpleasant. They can become meaningful only if the neighbors talk to each other, try to get to know or to recognize each other, however slightly, as the person that each one is or wants to be.

A meeting in the real sense assumes that people express themselves in accordance with some aspect of their own truth and so become freely present the one to the other. Such a meeting, modest as it may be and perhaps far removed from an offer of love, modifies those who have met. They are no longer exactly the same after the meeting. If they are capable of observing themselves, they may be aware of what has changed *in them,* albeit maybe for only a very short time.

Some people imagine that, through the change they feel in themselves, they have already acquired a knowledge of the other. Although this is sometimes the case, either through understanding listening or through a spontaneous inclination that opens the door to friendship or love, such a claim is far from always confirmed. It is even the source of countless confusions and misunderstandings both in love and in religion. The repercussion of an experience of meeting may be the result of largely egocentric wishes leading to a deafness to the wishes of the other.

As some young people scrawled recently on the wall of the religious house where I live: "Your sexuality will not make you ill, but it can make you deaf!" No doubt there were some girls in the gang.

Immediacy and interpretation

So immediacy is a privilege of sensation: an odor, a contact. All perception is thus a construction. A cubic object is not perceived but constructed mentally by completing the part that is not seen.

As for the experience of a meaningful relationship between two beings, it assumes that they talk and that they know what talking means—that is, that they interpret and, at times, verify. This brush with each other is very real and immediate. But is it a caress? And what about the other person's wish, if it is indeed a caress? Are a child's piercing cries an appeal? And if so, what about his wish?

If that is how things stand with human relations, how will they stand with experiences of God? Every religion offers paths leading to some experience of God, a founding experience in the past or the prospect of a future experience. What has the Christian tradition to say about the Christian experience of God?

"Seeing the man and believing in the God"

What a curious experience is the Christian faith! In the early days of Christianity there are men and woman, mainly Jews, who have *met* a man called Jesus; they have seen him, listened to him, attacked, loved, more or less understood him, and some have followed him. Had they met God? What has the traditional language to say on this subject as it tries to explain this encounter, followed sometimes by faith? Taking their cue from St. Augustine, theologians repeat that the apostles of Jesus of Nazareth "saw the man and believed in the God" (in Ioan., 79,1). Their experience of God was *a synthesis, actively established and maintained* between a perception, a human meeting (in the deep sense) and an interpretation born of trust, of a faith that went beyond the perception and the meeting. Maintaining this active synthesis involved considerable consequences in their practice and their life commitments.

But what about experience of the inner God, of the Spirit? Without anticipating the third part of this volume, in which the benefit of a movement of faith thus defined will become fully apparent, we maintain here, by way of hypothesis, that it cannot be otherwise. Experience of the inner God or recognition of the

Spirit is always indirect, mediated by signs which in the end are interpreted in faith. It is a synthesis, actively established and maintained in its integrity, in other words, the highest and most complete form of experience accessible to man, whether in religion or in love.[1]

Experiences and experience

But there must still be real experience: an affective and dynamic mode of knowledge, richer than notional learning, more lasting than mere emotion. Now, the notion of experience is one of the most ambiguous in both everyday vocabulary and the language of philosophy. To speak of human experience, completely formed in connection with a perceptible phenomenon, is normally to presuppose attention plus awareness, judgment plus interpretation and, sometimes, the formation of lasting attitude taken in regard to the object of the experience. But experience will often be spoken of when the whole range of these properties is not present or even in order to stress one of them: It may be the empirical (even immediate) component of the perception-enriching knowledge (or sensation), which would be known as *Erfahrung* in German; or it may be the intense, possibly entirely internal, component which makes it a deeply impressive "state of mind," which is felt to be "received" and would be called *Erlebnis* in German. Our language has only the one word "experience" at its disposal, which thereby falls into ambiguity.

Ambiguity of the word "experience"

Read these two statements:

— "In this grave situation we are appealing to someone to *use* all his *experience* in order to understand and resolve the difficulty." This could be any experienced person—electrician, surgeon, lawyer, psychologist—as the case may be. Each of them will make a synthesis between his competence, a sort of acquired wisdom available inside him, and a difficult situation. By applying it, he will display it, test it, and perhaps develop it.

— "We are living, presently, through a period that is much more upsetting than we had thought. *What an experience!*" This may be a bereavement, a love affair, an accident, financial ruin, a journey, a conflict. These are trying situations and to live through them is to be a prey to the accompanying emotion.

No doubt you realize that the word "experience" does not have the same meaning, is not unequivocal, in these two sentences. But you may think that in both cases it is referring to something all-inclusive which mobilizes or affects the whole personality.[2] But we still have to spell out how that all-inclusiveness comes into play. For want of a good comparison, let us say that the active-synthesis-experience in the first sentence and the passive-emotional-experience are designated by the same word which, out of context, would be truly ambiguous.

It is true that the active component of acquired and readily available knowledge does not exclude the passive component (repercussion from an emotion suffered) in individuals or in groups of humans. But when it is a question of God or of love, it is essential to remove the ambiguity and grasp the distance between *consciousness,* as vivid as you like, and *awareness.*[3] As will become clearer later on, the emotional intensity accompanying peak experiences or the suddennesses of transformations, associated psychologically with certain privileged experiences, are not *of themselves* proportionate to the openness to the other, or Other, which may occur at the same time. In this respect, the ambiguity of the word "experience" can poison certain discussions among those who manifest a fairly lively taste and renewed appetite for the irrational in contemporary counter-cultural groups, provided there are affectively rich experiences and other people who mistrust verbal trickery. There may be a lot of facile talk about love when all they really mean is experience of self.

Religious·experience suspect . . .

The ambiguous nature of the term *experience* continues to weigh heavily in the suspicious attitudes of many adults, religious or not, to experience of God. This is how Antoine Vergote sums up his observations on this point:

> Some people acknowledge having had some "experience" of God in adolescence, but looking back on it, they regard it as empty fancies with no guarantee of truth. The word "mystic" conjures up the same idea. . . . Experience (for these people) has come to be analogous to a subjective state where man finds himself in a *tête-à-tête* with himself, with the blissful feeling of being open to the Other. . . . We can recognize four characteristic traits typical of adults in this refusal: a) Modern man has discovered sentiment as such from a broader outlook, reflective and self-critical, which is one of the universal characteristics of our times; b) in Christian circles, they speak of the immense difficulty in integrating belief in the mystery of a personal God, not easily lending himself to experience because human experience bears on the palpable; c) Many think faith and experience are in opposition, so they think that faith takes root on another level from affectivity; d) finally, for the greater number of these subjects, the world has ceased to be a direct sign of God. It has largely lost any referential value to a God withdrawn from the cosmos. . . . It is no longer God who hides himself (Isaiah 45:15), but the world which closes in upon him. . . .
>
> (Thus) the question of religious experience has often been placed in a false light because those who dealt with it took as their model societies which had not yet reached this stage of maturity, not taking into account the profound change which has affected the link between man and nature.[4]

. . . but still fascinating

The loss of an experience of the divine through cosmic reality and the mistrust of any religious experience described as *"Erlebnis"* (emotion felt) are culturally inevitable but are a cause for regret. Many people in our culture who have become or remained nonbelievers turn, with a fascination which reveals their wish to believe in them, to reputedly marvelous phenomena: unidentified flying objects (UFOs), astrology, looking into the future through "clairvoyant" experiences, spiritualism, cures hastily designated as miraculous because they occur outside the framework of medicine and "legally" applied sciences, that is, those based on the study of conditioning. How lovely to catch nature at fault (she often is, but not in the circumstances we would wish) and so get our own back on her.

As for those who remain faithful to the teachings of the churches, many are pained to find orthodoxy, which governs the statements of a system of beliefs to which their faith remains tied, contrasting with an inner barrenness or affective dryness which encourages doubts and renunciations they do not want. Interpretations of the Christian message centered on revaluations of the "terrestrial realities," on the moral, social, or even political meaning of the gospels, have a certain vogue but often appear to be peripheral ideologies. In fact these interpretations, cut off from the environments that gave them birth (working environment, underprivileged regions or social classes), do little to galvanize the activity, thought, or affectivity of those who do not belong there. The more so as they are often presented as orthodoxies by institutions or authorities (churches or parties, sects or militant cells) in abstruse or obscure language which is somewhat argumentative and does little to stimulate creativity. Only someone who has been a prisoner, who has been oppressed or unjustly treated, can respond emotionally to a theology of liberation, however evangelical it may be.

So nostalgia for a variety of all-inclusive, integral, and pacifying experiences persists; a direct divine presence would transform doubts into certainty, anxieties into peace of mind, fragments into firm rock, sexual surrenders into permanent guaranteed love. This aspiration to live affectively experiences that gratify instinctive needs while bypassing the laborious and sometimes crucifying mediations of the progress, reflections, or dialogues of everyday life, reveals the most ancient and fundamental *lack,* the one that pushes the child to begin to exist on a human level by discarding in succession the maternal mantle, then that of the family, the group, society, and even the church.

So this aspiration will always be there, ready to obtain by cajolery the chance of some promised, transitory satisfactions, even ones that are regressive or childish. This aspiration is the remote *source* which makes mystic experience possible and empowers it, Christian or not, but it should not be confused with Christian experience, mystical or not. We shall come back to this in the last two chapters of this book.

Four types of privileged experience

Psychologically, four (possibly cumulative) aspects of an experience can bestow on it a privileged and fascinating quality with regard to the fundamental aspiration we have just been considering:

The suddenness, subjectively experienced, of an inner transformation. This feature is stressed in many accounts of conversions.

The intensity of emotions experienced unexpectedly (the "peak-experiences") or systematically researched (sometimes by means of drugs, possibly even a "sacred" drug).

The unifying joy of the group unit, experienced subjectively and collectively in a crowd, a meeting or a community where the organized intention is, among other things, to produce this effect.

The excitement of conflict in large or small groups also produces affective states which are subjectively very intense and confer a kind of absolute value on commitments shared or undertaken there.

These features, not in themselves religious, are discovered, sustained or stimulated nowadays in order to establish and justify the claim that these are not merely religious experiences but really experiences of God. They will be the subject of observations and reflections in the next four chapters.

Notes

1. At least this is true of experiences in the religious traditions found-ed on a relationship with a so-called "personal" God. For there are others, particularly in the Far East. They have even been spoken of as religions without God. In *The Christian Experience* (London and New York, Sheed & Ward, 1955), the theologian, Jean Mouroux, defines religious experience right away as linking man "with the sacred Being as such" and then immediately describes that Being as a person, creator, object of love, final arbiter. His work thus neglects the religious experi-ence in certain oriental traditions and also the spiritual life of great human atheists, those "mystics without God" that Madame Teste, in her anxiety about her husband, asks Abbé Bremond about (Paul Valéry, *Monsieur Teste*, Gallimard, 1946, p. 51).

2. All-inclusiveness is the term used by Jean Mouroux to designate the *experiential* category, which he rightly distinguished from the *empiri-cal* (uncritical and piecemeal experience) and the *experimental* (contrived experience). But, preoccupied as he was with showing the integral and integrating aspect of religious experience (on the subject's experiential plane), he provided a definition of this "experiential" plane which, all things considered, is rather vague: "experience taken in its personal entirety, which all its structural elements and all its principles of move-ment. . . , experience built up and grasped in the lucidity of a self possessed consciousness and the generosity of a self-giving love" (French ed. Paris, Aubier, 1952, p. 24). Since he failed to make a clearer distinc-tion between the "passive and receiving side" and the "active" side of this experience in the case of the Christian religion, Jean Mouroux was led several times to apply his "experiential" category (which many Chris-tian writers took over from him) with an orientation toward a spiritual-izing inner quality which is not without ambiguity. His mistrust at the outset of "constructive" or "self-committing" activities of the mind (sus-pected of "rationalism" for example, p. 20) limits the import of this work, which nevertheless remains masterly and unique in its time. Con-cretely, for the perception of situations, emotions, and commitments designated as Christian experiences of God, the vague notion "experien-tial" can be of little use. It has an uneasy stance in the face of certain critiques of religious experience as the fruit or effect of wishes (Freud). Oliver Rabut, in *L'expérience religieuse fondamentale* (Paris and Tournai, Casterman, 1969), is tempted at first by this same spiritualism when he postulates a psychic structure including a specifically religious spiritual function (especially pp. 54-62). But he extricates himself vigorously further on, introducing historical reality and presenting religious expe-rience as creating sense ("Union with God makes me a giver of mean-

ing," p. 150). But he remains trapped in the ambiguity of the word "experience." Much more precise and useful is the "Note sur l'usage du terme expérience," by Fathers Jacquemont, Jossua, and Quelquejeu in *Une foi exposée* (Paris, Cerf, 1972) despite their insistence on interpretation "after the event."

3. On the subject of this "distance" and the dynamic and reflective movements which bridge it, in part, there are interesting developments to be found in François Duyckaerts, *Conscience et prise de conscience* (Brussels, Dessart, 1974).

4. A. Vergote, *The Religious Man* (Dublin, Gill and Macmillan, 1969), pp. 58-59; and "Religious Experience," in *From Religious Experience to a Religious Attitude* (Brussels, Lumen Vitae, 1964), p. 45-46.

2

Sudden Conversions

Suddenly I met God . . .

The sudden feeling of an inner transformation attracts attention because it is interpreted as an effect of direct action by God. Witnesses who are asked, or are driven spontaneously, to proclaim their conversion verbally or in writing describe sudden and transforming experiences. These receive more attention because we tend to forget the much more numerous conversions resulting from a slow and progressive change.

Sudden conversions and "deversions"

The sudden nature of a transformation is obviously not religious in itself. Furthermore it is also apparent in abrupt changes of values, beliefs, and attitudes leading to "deversion" (abandonment of religious faith or membership of religious groups). Here are two short descriptions of such a kind.

Nothing had prepared me for this sudden obvious fact. I was finishing my university training after being brought up in a Catholic family: my father and mother were practicing believers, not particularly devout, certainly not bigoted; just straightforward, sincere, traditional Catholics. I went as a boarder to a Catholic school which was liberal enough to allow discussion among students, even in religion classes. It seems to me that many of my companions discussed the church rather than God. For my part, I took God for granted. As for the gospel, it had often been wrongly applied. But that did not

stop me from belonging to a fairly fervent prayer group. . . .
My fiancee was a Catholic herself and certainly didn't expect
what happened to me, anymore than I did. One evening, at
the end of a winter sports trip, I was looking at the sky, weary
after several downhill runs. Countless stars were shining. I was
thinking of going home to my girlfriend who would soon be
my wife. Suddenly a certainty thrust itself upon me. God did
not exist, either as a superior power or as a love different from
the love we had for each other. That would all have to finish
one day, since we should have to die one day and that was fine.
After all, life was so sweet in itself that there was no need for it
to be explained and even prolonged. I went back to the hotel
wondering if I was really thinking what I was experiencing: a
kind of immense relief.

The next day, when I woke, I knew that I had staked everything. God was useless, another life even more so. The sky was
blue, but there was no paradise beyond it and the clouds only
made it more beautiful. It wasn't necessary to believe or to
practice a religion in order to be good or to love. Nothing
overhead any more. Nothing in front of me except an as yet
nonexistent road which I would draw for myself. I drew a
deep breath. I was free.[1]

When I was fourteen I made my first profession of agnosti-
cism. I was at a cadet camp. One day I set out on a long walk
with another cadet, and we spent the whole afternoon together arguing strongly for and against religious belief. To my
satisfaction, I heard myself proving that there were no
grounds for believing, asking why, therefore, I believed and he
believed, doubting whether there was a God since there were
no serious arguments in favor and finally declaring that in all
truth I did not believe in God. I had burned my boats that day
and all I could do was go forward to meet the unknown.[2]

In reporting this second episode of "sudden deversion" Gustav
Jahoda also draws some conclusions from his research on the
genesis of nonbelief, based on 500 accounts of the development of
religious beliefs, of which 233 came from nonbelievers.[3] The

suddenness is rarer in "deversion" than in conversion. On the emotional plane, the course and the outcome are not the same, either in their steady progress or their sudden leaps. In conversion, feelings that were hitherto multifarious and varied in their object (love, friendship, anxiety, doubt, enthusiasm, sociability) come together and unite around a religious pole. Conversion leads to new or renewed membership of groups or churches, established institutions. Deversion, on the other hand, is accompanied by a splitting up of the affective life which is increasingly differentiated into objects perceived more clearly on account of their diversification. The new religious nonbeliever is deprived of the social references provided by religious institutions.

The character of a change in beliefs, faith, abandonment of or return to religious faith, whether sudden *or* progressive, cannot be linked directly with a kind of divine intervention (stimulation psychologically present, in the form of evangelical or religious texts, of the testimony of great religious or other personalities, both in the slow progress towards faith and in the other) nor with a sort of "divine withdrawal" which would be the equivalent in the transition to atheism. "Sudden conversions" should be ascribed rather to character traits in the personality of the converts.[4]

"God exists: I have met him"

All the same, the description of an experience presented as an immediate contact with God followed by wholesale transformation has a certain fascination. It responds to the ancient aspiration already referred to.

When André Frossard, in 1969, published the account of a sudden illumination thirty years after the event, he chose the title *God Exists: I Have Met Him.*[5] He immediately achieved his most successful sale and his book remained at the top of the bestsellers list for several weeks. This is very revealing of the psychologically latent *wish* of thousands of readers. To be transformed in a wholesale and direct manner by God in person: what a dream!

And what a brilliant, second-hand escape from the dreary grayness of everyday life of both believers and nonbelievers . . .

Is this dream-like wish disappointed or fulfilled by reading the book?

Someone wrote that he would have preferred a different title: *God Exists, I Have Not Met Him!* The ironic tone of this remark should not hide its relevance. It reminds us that any metaphor is ambiguous when designating God or the action of God in man. But a peevish criticism does not deprive Frossard's title of its undoubted popularity nor his testimony of its sincerity.

His very success, however, invites us to comment first on the far-reaching waves produced by this shock effect.

To see God and go on living

While preparing this chapter, I spoke to a group of some ten "ordinary" Christians, who were neither theologians nor psychologists by profession nor by their reading. Had they heard of a relatively recent book in which someone had met God? Half of them had heard of some such work. Only one could name the author because he had read it. As I expressed my astonishment that a Christian could "have seen" God, they mentioned some other witnesses which I list here: Moses (twice), St. Paul (twice), St. Francis, "a mystic Spanish nun" (this, the great St. Teresa), and Claudel (twice). These ten Christians were between thirty-five and sixty-five years old; their tastes and professions were mainly literary or legal.

The presence of Moses in their associations is fairly typical of an interesting distortion. Popular imagination has seized on him and drawn sustenance from him as a person who went up to Mount Sinai and saw God. Now, at least one of the writers of the book of Exodus shows Moses having almost the opposite spiritual experience. When Moses *asks* Yahweh: "Lord, let me see your face," he hears the reply: "You cannot see my face for no man can see me and live." However he adds: "Go into the cleft of the rock and you shall see me, as it were from behind" (Exodus 33:

23-30). And Moses saw the great shadow of God stretched in front of him like a silhouette of deep sapphire blue, probably on the yellow sand at the foot of the mountain.

This confirms the psychological reflection made above: the aspiration to see a supreme being, the direct contemplation of whose person would sum up the meaning of life, is a seductive wish, against which the God of Moses seems to warn us. If there is a meeting with God, at least in the case of Moses, it is through words, messages, in a dialogue, or possibly in orders that are difficult to execute.

No man can see God and live. So it would be amazing if anyone could meet God and continue to talk. Yet, as thousands of witnesses have done just that, have talked and even written of it, we must ask ourselves *what is the import of such accounts for the listener and the reader.*

Talking about the other in his absence

First, we do not normally talk about another (or the Other) except in his absence. If a Claudel or a Frossard talk, or rather, write about their meeting with God, the reader, fascinated as he may be, does not meet God. At the very most, in the best cases, he hears tell of him. What the reader meets is an account, an expression of their experience. He does not live their experience.

So, *of whom, exactly, does he hear tell?*

Experience of the other

The person who describes his encounter with another person may be so wrapped up in himself that, as he speaks or writes of those privileged moments, he retains primarily his own emotive states and in fact reveals nothing, or almost nothing, of that other to whom he really wanted to bear witness.

Anyone who has never known "love at first sight" will be intrigued by a story of this particular happening, one that is not essential to all love. It will be easy to rouse his interest, even enthusiasm, by a good description of the circumstances and excitement of such a happy moment in the life of a man or woman. But what does it tell him about the beloved? Someone madly in love can invite me to leap and dance for joy with him; but how much wiser shall I be concerning the other, or even the ways of love?

A story of religious conversion is open to the same question, at least if its readers are anxious not to avoid the question of God. When the other is absent, the speaker or writer may be so concerned with telling his life history and his feelings at the time of his experience of God that he says nothing, or almost nothing, about that Other. Many often poignant stories are brim-full of the description of a life, that of the witness. So we can count up the pages of autobiography and even some which have little to do with the conversion.

What is more, in the case of sudden conversions, countless autobiographical chapters are thought to be justified because they show the reader that the witness was totally ignorant of God in his life until a certain day when. . . .

> If I feel compelled to talk at some length about my child-hood, please believe that it is not in order to glory in my antecedents, but so as to establish firmly that nothing had prepared me for what happened. . . . It is not enough to say so, it has to be proved. Here are the facts.[6]

With due respect to Frossard, it is impossible to give such proof, at least from the reader's point of view. Furthermore the project is immediately suspect to any thinking person. All autobiography involves selection; it is written with an object in view.

The reader faces a *reconstruction* of the past. The often unconscious tendency to emphasize the break between "before" and "after" is always perceptible in this kind of literature. Charles L. Harper, examining the structure of the religious autobiographies of twenty-five new members of Catholic charismatic groups in the United States, discovered amazing simplifications in their presentation of the crisis preceding their charismatic affiliation, notably an underestimate of the Christian life these people had led before their "conversion."[7] Objective historical cross-checking is always possible, but it is not always accessible to investigators.

Who would have thought that the effect of suddenness—which is so striking in the admirable story of his conversion Claudel composed shortly after the emotion seized him one Christmas night at Notre Dame in Paris (1886)—was largely the result of literary composition? The very fame of the convert had long ago made public the laborious work he had performed in previous years in discovering and learning about Christianity. But patient research, inner decision, and its expression in literary creations are different things. We know now that *four months before* describing the emotion that seized him near the second pillar on the right, at the entrance to the choir in Notre Dame during the singing of the "Magnificat" and the "Adeste fideles," Claudel had already written *Pour la messe des hommes,* which he was to recognize later, quite frankly, as already "Catholic in character." In this lyric poem, Christ speaks to men in a "country cathedral" while outside branches brush against the "stained glass windows with their angels" and within "the hearts of men in song are silent before this strange revelation."[8] The semantic and structural similarities of the poem and the story in prose are particularly striking.

Anticipated changes

Stories of conversion take account of changes and transformations as a result of this experience of God. In Frossard, beyond the joy, light, and sweetness ("the miracle lasted a month"), the modification lies in religious certainty: "God exists and it is all true"; in a new grasp of the world: "There is an order in the universe and at its head, beyond the dazzling veil of mist, is evidence of God, evidence which has become presence"; lastly in a readiness to be taught and to believe: "The teaching of the church was true to the last comma."[9]

With regard to alleged changes, André Billette maintains, on the basis of sixty-eight stories of conversions (seventeen of them studied searchingly in very many interviews), that talk about conversion is both "formed and forming."[10] The transformations are largely anticipated and often correspond to previous, possibly discernable, wishes. The function of the talk is precisely to strengthen and maintain them. In other words, the witness also needs listeners or readers to confirm him in his conversion. Moreover this will appear psychologically normal in all spheres of life but will invite a return to the obviously alluring idea of conversion as an abrupt, wholesale, largely inexplicable transformation. "As a phenomenon of the word, reinterpreting and making decisions, the first change in a conversion is in the word, the confession, the profession of faith, and, consequently, the anticipation. The change anticipated in the discourse is not yet quite in existence, perhaps never will be. The theme of "reconciliation," so frequent in stories of conversion, is not accomplished in fact, despite very positive affirmations; this personal fulfillment can only be fully realized by resolving real contradictions . . ."[11] on the relational and collective level. It may even happen, adds Billette, that the anticipatory discourse, instead of setting real change in motion, becomes an obstacle to it, notably through its spiritualizing, abstract, or exclusively emotional content.

When it is the other who speaks

But there are cases, too, in which the one who talks about his encounters with the other is so little aware of himself that he obliterates himself and speaks only of that other and his wishes. So he becomes the other's voice in talk of love, or the Voice of the Other in religious talk.

Moses, indeed, returns from Mount Sinai with the Tables of the Law and breaks them in indignant protest at certain compromises under Aaron's leadership. He obliterates himself behind the words and acts which founded the religion of Judaism.

That is the origin of the prophetic *style:* when the prophets speak of God, it is God himself who speaks through them. Their personal autobiography or their "states of mind" count for little except to groan and complain frequently about the tasks God entrusts to them.

St. Paul, a sudden convert, gives Christian communities their first theology in which the episode on the Damascus road figures only very discreetly. St. Francis, St. Teresa, St. John of the Cross only speak of themselves in order to show us trails, roads, paths, or ladders which might be of use to others on a journey, a march, or a climb toward the Ineffable, beyond not only all visual representation but even beyond all words. In Greek, the mystic is a "mute."

In short, the difference is considerable between certain stories of conversions (Claudel, Frossard) and the spiritual writings on which religions are based (Moses, St. Paul) or spiritual families (whether they look to Assisi or Carmel). The first give rise to an initial shiver at the approach of an inexplicably transforming Ineffable; the second open up the austere roads of ascesis, sing hymns of hope, elaborate laborious channels of charity. "It is not those who see God who are saints, it is those who believe in him," wrote St. Teresa of Avila. Perhaps we must *learn* to lean on each other. A few indications in that direction will be offered by way of conclusion.

CONCLUSION

Not all converts claim to have had a personal experience of God. But if a story of conversion is presented on the basis of such an experience, the preceding reflections will invite us to raise the following questions:

1) How much of the story is devoted to an autobiography of the author and how much to the divine encounter proper?[12]

2) In the description given of the encounter with God, do we have solely or mainly an emotional reverberation? Do we also have consequences in the life of the convert that flow from a new grasp of the divine mystery?

3) Which particular features of the divine mystery are shown

in a new light? Does the author tackle it by means of a particular vocabulary or style? Is he an innovator?[13]

4) Lastly, does the story suggest a spiritual trail, an approach or method of prayer which would allow the readers, in their turn, to make some aspects of the convert's experience their own?

The more the author focuses attention on his own life without presenting anything that might renew and enrich the image each one has of God, the more religiously insignificant his story is. In an extreme case, it would no longer be a question of God at all; it would flatter the reader's wish without drawing him toward the reality it claims to talk about. As for suddenness, real or pretended, it has *no* valid claim to be a criterion in discerning an experience of God. Sudden or not, this experience is only said to be "of God" by an interpretation that must seek justification elsewhere. It remains true that to be approached by God, directly transformed by God, will always keep a kind of dream flavor for that is its fascination for psychologically natural religiosity: "the divine ambush" (Frossard) of a God who has nothing to do with human methods.

Notes

1. *Comment je suis devenu athée,* a ten-page manuscript (1975); a personal communication with permission to use it. At the time the author was twenty-four.

2. Gustav Jahoda, *The Genesis of Non-belief,* a fifty-two page manuscript, partially published in *New Outlook* (1957). The episode reproduced is on p. 13 of the complete text.

3. The English sample comes from questionnaires handed out in the Worker's Educational Association. Most of the respondents belonged to the middle class. The questionnaire consisted of three open questions on changes in beliefs or attitudes in the course of life—when, why, and under what influence they happened.

4. From this point of view, John Kildahl compared the personality traits (by the "Multiphasic Minnesota" questionnaire) of forty Lutheran theology students carefully paired by social coordinates. He found that each of the twenty "sudden converts" was relatively less intelligent but particularly more hysteroid (slightly extrovert with a tendency toward

expressive self-display) than each of the other twenty with *no* conversion in their religious past ("Personality Correlates of Sudden Religious Converts Contrasted with Persons of Gradual Development," paper given at the Annual Conference of the Society for the Scientific Study of Religion, 12 April, 1958, *Abstract,* pp. 3-4, using a dissertation for a doctorate in clinical psychology, University of New York, 1957). It should be noted, however, that "conversion" has long been a more or less institutionalized stage in religious growth in adolescence in Protestant environments. All told, the knowledge of psychological traits peculiar to "sudden converts" was not studied in much depth, in spite of two clinically interesting chapters in G. Berguer, *Traité de psychologie de la religion* (Lausanne: Payot, 1946).

5. André Frossard, *Dieu existe, je l'ai rencontré* (Paris: Fayard, 1969).

6. Ibid., pp. 14 and 15.

7. Charles L. Harper, "Spirit-filled Catholics: Some Biographical Comparisons," in *Social Compass* XXI, 3 (1974), pp. 311-324.

8. Henri Guillemin, *Le converti Paul Claudel* (Paris: Gallimard, 1968).

9. Frossard, *Dieu existe,* pp. 166-170. So the readers will know no more about this "encounter with God" which very mysteriously refers them to the church after the previous 150 pages sought to "prove" the church was totally ignored, unknown, and absent. St. Paul's report to the early Christian communities was less secretive, since the story tells us that "he persecuted them." But for the convert Frossard, God *has to* come from nothing. That is the trick.

10. André Billette, *Récits et réalités d'une conversion* (Montreal: Presses de l'Université, 1975). A recent and refreshing emphasis on "knowing as transforming event" (the cognitive aspect in conversion), is introduced by J. E. Loder, *The Transforming Moment: Understanding Convictional Experience* (San Francisco: Harper & Row, 1981). Interesting information from a religious and pastoral angle could be found also (with an excellent bibliography) in V. B. Gillespie, *Religious Conversion and Personal Identity: How and Why People Change* (Birmingham, Ala: Religious Education Press, 1979).

11. Ibid., p. 217. A discussion that coincides with this conclusion of Billette's studies had been presented a few years earlier by Jean-Francois Six, "Sur le livre d'André Frossard," in *Informations Catholiques Internationales* (15 October, 1969), p. 23.

12. It is enough, then, to count the pages in the two categories to obtain a first quantitative assessment of the religious significance or insignificance of a publication of this type. For André Frossard (*Dieu existe je l'ai rencontré*), this count reveals 160 exclusively autobiographical pages in a volume of 170 pages. There are *three* on the encounter itself and *seven* on the wholesale consequences of this experience ("The teach-

ing of the Church was true to the last comma," p. 171). By way of contrast we could point to the book of the convert J. P. Jossua, *Un homme cherche Dieu* (Paris: Cerf, 1979, 115 pages). We find seven *lines* on the fulgurating experience ("The universe being suddenly inhabited, my life turned round on itself. . . . Yes, I was visited. But at present I am trying to discover *by whom*, with the patience that only writing allows," p. 7). All the rest is research, discoveries and doubts, expectations and certainties, discussions and details, frontiers accepted and frontiers pushed back for the building of better towns. An amazing volume, with its rigor and fidelity, its fervor and serene humor: "All the reworkings are possible, but not all the origins" (p. 69). Unlike the first story, this one offers opportunities for maximal Christian meaning. On the other hand, if the former, broadly supported by the latent wish of a spontaneous religiosity, can hope to sell almost 100,000 copies, the latter has little chance of getting beyond 10,000. The voice of the Other, with its wishes for the world, is not so easy to listen to, since it would arouse us from our dreams.

13. But, you will ask, what can a convert say about God that is new? And from a Christian point of view is not revelation closed forever? This is a false problem, seeming to suppose as it does that a semantic area can ever be closed when dealing with God, whether the Christian one or others. The vast unbridgeable gulf that yawns in matters concerning God, on the contrary, invites a surge of creativity in theologies, liturgies, poetry, constantly reconstructing once more the tenuous link that binds each man, each group, each culture to the God (or gods) in question. Semantically, it should be possible to designate God by the greatest number of words in the linguistic repertory, of concepts in a philosophical repertory, of metaphorical images in an artistic repertory. Of course we are a long way from that, and indeed the opposite is true (see J. P. Deconchy, *L'orthodoxie*, pp. 57-114). God and the gods are much too powerful for men not to cage them, even semantically, in verbal enclosures. Should we not expect "converts," especially if they have "met God," to destroy such gags when they are writers, poets, theologians, journalists, orators? At any rate, those are the criteria that could be used to appreciate their books.

3

Intense Experiences

"Moment, stay; thou art so fair." It is sometimes said that this phrase of Goethe is a wish for eternity. But has the wish for time to stand still anything to do with the eternity of God and the philosophers? Or anything to do with the Judeo-Christian God intervening in the history of man? In this chapter and the next we shall be considering intense experiences: sudden, unforeseen peak-experiences or laboriously induced emotions which seem to offer a view, beyond the different appearances, on to the stable core, transcendent or immanent, which makes the unity of the world.

"You pray in your distress and in your need. May you pray, too, in the fullness of your joy and your days of abundance," wrote the poet Kahlil Gibran.[1] And Baudelaire, that magician with words, spoke of those privileged moments as "true favors" holding up a "magic mirror in which man is invited to see himself in the beauty that should and could be his: a kind of angelic excitement, a call to order in the form of a compliment" (quoted by Gilbert Maire).[2]

In your own existence, have you known certain privileged moments after which your life seemed to take on a new value? Is there not something divine, at least potentially, in these intense and bewildering emotions?

PEAK-EXPERIENCES

Twenty-five years ago, American psychology nearly underwent a revolution. A psychologist had discovered happy people and was endeavoring to understand them by distinguishing them from the rest or, more precisely, by recognizing a special dynamic peculiar to them. A revolution, because scientific psychology is accustomed to studying conduct based on needs, wants, deficiencies and is more familiar with the milestones along the road toward a problematical maturity than with manifestations of that maturity itself, if by chance it is to be found.

Abraham Maslow had just been elected president of the Personality and Social Psychology division of the American Psychology Association. On the first of September, 1956, in his presidential address, Maslow declared that the so-called "psychological laws" must be completely revised. They had been worked out from a study of human beings during growth (children and adolescents), in a state of deficiency (sickly, neurotic), or more generally in a state of development. The study of motivations in particular always assumed the idea of a goal to be attained, an action with the hallmark, more or less, of dissatisfaction or fear of not attaining the goal; in short, ordinarily it reflected some dissatisfaction, at least relative. Conative behavior had been studied to the detriment of expressive behavior.

Once Maslow began to question people who were successful in life, concentrating on certain peak-experiences which had inspired or marked out their lives, he discovered that their motivations and modes of perception of the universe, of things, of people involved characteristics hitherto unknown in general psychology. Several of these characteristics could easily figure as "religious" although found in profane achievements of existence: success in sport (athletic), intellectual or therapeutic intuitions, artistic creativity, sexual or parental activities, "oceanic" emotions (mystical), etc.

Maslow's subsequent work may perhaps have revolutionized only the department of psychology at Brandeis University (Waltham, Massachusetts, USA) where he taught. Even so, it will have left a permanent mark in the field of psychology. It raised the question of religious experience,[3] specific or not, in terms different from those of William James whose research, stamped with the hypothesis of the specific nature of religious experience, had opened a road which, in the long run, had seemed to lead nowhere.[4]

After prolonged interrogation of personalities typified by their happy success in various spheres, Maslow analyzed their descriptions of those peak-experiences and moments of high accomplishment that had remained in their memory. From among some twenty features peculiar to these peak-experiences, we shall single out those most frequently alluded to and designated by Maslow as taking on a religious value.[5]

The "basis" of existence

The peak-experience, or its object, is seen as an *absolute* in itself: it brings its own justification and is totally nonutilitarian. It is revealed as an end, a temporary one, at least, and no longer as a means to something else. This object (which may be an entirely inward affective state), all-embracing and captivating, depending on how it is perceived, somehow unveils the "basis" of existence while everything else is reorganized as figures, episodes, or parts of the decor, which derive their unity and are recognized as significant thanks only to that experience. The same is true, for example, of falling in love; all previous friendships are reorganized and fulfilled in that one.

A "value" in life

On the basis of the peak-experience and with reference to it, everyday life is *worth* living, even though ideas of death may feature in certain cases, not as a suicidal movement but rather as a wish to make time stand still so that the experience blends into an eternal present. The same is true of esthetic or religious contemplation (Maslow calls it "oceanic"), in which the subject subordinates himself completely to the "value" thus shared: this is the absolute, the totality which is imposed on everything else and reorganizes it.

An actively received "gift"

The relationship to the object (or the vivid awareness of the inner emotion) in the peak-experience is lived in joy and ineffable admiration, but also with a kind of *wonder* "as for a gift actively received, with a kind of humility, awe, and a sense of personal unworthiness" (pp. 15-16). This can also be true, it must be said, of the moment when a record is arduously broken in sport, or of a scientific discovery, a poetic or musical work. In those cases, is there not talk of inspiration as from a muse or visiting angel? The impression that the peak-experience is received with the feeling "I don't deserve this" is particularly striking in the observations of Maslow's respondents because they have felt it spontaneously, and in spheres where it is not suggested by interpretative or learned religious language. This prereligious feature is an observation of great interest.

The release of defenses and cure

The effects of these experiences are that *fears are allayed,* defenses, inhibitions, and checks are reduced, a state of empathy or sympathy is created, bringing with it an outgoing, tolerant, forgiving attitude. "I met two subjects who, because of such an experience, were totally, immediately, and permanently cured of a chronic anxiety neurosis (in one case) and, in the other case, of strong obsessional thoughts of suicide."[6]

Capacity for "regression to a playful mode"

With the benefit of the peak-experience, certain people become capable of behaving "regressively" by way of expressing the fulfillment currently being felt. "The person incapable of abandoning himself like a child in the arms of another," wrote one, "will never be able to know the deepest joys of love." Or might it be love that allows regression into sexual play? In the peak-experience (love, art, religion) regressive conduct is presented neither as pathological behavior (unconsciously conditioned) nor as the effect of an effort of will (as would be the case in a psychodrama with a therapeutic purpose). Rather it is an excessive feeling of happiness bursting forth into expressiveness, particularly of a bodily kind.

Experiences accessible to the greatest number

In time, Maslow discovered that a large number of people had known such privileged moments, at least in one sphere, even if their success remained socially modest and almost unknown outside their immediate circle. Finally, he turned his attention to people who denied having known these moments of fulfillment; he became convinced that they had come very close to such occurrences but had side-stepped them out of some kind of fear of the irrational, of such a blossoming out in affective abandon, or indeed for fear of using childish (regressive) expressions as a means of making them manifest or talking about them.

Religious experiences?

We must bear in mind that Maslow uses the term to describe the general components of a rediscovered "state of grace," whatever the sphere in which the privileged peak-experience occurs: the athlete accepts his record as a gift "granted him," however much effort he may have put into training; the poet receives gratuitous inspiration; the lover starts living for love of the other; the mystic feels himself to be a passive recipient of illumination or movement. The impression of fulfillment goes hand-in-hand with that of a *received* fulfillment. That is probably a very important feature of the highest human experiences in which a philosopher might read their profound intentionality.

In fact, these privileged moments can be *interpreted* as religious and believers regularly do so. But Maslow understands them, if we may use the expression, on a lower level than these conscious interpretations. He brings together all the common features, the main ones of which we have just reviewed, and analyzes them from a humanist, possibly gnostic point of view, so he is not looking for a specific religious quality (Christian, Buddhist, etc.). Such a quality would even be played down. For Maslow, there is neither prophet nor word of God.

He acknowledges, too, that he has not sought descriptions of another category of "abyss"-experiences, sometimes mentioned by the same subjects: a vivid awareness of the inevitability of death, of individual solitude at moments of major decisions incurring responsibility, of distress at the cold impersonality of nature, of the strangeness of our own unconscious, of revolt in the face of insuperable injustice. Maslow dismisses these, perhaps too easily, as provisional situations, as if experiences of the "void" (the absurd, nausea, vertigo) were not also capable of revealing a fundamental aspect of existence.

According to Maslow, the most religious feature of the various peak-experiences would be "the lively perception that the entire universe is an integrated and unified whole" (1964, p. 69). He adds shrewdly that "many rigidly orthodox believers would be so alarmed at abandoning the idea that the universe derives its unity and meaning from the fact that it is created by God, or governed by God, or even that it is God himself (according to different beliefs), that their only alternative would be to perceive it as chaos, incapable of any integration at all" (p. 60).

That a peak-experience might be transforming and that it refers to a transformation to be actively introduced into the world, these are possibilities that Maslow does not consider. Peak-experiences for him are moments of completeness and are self-justifying. So he is looking only at the passive-emotion-experiences with a few automatic deconditioning effects in operation (cures). He himself is convinced that if organized religions do not aim to communicate and multiply such peak-experiences they will destroy themselves through failing to achieve what he sees as their main task. He is saying, in the clearest possible way, that religious organizations can only survive by becoming "functional" and satisfying the religiosity that spontaneously expects these privileged moments.

SO-CALLED TRANSCENDENT EMOTIONS

If we consider with Maslow that the most religious feature of peak-experiences is a vivid awareness that the entire universe is an integrated and unified whole, we cannot avoid a brief examination of certain ecstatic states that are systematically induced to that end. These "experimental" attempts have tempted psychologists of religion for a long time. As early as 1902, William James was writing that by the use of nitrous oxide he experienced "a vivid feeling of reconciliation . . . as if the opposites of the world, whose contradictoriness and conflict make all our difficulties and troubles, were melted into unity."[7] The use of LSD-25 (lysergic acid) gave a new impetus to these experiments some fifteen years ago. In minute doses, possibly under medical supervision, LSD has an interesting characteristic: It gives many experimenters, not only the impression of "standing off from oneself" with wonderful visions such as other hallucinogens produce, but rather the impression of being "at the core of one's being" of having never been "so fully oneself." In spite of some regrettable excesses on the part of one of the American promoters (Timothy Leary), LSD (a formidable drug in large doses) is not in itself addictive and the contemplative state it releases has, according to certain authors, a lasting beneficial effect.

Joseph Havens has provided a first critical examination of research published up to 1964. These are the conclusions he reached:

1. The states produced by LSD and the effects of the experience vary widely, from blissful contemplation to psychotic dissociations, from a feeling of intense love to discordantly aggressive urges, from joy to feelings of panic terror.

2. The religious orientation of the states provoked depends largely on the previous personality of the subject, but not on his expectations immediately before the experience.

3. Of eighty-two subjects at Harvard, more than half experienced principally certain feelings characteristic of mysticism,

according to W. T. Stace[8]: unitary consciousness integrating various functional levels (even regressive) into an all-encompassing, blissful emotion; loss of time sense; a richer, fuller, more colorful perception of objects; extreme pleasure, ecstasy, cosmic joy; an impression of being at the center where all things are "one" and of recognizing their profound unity; the indescribable nature of the experience.

4. With ten subjects studied individually with great care, almost all mentioned a permanent change in their subsequent life.[9]

Havens refuses to make a distinction, in this connection, between so-called subjective states and a pseudo-objective reality: the novelty of the affective contact, intensified, *is a fact* which is immediately enriched, if only in the mind of the subject, by metaphorical or symbolic *interpretations* which give it a social or religious bearing. Indeed, this seems to be of capital importance in order to go beyond subjectivism and approach the formally religious perspective of these vivid experiences, without abandoning the scientific approach.

The richness of this new emotional experience produced by LSD exposes the subject to two dangers, as Havens points out: a) accentuating a notion of religion as withdrawal from the world, with a weakening of the will to work effectively in it; b) developing a sort of cult centered on the ecstatic experience itself. It is known that drug smokers develop complicated rituals according to which they light the grass, pass the reefers round, swap recipes. On the same lines, we may recall that the Indians of Mexico and South America finished by making the *peyotl* plant itself sacred, just as the Indians and the Iranians did with the *soma* plant (or *haoma* in the hymns of the Rig-Veda).

Another examination of experiences based on drugs and a discussion of their implications was presented by Walter Houston Clark, a psychologist of religion and author of a well-known manual of religious psychology.[10]

Lasting religious effects

Clark described in detail what he himself experienced in the course of well-controlled experiments using lysergic acid. These are his conclusions from the religious point of view.

Although my experience had nothing specifically theological in its content, and I did not have the impression of having met God, it seemed to me to be profoundly religious for four reasons: a) I had been in contact with a new, ultraterrestrial domain with a horizon opening on to eternity and beyond; b) I had been through a sort of conversion which had modified me and helped to make me more integrated; c) I had experienced a feeling of belonging to the human community far deeper than any I had known in my church community; d) I had considerably extended my capacity to grasp the language of religion and understand the nature of the religious mentality.[11]

Clark's descriptive evidence shows clearly that the intense experience produced by LSD *becomes* religious only when set in a symbolic context, that of the language habitually used by the churches: conversion to something ultraterrestrial, a source of light and strength, the possibility of making this new contact permanent by active attitudes in daily life.

Discussion

It is difficult to challenge *a priori* the analysis of the states produced by LSD and the religious transformations resulting from experiments as well-controlled as Clark's. Nobody disputes that these are artificially induced emotions, like those achieved by shamans and whirling dervishes in order to reach a state of trance. The Tibetan liturgy, too, uses resins from hallucinogenic plants in order to enable their soothsayer-priests to pronounce oracles,[12] unintelligible words that others must interpret for the worshipers. Is it not a Christian tradition to use intermediaries like music, incense, architecture, prolonged silence, or fasting to produce devotional states? It is true that ordinarily the Christian neither wants nor claims to use these devotional states to achieve an encounter with God that can then be told, transposed into a useful tale for Christians. He would be much more inclined to wait for such states as unpredictable gifts from God (the "gift of tears" for example). Difficult though it may be, it is nevertheless essential to make a distinction between intense emotion, ecstasy with or without trance, trance with or without possession, and possession that is mute or issued forth in speech that may or may not be intelligible without interpretation. But, elementary as these distinctions are, they lie outside the scope of this chapter.[13]

The similarities pointed out by Havens and Clark between the expressions used by the subjects in these experiments and the verbal categories often used by mystics (according to W. T. Stace) are of obvious interest. However, we may hesitate to subscribe to Stace's assertion that: "*If* the phenomenological descriptions of the two experiences [with or without drugs] are indistinguishable, so far as can be ascertained, then it cannot be denied that if one is a genuine mystical experience the other is also."[14] This principle, which he calls "causal indifference" should be treated, if not with reservation, at least with flexibility when dealing with observations in the human sciences.

In the first place these observations simply show that under the influence of LSD-induced emotions and impressions the only language available to most of the subjects at Harvard in which to describe what they were experiencing was religious and even, in other contexts, mystical. In short, the situation was the opposite of that of certain nonexperimental mystics when they use the language of love to describe their feelings during contemplation. Would the methodological position of "causal indifference" lead us equally to say that these mystics are having an "authentically amorous" experience—no more and no less?

Next, on the subject of the language produced, no psychologist can fail to examine the social context and, above all, that of the psychological motivations underlying and encompassing these LSD experiences. Is the social context one of pleasure? of psychological research or experiment? of moral reeducation, as in the case of certain delinquents? Is the psychological motivation one of psychological experimentation undertaken in a scientific or humanist frame of mind? Or, as in the case of W. H. Clark, has it already a religious orientation? And if so, is it slanted more toward reaching some understanding of mystical psychology or is it rather a possibly ambiguous means of getting in touch with the absolute, the sacred, the divine?[15] These are some of the questions that, psychologically, must be asked before proclaiming, in the name of the "causal indifference" principle, that the states obtained are authentically mystical. We must compare like with like; a prolonged fast might well have conscious and unconscious connotations very different from the absorption of a drug. Their implications for the language used to describe the states experienced would be intricate.

Lastly—and this perhaps is what is at stake in these experiments—anything resembling a psychic state, experimentally induced and then described by comparison with a vocabulary recognized as mystical in primitive cultures, in Christian literature or oriental traditions, calls for a clearer idea of what a formally religious experience may be: not a passively experienced "state of mind" but a personal reaction in, about, or on the basis of that state. This reaction begins the moment what is "lived" takes shape in what is "spoken."

CONCLUSION

Reflection on peak-experiences and on intense experiences, whether spontaneous or experimental, brings out more clearly the conditions in which other experiences, felt internally, can be said to be divine:

a) They must first be *interpreted* in a religious manner. This interpretation bears, of necessity, the mark of the surrounding culture and the education received. Any state experienced will, as such, always be ambiguous: there must be a veil in relation to the Transcendent, but unveiling may be possible. There can be no mystic experiences without linguistic, and so hermeneutic, activity, however modest. Once told, these experiences become significant.

b) They must be *accepted* according to their meaning and *mediated* in an attitude leaning towards commitment, which is the only means of ensuring that their value is permanently inscribed in the subject's existence and leaves a mark on society. No *mystic* experience exists without a reaction of liberty so as to outstrip the moment and inscribe the promise or invitation into conduct of daily life. By analogy with the movements of sexuality whose discontinuous impulses are transformed into a stable and lasting love, religiosity and its occasionally intense experiences expect to be actively built into faithfulness.

To sum up: No "pathic" experience, which is manifested affectively, constitutes an unambiguous revelation of the divine. Any experience of that kind, whether spontaneous or artificially induced, enjoys the same status: it appeals to or awakens an *intentionality* inherent in human existence, a polymorphous intentionality which tends to manifest itself in the ambiguity or intense experiences that are immediately picked up and shaped by the culture or religions *in situ*.

An awakening of religious intentionality: This is the interest of the experiences in religious and Christian revivalist groups which will be analyzed psychologically in the next two chapters.

Notes

For some years now psycho-physiological research into cerebral states induced by contemplative ascesis has provided unexpected observations that stimulate reflection. They concern differential encephalographic tracings obtained from people who have steadfastly followed the methods of contemplation practiced in certain spiritual traditions.

As early as 1969 Charles T. Tart published *Altered States of Consciousness* (New York: Wiley, 1969). In it there is a good selection of thirty-four pieces of experimental research, ranging from states induced by hypnosis or drugs to dream manifestations, four of which concern the cerebral, neurological peculiarities of people trained in various methods of meditation. Zen Buddhist meditation is accompanied by a predominance of Alpha rhythms, frequent and slow, with the eyes open, indicating psychomotor relaxation with the consciousness in a state of great vigilance and in contact with the outside world. Those qualified in the Kriya-Yoga method of meditation display a predominance of rapid Theta waves, with eyes closed but not asleep, indicating a state of great excitement but without response to external stimuli. These differentiations are summed up and discussed in *The Electroencephalogram, Meditation and Mysticism,* supplied in a double number of the Bucke Memorial Society *Newsletter-Review* V, 1-2 (Montreal, Spring, 1972). The articles by Victor F. Emerson and Thomas B. Mulholland show the interest of this bioneurological approach for a new classification of so-called "mystic" states. Note that the electroencephalograms are very different in states induced by LSD or other drugs.

These studies are mentioned here simply for information. What can they lead to? Do not hitherto unsuspected modifications introduced by meditation into the cerebral functioning direct attention to rather futile transformations? Do not these psychic states, researched during hundreds of hours of relaxation or concentration, as the case may be, appear religiously insignificant? Now that biofeedback apparatus allows us to obtain from ourselves, in a few hours, countless Alpha and Theta rhythms with their psychological concomitants—much more efficiently, or at least more rapidly than through the initiations of Zen or the Maharishi Mahesh Yogi or the school of St. Ignatius—are we not forced at last to open our eyes to the religious meaning of it all: enjoyment of an anticipated nirvana, far removed from the world? acquisition of a new, humanist mastery over the production of our own affective states? the claim of a way to God? to what God? All told, those questions are not foreign to the subject matter of this book. Indeed they take on a certain sharpness which makes this digression worthwhile.

1. Kahlil Gibran, *Le Prophète* (Brussels, Universelle, Cahiers des Poètes catholiques, 1940, original edition, p. 66. New translation: Paris and Tournai: Casterman, 1956).

2. Gilbert Maire, *Les instants privilégiés* (Paris: Aubier, 1962), pp. 13-16.

3. Abraham Maslow, *Religion, Values and Peak-Experiences* (Columbus: Ohio State University Press, 1964). Maslow clarifies certain of his differentiations in mystic states, with reference to Buddhism and regressive states, in "Notes toward a Psychology of Being" in *Report No. 7* (12 pages, 26 July 1961), Western Behavioral Sciences Institute, La Jolla, California, 1961.

4. In this connection, see J. P. Deconchy, "La définition de la religion chez W. James," in *Archives de Sociologie des Religions* 27 (1969), pp. 51-70.

5. The following summary and quotations come from the 1956 presidential address, "Cognition of Being in the Peak-Experiences." A slightly expanded but sometimes less incisive version can be found in A. Maslow, *Towards a Psychology of Being* (New York: Van Nostrand, 1962), chapter 6, pp. 67-96.

6. Maslow, *Religions, Values and Peak-Experiences*, p. 59.

7. William James, *The Varieties of Religious Experience* (New York: Longmans, 1902), p. 387 of the undated reedition, New York, Modern Library.

8. W. T. Stace, *Mysticism and Philosophy* (Philadelphia: Lippincott, 1960).

9. Joseph Havens, "Memo on the Religious Implications of the Consciousness-Changing Drugs," in *Journal for the Scientific Study of Religion* III (1964), pp. 216-226.

10. W. H. Clark, *The Psychology of Religion* (New York: Macmillan, 1958). His main study of induced ecstatic states is *Chemical Ecstasy* (New York: Sheed and Ward, 1969). Comparisons between the results of the experimenters (W. N. Pahnke, S. M. Unger, for example) and analyses of the language of the mystics (conducted by R. C. Zaehner and W. T. Stace) can be found in his article "Mysticism as a Basic Concept" in *From Religious Experience to a Religious Attitude* (Brussels: Lumen Vitae, 1964), pp. 47-58. W. H. Clark figures among the authors of nine contributions on the use of drugs in a socially organized religious context (notably in Peru) in a booklet with a very good introduction by D. H. Salman (co-editor with R. H. Prince), *Do Psychedelics Have Religious Implications?* (Montreal: Bucke Memorial Society, 1969). There are also three good accounts by W. H. Clark, in reply to some excellent opponents (notably the anthropologist, A. R. Tippett) in the volume *Religious Experience: Its Nature and Function in the Human Psyche* (The First John G. Finch Symposium on Psychology and Religion; Springfield, Illinois, Charles Thomas, 1973). These last two publications give the best theoretical discussions on the whole question of religious experiences, individual and induced.

11. W. H. Clark, "Religion and the Consciousness-Expanding Substances," in *Religion Ponders Science*, ed. Edwin Booth (New York: Appleton-Century, 1964), pp. 3-16 (quotation p. 10).

12. Exceptionally interesting interviews with five soothsayer-priests, recently emigrated from Tibet to northern India, are reported and commented on by Günter Schüttler, *Die letzten tibetischen Orakelpriester* (Wiesbaden: Franz Steiner Vg.; Collection "Forschungen zur Ekstase,"

1971). Once there is an oracle, and so speech, however, we are outside the limits of this chapter on intense experiences as transcendent *emotions*. In reality discontinuities tend to be effaced: What is "possession" if not a state of ecstasy or trance *interpreted* as such?

13. These different states of the psychism would be found a prey to religious emotions that are well studied and distinguished (as far as possible) in *Trance and Possession States*, ed. R. Prince (Montreal: Bucke Memorial Society, 1968). A world distribution map of these states, whether interpreted as "possession" or not, is presented by Erika Bourguignon, "World Distribution and Pattern of Possession States," pp. 3-34.

14. Stace, *Mysticism and Philosophy*, pp. 29-30.

15. The undeniable popularity of these drug-reinforced, transcendent emotions probably stems from the fact that they prolong and seem to promise an outcome to small, fleeting experiences, typical of spontaneous religiosity. Who would have thought, before a sociological survey was made, that, of a representative sample in the United States (1400 persons), 35 percent would reply "yes" to the following question: "Have you sometimes felt that you were very close to a powerful spiritual force that seemed about to lift you out of yourself?" Half these people even specified that it had happened "several times" or "often." The groups in which this feeling was affirmed more particularly included, with significant differences, men, over forty years old, those who had pursued their studies at least up to college level and had incomes of more than $10,000. A. M. Greeley and W. C. McReady, *The Sociology of Mystical Ecstasy* (Some Preliminary Notes; Chicago: National Opinion Research Center, 1975). Extracts presented prior to publication in Bucke Memorial Society *Newsletter-Review* VII, 1-2 (Spring, 1974), pp. 61-65.

4

Fusional Joy as an Experience of the Spirit

(Charismatic Groups)

Concerning religious experiences and addressing himself to the church authorities, Abraham Maslow wrote:

> Any religion, whether liberal or orthodox, theist or not, must be not only intellectually credible and morally worthy of respect but also emotionally satisfying. And I mean to include here emotions of the transcendent type corresponding to the need for respect, for giving, for humility, for worship, for sacrifice. . . . (Without this) all we now get is a vague, cold philosophy of life, colorless, dull, unexciting, unemotional, which fails to do what traditional religions accomplished in their great days . . . including wild, joyful, eruptive, emotionally satisfying experiences.[1]

A Christianity that is "not only credible but emotionally satisfying"; at present this request of Maslow's seems to be met by the vivid and joyous, pentecostal type of spiritual experience being practiced nowadays in Catholic and ecumenical prayer groups by the so-called charismatic revival. The typical features of the peak-experience, taken from Maslow in the preceding chapter, are being re-introduced by the Pentecostalists and Charismatics as group experiences in which the Holy Spirit becomes perceptible to the heart. In that case, "how can we not be charismatics?"

100

That is the question posed by André Méhat at the beginning of his autobiography.[2] And his answer oscillates between "how could I not have been?" and "haven't I always been?"

Indeed, there is nothing to prevent anybody from attributing these lively experiences to the action of the Spirit, by an interpretation based on faith. But when aroused and lived communally the charismatic experience has other interesting connotations. It develops in a climate of programed spontaneity which is manifestly due to a certain type of leadership that responds to expectations or wishes latent in certain strata of the Christian population in Western culture.

Starting from the belief, undoubtedly fundamental to Christianity, that union between men and God is possible because it is already there in Jesus Christ and the mystery of the Trinity, the pentecostal element in the charismatic revival develops prayer meetings and a few communes centered on praise. The theme or feeling is of Christ "with us here and now"; any witness is welcome so long as it reinforces this conviction or experience, and living incidents, often very moving, are told in abundance; they are immediately celebrated, but rarely is their interpretation discussed. Is it not obviously the work of the Holy Spirit? Is the witness not corroborated by a climate of spontaneous prayer and a freedom of bodily gestures in the service of prayer? Is it not expressed in the graciousness of the welcome, suggested in the friendly audacity of a joyous proselytism, confirmed, in a word, by a *living faith*? Moreover, how is the idea of an *immediacy* in the action of the Spirit to be resisted in view of the superabundance of demonstrations of it, reminiscent of the charisms considered typical of primitive communities: individuals speaking in tongues and yet, in many French-speaking groups, blending into collectively modulated murmurs; spiritual or prophetic interpretations based on these glossolalias or on texts from the scriptures; layings on of hands, restoring, if not health, at least inner peace; various adorcisms of the Spirit (liturgies renewing baptism) and some exorcisms of the Evil One, the latter very rare in France but more frequent in Switzerland and Canada. How can it be denied that they offer the fruits of the Spirit to whoever is willing to lay hold of them in the group itself?

THE CHARISMATIC EXPLOSION

The results of this encounter between experience lived by the participants and a traditional theological language were not long in coming. To go from *six* Catholics receiving an effusion of the Spirit in January 1967 at Duquesne University, in Pennsylvania, to *six hundred thousand* Catholic members in the United States (one hundred and fifty thousand elsewhere) joining in regular organized prayer meetings ten years later is indeed a remarkable achievement. It did not fail to attract the attention of sociologists. We shall look at some of their data with a more directly psychological import.[3]

JUDGMENT OF CHARISMATICS ON THEIR LIVES BEFORE JOINING THE MOVEMENT

Before joining the movement
(455 neo-pentecostal Catholics—1974)

"My life was without meaning/purpose" 31%

"I was uncertain as to the values to pursue" 45%

"I had gone through a personal crisis
shortly before" 47%

(Among charismatics who speak in tongues, interviewed
by J. P. Kildahl in 1972, this last affirmation
was made by . . . . 85%)

These responses, obtained by B. J. Mawn in the United States are certainly numerically more than a population of nonpentecostal Catholics would give. Moreover, Mary Ellen Greeley developed the comparison using an index *of cultural isolation,* a complex measurement consisting of several features: a negative judgment on the life led by most men, a conviction that existence is full of threats and frustrations, a distaste for the most popular national pastimes.

These dispositions must certainly be related to the cultural crisis of our age: breakdown of the social network, pluralism and confrontations of opinion, ideological and political disputes of all kinds (bitter disappointment of a generation of politically committed youth in the United States whose "campus revolt" had ended tragically in volleys of fire from armed soldiers), a loss of influence by ecclesiastical institutions, aspirations on the part of the laity to take on wider responsibilities in the churches.[4]

DEGREE OF CULTURAL ISOLATION
BEFORE JOINING

Score on the index of isolation	CATHOLICS	
	216 Pentecostals	203 Non-P
High	39%	17%
Medium	40%	37%
Low	21%	46%

By means of qualitative individual psychological interviews, other researchers have established that recruitment to the charismatic groups takes place among Catholics of the middle and upper social strata, whose initial religious fervor was gradually undermined by liturgical formalism, a lack of feeling in prayer, the difficulty of translating into concrete commitments the sometimes innovative themes of a theology which, since Vatican II, was more concerned with deeper research than with consolidation through apologetics.[5]

Effects of the pentecostal experience

Membership in charismatic prayer groups entails an emotional experience that renews a sense of divine presence and action on the part of the participants.

The table (on page 105) shows some changes produced by the religious experience of pentecostal Catholics, according to the researcher already quoted (B. J. Mawn). He also tells us that "while 96 percent of the Catholic pentecostals studied gave an intellectual assent to the Catholic belief system prior to their pentecostal experience, one-third believed without conviction and two-thirds believed without any personal experience."[6]

The conduct of meetings

But *how* does the charismatic movement obtain this renewed sense of divine presence? We can identify certain specific features in the way the meetings are led, in the predominance of interpretation, and in the general structures of the organization of the movement.

PRAYER MEETINGS

Participatory observation at prayer meetings contributes to an understanding of some features of their leadership, given a willingness to ponder the matter afterwards.

Interrupted verbal contributions

Unlike official liturgies in the churches, a charismatic prayer meeting consists of a host of spontaneous contributions (testimonies, prophecies and spiritual messages, words and songs "in tongues," that is, glossolalia followed or not by interpretations, laying on of hands with prayer, etc.). These interventions seem to come one after another, the gaps between being filled with singing of brief invocations (praise, requests). It soon becomes apparent that the object of these contributions is to "build up the group," to

CHANGES IN EXPERIENCE OF GOD
AFTER JOINING CHARISMATIC GROUPS

(B. J. Mawn—455 respondents)

CONFIRMING EXPERIENCE
A vivid and frequent awareness of the divine presence:

"Have you had a feeling of the divine presence in your life?"

	YES	FREQUENTLY
—Before becoming a pentecostal	60%	10%
—After the outpouring of the Spirit	90%	43%

RELATIONAL EXPERIENCE
A feeling that God is active on my behalf: "Have you in your
life had the impression of being saved by Christ?"

	YES
—Before becoming a pentecostal	38%
—After the baptism in the Spirit	91%
(Answers to the same questions asked by Glock and Stark in 1964 of a representative sample of American Catholics	26%)

RELIGIOUSLY MODIFYING EXPERIENCE
A change in an attitude of spontaneous religiosity: "Have you
experienced punishment by God for wrongdoing?"

	YES
—Before becoming a pentecostal	41%
—After baptism in the Spirit	15%

open it to "receive the Spirit," to encourage "availability" by maintaining as far as possible a nonconflictual consensus among the participants. These expressions in quotation marks are the ones used by all the qualified leaders. They can be found too in the Team Manuals produced in America between 1969 and 1972 and quickly translated for wide distribution in various countries where these prayer meetings were beginning to develop.

Free from conflict

The leaders' intention to obtain a climate of prayer in consensus, by reducing demands for detailed examination to a minimum (e.g., with a testimony) or by deflecting attempts at discussion (e.g., with an interpretation of the scripture or of a prophecy) is confirmed in some ten personal interviews with particularly successful charismatic leaders in the United States, Canada, France, and Belgium.[7]

This intention to build up the group "in unity" (not just in union) has another consequence, not always consciously willed but very tangible to the observer. Since most of the variety in opinions, attitudes, and interpretations arises from the participants' background, their readings, and above all the actions they undertake in a divided or professionally compartmentalized society, the precise problems resulting from these family, professional, or social commitments are rarely mentioned in the prayer group. The preferred testimonies tell of "solutions that are more or less sudden and miraculous (chance happenings resolving an otherwise impossible situation) or more or less illusory (generous impulses with no serious analysis of the situations). Political questions are probably the most dangerous to unanimity in prayer: they are practically ignored, as are sexual or financial questions. So the apparent unity is achieved psychologically by keeping silent on a great number of questions relating to life outside the group. If changes are expected there, they are assumed to result from a change of heart and not from a better understanding of the current situations which confront men and women in history and society. In short, class conflicts or structural reforms are seen as concepts that change with fashion and are to be treated with suspicion or simply ignored. A well-known charismatic leader spoke of politics as a virus.

Some may feel this lapse into silence is a very heavy price to pay. But the restoration of a unifying climate is so precious that most people forget the cost or consider it of little importance.

SYSTEM OF INTERPRETATION

This twofold cut-off (contributions interrupted before being adequately explained; avoidance of disagreement by erecting a kind of barrier against the realities of the outside world) encourages a climate of warm unanimity, of spiritual internalization, and the joyful expression of restored unity.

"Immediate" presence of the Spirit

Praise and gratitude find a perfectly natural place, in prayer and singing, once laborious intellectual discourses are circumvented in favor of a collective experience *(Erlebnis)* interpreted as the "immediate" presence of the Spirit. In fact what is immediate is a certain jubilation such as is found at least occasionally in any group where emotionalism is dominant and intellectual communication is reduced. For it to be *interpreted* as a gift of the Spirit is a transition from the sign (here entirely internal and emotional but experienced in the group) to the signification: an experience by active synthesis, which was mentioned in the introduction to this second part. Such a transition is clearly legitimate when experienced in faith. The majority of theologically trained charismatic leaders recognize it as such. But many of the participants are content to live this restored joy and security as a *direct* gift of the Spirit. That they could be the direct effects of a certain type of leadership in the meetings, effects which can be interpreted in faith, is an idea which hardly occurs to them, except to attribute it to the reductionism of the human sciences.

Still less does the idea of human mediation in the service of the Spirit (under certain conditions) occur to them in connection with the phenomenon of glossolalia or of cures by laying on of hands. Excellent articles have examined glossolalia, not as a kind of miracle consisting in speaking a foreign language that has never been learned (this should be called "xenolalia"), but as a phonetic and linguistic activity corresponding to certain laws that are becoming increasingly well understood.[8] In spite of this, participants at reunions where glossolalia is still popular[9] glory in it as an intervention by which the active presence of the Spirit is made manifest: did people not speak in Greek, in Hebrew, perhaps even in Aramaic this evening? The same contrast between the position taken by the leaders and the enthusiasm of the crowd for "miracle cures," when what takes place is spiritual solace with a more or less lasting bodily effect, occurs at large or small healing ceremonies. These ambiguities are openly encouraged, it must be said, not only by certain leaders (they can be excused for being taken in by their own trick!), but by the organization of the major national and international charismatic congresses.[10]

A discontinuous spiritual time

The systematic avoidance of disagreement after contributions has already been pointed out in regard to the conduct of meetings. This is accomplished by a constant movement between the events reported by testimonies (constituting a surprise happening, awaited and much appreciated by the participants at the prayer meeting) and the intervention of the leader whose vocabulary is restricted to a few prestigious words *(praise, love, joy, forgiveness, faith, trust),* and a few interpretative concepts *(providence, fatherhood, brotherhood, outpouring of the Spirit, miracle, salvation, unity, faithfulness, spirit).* What these words and concepts have in common is that they are ahistorical, outside time, sufficiently general to be always true and indisputable. For who would want to speak against love or peace? The very concrete and historically determined situations reported by the witnesses in their contributions thus reveal a relatively simple, latent but constantly recurring, atemporal meaning.

This cut-off by the leader, who superimposes an atemporal language on contributions whose historical concreteness is neither analyzed nor studied in depth, succeeds in structuring a curiously discontinuous spiritual time. The actions of the Spirit, both in the group and in the reported incidents in the lives of individuals, are often designated in sudden, tangential, or scattered happenings which are brought together in this way by the dominant interpretation (mentioning here and there these interventions of the Spirit) so that they shall be recognized. This spiritual discourse is floating above the concrete events more than penetrating them.

The participants in these charismatic assemblies normally live in the history common to all people, but in the long run divine action is experienced as discontinuous, sudden, and irruptive. At least the manner of interpretation tends to show the course of events in this way: a series of momentary but wonderful interventions by the Spirit.[11]

In certain groups, the use of the scriptures by selecting brief passages out of context (sometimes even opening the book at random, a very ancient pentecostal practice) reinforces this particular way of living time spiritually. This is not the place to examine the theological credentials of such a practice. We need only indicate how the discontinuous time of the charismatic experience is built up or how it is reinforced. Indeed it seems that the expectation of timely interventions of divine origin and the interpretation of events on the basis of that expectation are typical of spontaneous religiosity (described in our first part). In this respect the charismatic discourse would be very functional. On the whole it restores features of spontaneous religiosity.

Discussion

Observation of what happens and what is said in countless charismatic prayer meetings links up with one of the fears expressed by the theologian Yves Congar, revealing a theology of immediacy in both charismatic practice and the pentecostal practice which gave birth to it.

A response or solution is sought and found in a brief, immediate, personal account that cuts out long and difficult mediations such as an exegetic approach to the scriptures, analysis of social problems, formulation of questions raised by the crisis in the church linked with the incredible changes in the world."[12]

We must certainly listen to the reply of many charismatic leaders when they maintain that a time of prayer is not a time for discussion, intellectual investigation of the scriptures, or soliciting social commitments. But these other "times" should be made generously available in other places if there is an insistence on maintaining barriers in prayer groups that are not encouraged in other types of Christian revival (as we shall see in the next chapter). And in these other times and places provision should be made for the education of the charismatics through exegesis of the scriptures and sociological analysis of social structures and political changes. Examination of what happens regularly in these (rare) forums for discussion at national or international meetings seems to confirm a certain skepticism in that regard; multidisciplinary study of this type of problem is oddly curtailed or simplified for the benefit of participants who are anxious to resume the jubilant climate of prayer meetings, spiritual meditation on scriptural texts, and reaffirmation (on the basis of anecdotal testimony) of the certainty that all true revolution begins with a conversion of the heart and that the Spirit of Christ *is* the answer.[13]

The point of view of the theologian Congar leads us to suspect a latent theology in which the Spirit is thought to be immediately present in a primary spontaneous simplicity which is rediscovered in a certain innocence protected from the complications or incoherences of the intellectual mediations essential to adult thought and action. The psychologist will want to question leaders who are disposed to shelter Christians (particularly the young ones) from these distortions or risks at a moment in culture or history when they are already inclined to "camp out on the margins of the adults' city."[14] The adults' city—does that not include their Christian churches, riddled with crises that are crying out for reform? By side-stepping these questions or leaving the burden of response to the Spirit alone, what churches are they really reviving?

ORGANIZATIONAL STRUCTURES

To the cut-off typical of the leadership of the prayer group (avoidance of disagreements), which is reflected in various aspects of the main interpretative discourse (temporal discontinuity of the actions of the Spirit), a third must be added which runs through the organization of group life and recurs in the whole institutional structure of the pentecostal movement: who discriminates? Who decides how far the Spirit can be liberated without going . . . too far?

At group level

The organization of a prayer group is not a matter for deliberation, evaluation, or decision on the part of its participants. Even less so are the general orientation of the movement or the programing of activities at regional or national conferences.

A restricted group of elders or experts, acknowledged as possessing the charism of discernment, undertakes the delicate choices, painful decisions (such as the expulsion of a member), changes in leadership, and modifications both at the level of the practical program of the group and at that of the developing group structures. We are witnessing important changes in local or national control. In a few years some of the most charismatically esteemed leaders become undesirable (to whom?); if they are challenged, they are soon removed, even officially spurned by a regional or national committee against which there is no appeal. Their publications, for example, are not only censored but rejected by editorial boards which have become financially very powerful (books, pamphlets, and especially cassettes). For want of a procedure, these practices have become current and accepted in the majority of countries where it has been possible to carry out observations. The press has occasionally latched on to them but not often because the interested parties themselves go along with this state of affairs.

For the last ten or fifteen years, these small nuclei or committees of enlightened persons have undoubtedly often proceeded with caution and wisdom, always collegiately and praying together, sometimes even with the support of generous psychology and enlightened theology. It is nevertheless still true that "in spite of all ideological declarations to the contrary . . . the local assembly in which the 'gifts' are made manifest is not the seat of religious decision." And Jean Seguy went on: "This ambiguity is not merely functional, it is structural."[15]

At the level of the structure of renewal

This abandonment of active participation in decisions concerning the future, not just of each group but of the movement as a whole, is not unpleasing to the majority of charismatics. For many it means greater peace, increased security: "Spiritual availability" is fostered in "psychological docility" in a way which is not very different from that of monks or nuns making their vow of obedience. So it is not surprising that the charismatic renewal has been congratulating itself for some years on discovering, among the fairest fruits of the Spirit, the appearance of living communes ranging from shared prayer to cohabitation and sometimes a certain sharing of goods. They regroup lay people, married or single, drawn largely from the middle class and the liberal professions, around formulae for life that are still experimental and sometimes expressed in a sort of founding charter presented to a bishop for approval.[16] It is noticeable, too, that, once founded and approved, these new foundations develop original practices in prayer that are sometimes quite far removed from the neo-pentecostalism of the early days.

The abandonment of activities of discernment into the hands of a few, however wise and well-balanced, is not without repercussions on the Christian experience itself. If discernment figures in the list of charisms as a "gift" of superior quality, it contains a component of practical decision (active synthesis, as we have seen earlier, *Erfahrung*) which assumes that various intellectual mediations come into play in the concrete analysis of social or personal situations. Now, experiences of the Spirit based on lively emotion *(Erlebnis)* are hardly an adequate preparation for this. Several charismatic leaders lament the rarity of the charism of discernment, which according to them should be asked for in prayer and obtained by a much greater number, if not by all. They fail to see that it is the functioning of the present organization that prevents or reduces its dissemination: the places of prayer, in which (for a great many) the other "gifts" are made manifest, are separated, as J. Seguy noted, from the places of decision (reserved for a few).

There remains too the danger of a pervasive authoritarianism among certain local leaders, since the institutional structure provides neither for election nor for rotation of management. A rotation limiting the period of power for spiritual officers and leaders of national or regional committees would seem particularly desirable in a movement which appeals to communal values and collegiate practices. It might well have avoided certain abuses, only a few of which have filtered through into publications or the press.[17]

THE EXPERIENCE OF "SLAYING IN THE SPIRIT"

The uncertainties and ambiguities of a communal movement inspired by the Spirit (as clearly proclaimed by its ideology) and yet restoring submissive obedience (as emerges, poorly decoded, from its functioning in practice) have a fall-out in the limitations imposed on possible expansion of the religious experiences. A recent example will be of interest on this point.

For four years (1976-1979), groups of neo-pentecostal Catholics on both sides of the Atlantic saw a particularly spectacular bodily religious expression spread like wildfire; it was new to these groups but well-known for a long time in evangelical circles: the experience of "slaying in the spirit."[18]

> For the observer, it consists in a reaction to the laying on of hands: the recipient falls backward (supported by one or two assistants) and remains prone without loss of consciousness for two to ten minutes; this is followed by a feeling of profound psychic and moral well-being. This manifestation had become very popular in the United States, particularly among the Methodists, after Kathryn Kuhlman's healing sessions, and a few Catholic priests were also making use of it in this context. Described by most of those who have been through it as an experience of *abandon*, of loss of *self*-consciousness, of submission to God or the Spirit with a sensation of warmth, of weightlessness followed swiftly by a feeling of joy and peace, it was experienced by Father George Maloney, S.J., and reported in these terms: "After a few seconds I got up but I still had a sensation of being at peace and returned to my seat in calm contentment, feeling that, for a moment, I had been raised up outside space and that I would have liked to stay there longer. It was a truly religious experience for me. I would not wish to encourage it nor dissuade anyone from it, even though I am of the opinion that it should only be done in appropriate circumstances, with the right minister to bring people to that kind of thing."[19]

The experience accompanying the "slaying in the Spirit" behavior presents as a bodily manifestation charged with a symbolism analogous to that of "speaking in tongues" (abandonment of a function normally linked with self-control) or even of baptism by total immersion (involving a brief loss of breath: death-rebirth). It is not immediately clear why this practice, duly ritualized (like glossolalia or baptism) could not be embodied in the faith with a Christian meaning, that is to say in a complete, symbolic experience, a natural phenomenon with a spiritual meaning. Certainly falling in the Spirit, like glossolalia, can be experienced in a spiritual realism that is hard to justify, and with a fundamentalist interpretation according to which the touch of God is acting directly, in the first case to strike down and in the second to produce a language that can be decoded subsequently, thanks to a further intervention of the Spirit. But this way of understanding and experiencing falling in the Spirit or glossolalia, as a direct passive response to an imaginary Spirit[20], is obviously not the only one possible, whatever the emotional experience *(Erlebnis)* involved. To cooperate actively by giving it a meaning in faith with or without emotional overtones, as conduct pledged publicly in a religious liturgy, would be more in keeping with a complete symbolic experience *(Erfahrung)*, no more mystifying than, say, glossolalia.

However, the reaction of "the elders" of the Catholic charismatic renewal[21] has not been favorable. They were no doubt anxious to regulate behavior which does not figure in the lists of charisms or gifts of the Spirit (although these "falls" have several historical antecedents in the Judeo-Christian tradition)[22] and so, while lacking any institutionalized function, they frowned on this bodily manifestation. It probably lacked the respectability that would have made it socially acceptable. But was glossolalia so "respectable" in the days when Catholics smiled at or held aloof from pentecostal practices? Even if it is opportunist, the argument of nonrespectability is weak and does not go to the root of the matter; it can nullify the creativity of ceremonies in which experiences of the Spirit are celebrated charismatically.

It is obviously not easy, with a large public and varied cultural expectations, to organize prayer meetings that are constantly torn between expressive but primitive manifestations, in which certain participants display their emotional religious states, and the controlled liturgification of gestures or words that are in the process of being ritualized. There is also the danger that the vivid experience *(Erlebnis)* of the Spirit would be lost in deliberately restricting or programing interventions.[23] These frictions or oscillations are probably unavoidable in groups founded because they cling to their designation as "charismatic" without really knowing to what extent their faith in the Holy Spirit will allow them to become so, their charity will let them prove to be so, and their hope will let them remain so.

GROUP EXPERIENCES: PSYCHOLOGICAL CRITERIA

For some years the groups known as "charismatic" have been evolving differently in the different countries in which they are proliferating. Where they have agreed to acknowledge them, the regulatory function of the Christian churches has been exercised very unevenly.[24] Cultural variants and the different historical circumstances of the nations are very sensitive, too; sometimes they tend to prevent a pentecostalizing experience from taking root (Spain, Latin America, apart from certain exceptions like Chile), and sometimes they welcome it enthusiastically (Ireland, the United States, Australia); sometimes it is in order to slant it toward social action (certain American and French groups) and sometimes toward an internalization of the experience of personal prayer (French-speaking countries in general). In one and the same country, the United States or Italy, for example, varying tendencies are felt, tending to cause splits in the Renewal movement. The many notes in this chapter allude to this fact. In short, as Congar writes: "We know it is not possible to speak of the renewal as a homogeneous whole, equally reliable in all its groups and manifestations."[25]

By restricting ourselves to locating a few variants derived from the observable functioning of prayer groups or meetings, it is fairly simple, in the end, to discern the direction in which the experience offered to the participants in this or that group is moving psychologically. To that end four series of questions might prove useful to a participant-observer (psychologist) as well as to the charismatics themselves.

The ghetto?

How many verbal contributions (testimonies, for example) bring up or throw light on problems experienced *outside* the group? How many have a bearing *only* on internal (spiritual) events, interpretations, or movements? How many, lastly, endeavor to establish an active synthesis between these two aspects of reality as lived: a situation in the world outside to be *changed* (not merely condemned) and an inner inspiration instigating research and innovations? If these latter interventions are rare or brief, the group tends to function as a ghetto, isolating its members on the fringes of society. They feel cosy and decide to stay: That is fine! Explicit spiritual talk will in no way change the effects of this basic, easily observable way of functioning.

The sect?

How many interventions or prayers are concerned *solely* with people in the group, the friends of participants, or the group itself? How many express any preoccupation with the life of the church or even other groups, charismatic or not? If such preoccupations are rare, the group tends to function as a sect, a group of initiates to a certain type of prayer (for example after having received the outpouring of the Spirit), instinctively mistrustful of the noninitiated. A mere verbal reference to the mother church, which, moreover, they are careful not to criticize in any way, is not enough to correct this tendency to sectarianism.

Alienating docility?

How many questions concerning the life of the group are subjected to evaluation, discernment (individual and communal), or decision by all the members concerned? Or are such questions put aside in the interests of an emotional climate fostering pure availability to the Spirit with no attempt to educate all members to be discerning in these matters. If the latter is the case, the group tends to function in an alienating mode with no real awakening to a sense of responsibility. Explicit talk about "spiritual openness" is superimposed on a practice based on "psychological docility" (trust in the leader or the collegiate leadership on a higher, rather anonymous echelon of the organization). Possible justifications, drawn from ecclesiastical practices, may confirm some in their membership of a group like this, but they will not prevent the impoverishment of experiences of moral and Christian discernment.

Manipulated spontaneity?

How much time is devoted to emotively charged, even regressive demonstrations (successive glossolalias; authoritarian messages admitting no mitigation or reply; strange behavior, even behavior interpreted as signs of a demoniac presence; intimidation by the leader through allusion to participants who resist the invitations of the Spirit), all these demonstrations fostering the illusion of immediacy in precisely located, transitory interventions of the Spirit? The greater the proportion of time spent in this way rather than in silent prayer, listening to other, even critical contributions or a collective study of the evangelical texts of reference, the more the group will tend to function in a "fusional" mode in which a feeling of unity is obtained by reducing communication; the more, too, each participant runs the risk of (unconscious) conditioning or manipulation on the part of the group or its leaders. In these cases, joyful spontaneity departs from a spiritual experience that is in a very real way, transforming and liberating. Religious experience as an emotional state *(Erlebnis)* is intense as a direct effect of the leadership that produces it. If it is repeated, emphasized, built up in that direction, it nourishes a happiness due to the group illusion (acting as a drug) and few of the participants are led to the experience of liberty in the laborious ascetic and intellectual mediations that theologians are accustomed to call Christian experience in the Spirit.

A return to the Spirit (Ranaghan) or to Dionysius (Brun)[26]?

The above series of questions, with easily applied criteria, will offer a first step in discernment. If Dionysius offers spontaneity, the Spirit should offer liberation. But as Dionysius, after all, is not the Devil, no doubt there is here no real dilemma.

CONCLUSION

Only one of the many aspects of the Renewal in the Spirit demands our attention here. Thanks to it more than a million Catholics in fifteen years have rediscovered a taste for group prayer. This aspect is the charismatics' claim to a specific, immediate *experience* of the reality and the action of the Holy Spirit "not as a presence they simply believe in, but as a presence they experience in the most mysterious manner.[27]" Observation has illuminated several characteristics of that experience, both in its psychological effects and its modes of production.

1. The most frequently described experience, in which a feeling of joy predominates, is lived consciously as *Erlebnis* and, as such, can be ascribed to the Holy Spirit only by an interpretation in faith. It is in the novelty and intensity of these lived states, the suddenness of the modifications felt or even operated in others, that the success of the charismatic Renewal lies. To recognize that, like the majority of religious experiences, it is *Erlebnis* is not to devalue or destroy it.[28]

2. This group experience is *produced*, built up, like most psychologically observable charismas (glossolalias, healings). It is the result of a particular type of stimulation which has not only been described psychologically but also confirmed by the leaders themselves as an alternation between verbal contributions and the avoidance of disagreements, between allusions to historic situations and a rapid return to atemporal, spiritual discourse. What is felt emotionally is the effect of a group unanimity obtained in this way. All stimulation of this kind, even if it were profane, would have the same effects, including glossolalias, provided they were presented as desirable.[29] To be aware of this mode of production is not to depreciate it. The context of collec-

tive enthusiasm in which healers operate in no way diminishes the effects produced. But, on the contrary, this new light may enhance freedom of action, obviate mystifying imaginings, dispel naively literal or fundamentalist interpretations in favor of a realism in which natural factors would be neither ignored nor confused with direct and pinpointed interventions of the Spirit.

3. Looked at in this way, the experience known as charismatic is from many angles a *religious* one, very precious to those who have it. Moreover it contains many of the characteristics of spontaneous religiosity: providentialist interpretation, an interventionist conception of the gods (in this instance, the Spirit), an aspiration to be in a sense possessed by them (it), an identity that is seen affectively as acquired, deliverance obtained outside natural mediation, submission to a sacralized authority.[30] These characteristics (studied in chapter 1 of this book) are reanimated in Christians well on the way to losing them by the experience known as charismatic. And yet, on this level it functions only as a pre-Christian experience; healings, glossolalias, religious enthusiasm, ecstatic or even mystical states are religious phenomena which are not contained within the historic and social framework of the Judeo-Christian tradition. For some they are pre-Christian, for others para-Christian.

4. Finally, there is nothing to prevent these religious practices or emotions from being assumed according to faith in a Savior God, revealing his purpose for the world. And this is probably just what happens for a certain number of charismatic Christians in the same way as most of the manifestations of what is sometimes called "popular" religion can be absorbed. As described above, the experience known as charismatic *(Erlebnis)* may lend itself to an interpretation in the faith and, under certain conditions, may be fulfilled in a richer experience *(Erfahrung)* of Christian discernment, for example, or contemplation. The first condition, and not the least psychologically, is to recognize that an emotively intense experience *(Erlebnis)* or a practice like glossolalia cannot be immediate experiences of the Spirit, although they may become signs of it. Another condition of access to an experi-

ence as a synthesis actively built in faith and Christianly liberating would be that it should be more closely linked to the conduct and words of Jesus of Nazareth which reveal the Father's wishes in a man living in the situations and the religious (Jewish) society of his time. If the pneumatic side (relating to the Spirit) is enough to produce the unifying joy and allied manifestations that have been described, the Christocentric side (relating to the Son incarnate in history) is necessary if the Christian experience is to appear fully formed and faithful to the active synthesis that constitutes the Christian faith (as the last two chapters in this book will show more fully). A theologian will probably notice that these two sides complete each other and cannot be separated. From a normative angle, he is no doubt right. But concretely and psychologically, one side can be constructed without the other, sometimes even to the detriment of the other. All in all, charismatic practices frequently lie under (if not alongside) the theology which inspires "the elders" of the movement.

If it is to open out in that direction, the experience of Renewal can *either* throw overboard certain practices or interpretations that made it "charismatic," in the sense of being seized by timely and discontinuous (though well-programed) interventions of the Spirit, *or* it can adhere to them as practices that are in the process of ritualization, as mediations symbolizing a more total experience, an active synthesis between the sign produced (jubilation, inner changes, glossolalias) and the signified. This latter meaning can never be grasped as an immediate gift: as a response to a wish of God it requires the interval in which words can reverberate that are different from man's wishes. This requires laborious mediation if it is to be constantly understood, accepted, and inscribed anew in the twists and turns of history.

We can be reasonably certain that both these evolutionary paths will be tried. Along the first, the Renewal groups will no longer designate themselves as charismatics right away because by so doing they run the risk of never being so, or not for long. Along the second path the groups will try to ensure that the actively provoked religious experience is sufficiently symbolic to lead to commitments based on the needs of the world. Thus they will manage to avoid going round in circles with rapidly ritualized practices which will soon become incapable of producing any but a conventional jubilation. Otherwise these groups with a style so much their own will face the danger of disappearing altogether as several similar endeavors have done in the course of history.

Notes

1. A. Maslow, *Religions, Values and Peak-Experiences* (Columbus: Ohio State University Press, 1964), pp. 42-43.

2. André Méhat, *Comment peut-on être charismatique?* (Paris: Seuil, 1974).

3. The percentages in the three tables are taken from the remarkable, multidisciplinary work *The Catholic Pentecostal Movement,* a special issue of *Pro Mundi Vita* 60 (May 1976). The expression "Charismatic Renewal" has long been in circulation in the United States along with "Pentecostalism" or "Neo-pentecostalism" already in use for ten years to designate practices in prayer being progressively adopted (outside the churches, but with no protest from them) by Episcopalians (from 1958), Lutherans (from 1962), Presbyterians, and lastly Catholics (1967). It can be traced together with a historical synthesis and many useful details in René Laurentin's book entitled *Pentecôtisme chez les Catholiques* (Paris: Beauchesne, 1974). After much discussion and prayer, the members of the National Catholic Committee (American) decided in July 1973 to abandon the phrase "Catholic charismatics" in favor of "Charismatic Catholics," which, however was less ecumenical. The decision was not respected by everyone, expecially in prayer meetings attended by both Catholics and Protestants (where there was no celebration of the Last Supper or the Eucharist). In Europe, after various meetings in Malines-Brussels at the initiative of Cardinal Suenens, the name "charismatic Renewal" seemed to have won the day and replaced "Movement" (still used by Laurentin and many others); for internal use, just the word "Renewal" was common and recently there has been a drift toward "Renewal in the Spirit."

4. "The Catholic pentecostal movement asserts, contrary to the dominant practice so far, that certain lay persons can mediate the Spirit itself (in the laying on of hands, for example). . . . We feel that lay people are protesting in this way against a certain theory and practice of double priesthood" (Jean Séguy, *Les conflits du dialogue* [Paris: Cerf, 1973], pp.

73-74). This explanatory hypothesis seemed to Jean Seguy to lose its validity three years later. At least in the French-speaking countries, the organization of the charismatic renewal (general management, personnel, publications) remains largely in the hands of clergy and nuns. See his article "Charismatique (Renouveau)," in *Universalia*, Paris, *Encyclopaedia Universalis* (1976), pp. 189-193. But if the hypothesis of the protest is not confirmed explicitly and statistically, Jean Seguy has just given it a much more subtle and convincing value in "La protestation implicite: Groupes et communautés charismatique," in *Archives de Sciences Sociales des Religions* 48/2 (1979), pp. 187-212.

5. On factors motivating "conversion" to the charismatic movement in its early days, see Charles L. Harper, "Spirit-filled Catholics: Some Biographical Comparisons" in *Social Compass* XXI, 3 (1974), pp. 311-24.

6. B. Mawn, article quoted from *Pro Mundi Vita*, p. 17.

7. These interviews confirm the observations in a report at the thirteenth International Conference on Religious Sociology by A. Godin, "Moi perdu ou moi retrouvé dans l'expérience charismatique: perplexité des psychologues," in *Archives de Sciences Sociales des Religions* 40 (1975), pp. 31-52.

8. A summary of these phonetic and linguistic works (published before 1974) also figures in the report quoted in the previous note. No recording has ever confirmed speech in a foreign tongue that had not been learned. But similarities, especially phonetic, confirm the vocal specificity of glossolalic productions and distance them from known, modern, spoken languages. On this point, chapter IV of Laurentin's book, quoted above, calls for serious reservations: it is too indulgent to very suspect witnesses reporting anecdotes with little confirmation.

9. In some countries (France and Belgium), glossolalias, formerly much appreciated, are rapidly disappearing. But some regret this. René Laurentin noticed it too (p. 118) at a *parish* Mass in Houston. By presenting this "more discreet role" of glossolalias as the norm, he is probably generalizing too quickly. In fact the dominant practice varies considerably in different countries and continents. It is to be feared that, once the "miracle" of unlearned speech (in a foreign language: "xenolalia") is brushed aside, glossolalia will disappear as a consequence, despite its obvious symbolic potential: a surrender to the Ineffable by this use of phonetic devices. Similarly, great variations can be noted in the importance attached to healing, "deliverances," exorcisms which certain Italian bishops have forbidden in their dioceses. These trends may help to distinguish a more "primitive," sometimes more popular type of charismatic from one with a tendency to internalize. The latter is undoubtedly looked on more favorably by the Catholic Church. They may ultimately give rise to divisions, as in Italy where 10 percent of the groups

in the south have seceded under a more lay leadership. But is it so easy to control or master the Spirit, if indeed it is the Spirit that is at stake?

10. As early as 1974, a healing session on the occasion of an international conference at Notre Dame University (14-16 June) was reported in a way that made bad reading (*National Catholic Reporter* X, no. 34 (5 July 1974). "Pentecostals Claim Healing," pp. 1 and 4). The painful impression arose from the contrast between the serious reservations expressed by the leaders (Cardinal Suenens, Mgr. J. McKinney, Father H. Cohen) and the enthusiasm of the crowd or of certain witnesses (Father MacNutt, Mrs. B. Shlemon). In June 1977, the first great rally in French-speaking Canada ("Les Olympiques de l'Esprit") was held in the Olympic Stadium at Montreal and was an immense popular success (45,000 people at the closing session); it ended with a Eucharist followed by a procession of 900 priests who, at the invitation of Father Emilien Tardif, laid their hands on the sick and many healing effects were proclaimed. When assessing the rally, some *theologians*, themselves charismatics, seriously questioned and criticized a program which tended to magnify the "healings" spectacularly and make them "the climax of the day and the conference (thus wrote Jean-Marc Dufort in *Relations* (July 1977), pp. 195-7, also Jacques Custeau, in *La Vie des Communautés* (September 1977), pp. 206-11, Herman Giguère, and others). It might have been thought that the idea of programing healings *at the end* of the rally in 1979 would have been abandoned. Nothing of the sort; what is more the voice of the announcer at this show-ceremony proclaimed that he could "see" a healing taking place in a house in Montreal, over a mile from the Olympic Stadium. Thereafter, the voice of the theologians is quickly drowned in the hubbub of Christian people rejoicing.

11. Some interesting observations on these timely interventions by the Spirit are made by Colette Degive in *Le discours charismatique: perspectives sociologiques*, a master's thesis at the University of Louvain, Laboratoire d' Anthropologie Sociale et Culturelle, 1977, p. 80.

12. Quotation from Yves Congar, "Renouveau dans l' Esprit et institution ecclésiale," in *Revue d' Histoire et de Philosophie religieuses* 55, 1 (1975), p. 147. Since then, Father Congar has resumed his criticism of immediacy in the experience of the Spirit on a broader and more profound basis in volume II, part 3 "Le renouveau dans l'Esprit: promesses et interrogations" (pp. 187-239) of his latest work *Je crois en l'Esprit Saint* (Paris: Cerf, 1979) 3 volumes.

13. In the early days of charismatic proselytism, the walls of a small town in the United States were covered with slogans: "Jesus IS the answer!" A week later someone had superimposed: "But what IS the question?"—a sally that gives food for thought.

14. This is the key expression in a sociological survey *Les jeunes,*

l'avenir et la foi carried out among young French believers and non-believers in the fall of 1975 (Paris: Desclée De Brouwer, 1977).

15. Jean Séguy, "Pentecôtisme et néo-pentecôtisme: pour une interprétation macro-sociologique," in the Proceedings of the 12th International Conference on Religious Sociology, Lille, Secretariat C.I.S.R., 1973, pp. 273-83 (quotation p. 275).

16. On these new religious foundations in France, at least a dozen of them, there is an interesting report-testimony by Monique Hebrard, *Les nouveaux disciples: Voyage à travers les communautés* (Paris: Centurion, 1979). Jean Séguy gave a very interesting commentary on this book "La protestation implicite . . .", in the work quoted above, 1979, pp. 192-211.

17. The reaction against abuses in the United States was known in France through a little book by J. R. Bouchet and H. Caffarel, *Le Renouveau charismatique interpellé* (Paris: Editions du Feu nouveau, 1976). The danger of docility in structures that are confused, and so open to authoritarianism, does not figure among the rocks to be avoided in the so-called "Malines" document: *Theological and Pastoral Orientations on the Catholic Charismatic Renewal* (International colloquium summoned at Malines by Cardinal Suenens and bringing together a dozen charismatic leaders from seven countries in May 1974; the text was released after consultation with seven theologians) (Notre Dame, Indiana: Ave Maria Press, 1974). The reefs mentioned (such as elitism, fundamentalism, sentimentalism, spiritualism cut off from temporal commitment) are never related to an institutional analysis of the modes of functioning of the Renewal.

18. Good documentation in Morton Kelsey, *Discernment: A Study in Ecstasy and Evil* (New York: Paulist Press, 1978), chapter II "Slaying in the Spirit," pp. 10-50. Critical discussion in *Resting in the Spirit* by John Richards (with several contributions), (Addlestone, Weybridge, Surrey, Renewal Servicing, P. O. Box 366, 1982. In French, the spiritual experience is well described by Dr. Ph. Madre, *Le repos dans l'Esprit* (Paris: Pneumathèque, 1982).

19. Kelsey, *Discernment: A Study in Ecstasy and Evil*, pp. 16-17.

20. "The Lord prompted me," "The Spirit moved my tongue in my mouth" (speakers-in-tongues quoted by Kildahl in the work already mentioned, p. 67); "The Lord lifted me up," "Lifted by some force, then stretched out on the ground, I abandoned myself to God and felt wonderful" (quotations from Kelsey in the chapter quoted). But several authors (notably Maloney) react against these interpretations (or imaginations?) of direct interventions attributed to the Spirit or the Lord. By distinguishing some part, at least, attributable to psychic forces, they reestablish the possibility of discerning some other part attributable to

the Spirit (thus Maloney, quoted in Kelsey, p. 13). A distinction between the fact and its meaning may be preferable to this splitting into two parts; it would open more space to a free activity between awareness and the introduction of meaning. Thus experience as a natural phenomenon can become experience in the faith.

21. These "elders" are not always easy to identify. In the present case ("falling in the Spirit"), the team of counselors around Cardinal Suenens led him to express his disagreement as early as 1978) (*Oecuménisme et renouveau charismatique, Document de Malines 2* [Paris: Centurion], pp. 101-103). The team enjoys a well-deserved spiritual reputation and a strong influence through various regional or national bulletins of the Catholic pentecostal renewal. In certain, chiefly French-speaking, countries the "respondents" mandated by the bishops have an influence in the "support groups" (a Canadian expression); these groups are themselves composed of an elite of charismatic leaders who help to solve conflicts or arrive at difficult discernments in local groups. When it comes to practices like exorcisms or "falling in the Spirit," this direct or indirect influence of the mother church is not uniformly recognized and followed. Who will supervise the "charisms"? Does the mother church really want to? In the three addresses by Paul VI to charismatic Catholics (October 1973, October 1974, and May 1975) the expressions "charismatic movement," "charismatic renewal," and even the word "charism" are not used once. This may not be fortuitous. Elsewhere, in the diocese of Malines-Brussels, diocesan officials were "mandated . . . to follow and coordinate in my name the development of the Charismatic Renewal" (Cardinal Suenens, *Pastoralia,* 15 February 1976, and *Magnificat* III, 2 March 1976, p. 31) and communities claiming kinship with this Renewal were asked to contact these mandated authorities. So the authorities of the church are taking charge of these "charismatics," at least the Catholic ones. New vicissitudes for a nomenclature which is sometimes ignored (Paul VI), sometimes adopted by a bishop anxious to secure "the mystery of the church as one of unity in the complementarity and convergence of charisms" (*Magnificat* quoted above, p. 31).

22. On the antecedents of "falls" close to God in prayer, see M. Kelsey, quoted above, pp. 32-34.

23. On programed ritualization with the aim of producing various "gifts" of the Spirit (conversion, bonds of communal life) a reading of the following is recommended: James T. Richardson, *Organized Miracles* (New Brunswick, N.J. Rutgers University, Transaction Books, 1979); also Thomas J. Chordas and Steven J. Gross "The Healing of Memories: Psychotherapeutic Ritual among Catholic Pentecostals" in *Journal of Pastoral Care* XXX, 4 (4 December 1976 pp. 245-57, or Meredith B. McGuire, "The Social Context of Prophecy: Word-Gifts of the Spirit

among Catholic Pentecostals," in *Review of Religious Research* 18 (2) (Winter 1977), pp. 134-47. In a wider context the basic works in psychology are still those of Leslie D. Weatherhead, *Psychology, Religion and Healing* (London: Hodder and Stoughton, 1951), of J. D. Frank, *Persuasion and Healing* (Baltimore: Johns Hopkins University Press, 1973), and in theology that of Georges Crespy, *La guérison par la foi* (Neuchâtel: Delachaux, 1972).

24. Powerful and decisive action by Cardinal Suenens in the years 1972-76 avoided the possibility of charismatic Catholics finding themselves on the fringes of the church (for example in certain episcopal conferences which were preparing rather adverse statements). From his Belgian center (consisting of an international team of counselors), especially after the international conference at Rome (1975), he gave national groups the chance to unite, if not formally and institutionally, at least effectively through influence on various regional bulletins, publications, and translations. This influence tended toward a more internalized renewal with a social slant and less effervescence in charismatic demonstrations (individual glossolalias, exorcisms, and falling in the spirit, etc., disappear). As a consequence, particularly in French-speaking countries, the groups lost their attraction on a popular level, had no impact on nonbelievers, and drew their recruits almost entirely from already fervent Christians whose faith was showing signs of withering in the absence of a style of prayer in which joy and praise could replace the boredom of repeating formal rites. Of course this influence was felt very unevenly, especially when it attempted to reintroduce charismatics into the parish framework. Occasionally it produced partial schisms (Italy, United States). The recent transfer to Rome (1981) of the international secretariat completed formal integration without reducing the difficulties.

25. Yves Congar, *Je crois en l'Esprit Saint,* quoted above, volume II, p. 205.

26. K. and D. Ranaghan, *Le retour de l'Esprit* (Paris: Cerf, 1972). J. Brun, *Le retour de Dionysos* (Paris: Editions Les bergers et les Mages, 1976). These two titles are compared in an interesting study presented at the University of Geneva (Autonomous Faculty of Theology) by Francoise Van der Mensbrugghe, *Les mouvements de renouveau charismatique: retour de l'Esprit ou retour de Dionysos?* (Geneva: Institute of Applied Theology, 1978). In addition to a good multidisciplinary bibliography, the reader will find in these 133 often very novel pages observations from life, grouped together in the twenty pages of the "story of my research." His attention is drawn to the manipulations indulged in, often with the best intentions, by leaders determined to produce both outpouring of the Spirit and, in a well-programed way, the most common

charismas, all in the space of a few days in a retreat.

27. Albert Cartier, "Le renouveau charismatique: un témoignage," in *Les quatre fleuves,* no. 9 (1979), p. 96. He also writes: "The whittling away of all our protective layers by shared prayer makes each one and the community vulnerable to the presence and action of the Lord. . . . We touch God."

28. In a semantic analysis of twenty interviews with charismatic Catholics in Canada "divine" appears 1,225 times, "the Lord" (traditional term among all Catholics of this generation) is mentioned 406 times and "God," 370 times (320 of them in the form of various timely interventions). The Holy Spirit is named 133 times and the other names for the "divine" all have a frequency of less than 100. Paper presented by Robert Chagnon at the colloquium *"Sciences sociales et Eglises"* under the title of "Discours charismatique: essai de sémantique" (Quebec: Laval University, 1978) chapter 13 of the volume *Sciences Sociales et Eglises* (Montreal: Bellarmin, 1980), pp. 199-214.

29. On experimentally produced glossolalias in a profane context, see Werner Cohn, "A Movie of Experimentally Produced Glossolalia," in *Journal for the Scientific Study of Religion* VI, 2 (Fall 1967), p. 278.

30. "Obedience is demanded so that the Community may be a communion, the communion of the Holy Spirit. . . . More often, perhaps, than in many other traditional communities a Shepherd or an Elder may have more authority than most religious Superiors. . . . To love is to obey. We obey because we love." Père Jacob in *Lettre de la Théophanie,* no. 20 (June 1979), pp. 15 and 17. "At first I thought that God's happening for our generation *was* the charismatic Renewal. Then I understood that God's happening for this generation was the church itself. . . . Abandoning oneself to God *is* truly the center of the *experience* of the Renewal." J. Claude Sagne, in the volume *Présence du Renouveau* (Paris: Châlet, 1979), p. 9.

5

The Excitement of Conflict as an Experience of Hope

(Socio-political groups)

The aftermath of the Vatican Council has been marked by a revival of Christian communities, much less unified than the charismatic movement but still increasing in importance in many countries. They consist of assemblies of critical Christians, people meeting informally for research or a free exchange of ideas, political celebrations in prayer meetings, popular Christian communities (Spain), base communities (especially in Latin America), "grassroots" groups in almost every Christian country. The participants share very intense group experiences. Their atmosphere is so different from that analyzed in the previous chapter that a sociologist has spoken of "new cleavages between Christians."[1]

An extensive survey would be required to give a thorough examination of these "base communities" and their roles.[2] While eschewing charisms, they nevertheless feel "similar in many ways to the early Christian communities, particularly in their Christian solidarity."[3] It is noticeable that "the image of the base communities as a cognitive support for threatened beliefs," has a consolidating effect, even among those who do not take part in them. It has been possible to check this experimentally.[4] For many Christians, eager to find coherence again between their beliefs and the rationalism of the surrounding cultural environment, the idea that somewhere there are "base" communities, in which an *understanding* of the dogmas is being acquired, provides a large measure of indirect support these days. In the Middle Ages, the monasteries, or at least the image people had of them, were a kind of guarantee for people far removed from theological discussions and mystical orations. But there is one difference and a considerable one: this time the communities are proliferating from below (particularly in Latin America and here and there in Italy). One of their characteristics is the poverty of a large number of their members who have become *active* Christians through their *experience* of their beliefs, both in their actions and in their prayer meetings. This is such a startling novelty that they feel the need to cling to the vanished model of early Christian communities, if only by the one fundamental feature of solidarity, of which Christians obviously do not have a monopoly. What makes these groups specifically Christian, if indeed they are, lies elsewhere.

The study of base communities becomes more and more difficult because of the great diversity in their composition and practices as they spring up all over the world. But the purpose of this chapter is more modest: to determine and describe the particular operations that make them genuine meetings of Christian *experience*, especially in their prayer groups.

Inspiration and group climate[5]

A God who comes from the future. Firmly uplifted by the hope, fundamental in Christianity, that the kingdom of God, "always at hand and always to come" will come about in history only through the impetus of Jesus Christ, who died for his insurrection and lives in his resurrection by the power of the Spirit, these communities and prayer meetings develop a militant messianism. "Christ has no hands, he has only our hands to do his works today" (prayer of an anonymous Fleming of the fifteenth century).

The sharing of personal, if possible complete, experiences based on situations in daily life (work, family, politics, ideology) is the starting point for the exchanges. It tends to be organized by making strong connections or drawing rapid parallels with gospel stories presented as reactions by Jesus to his historic, political, and religious environment.[6] Contributions, confronted in this way by the Scriptures, take up much of the time at the meeting. Cases of oppression are presented in a framework of Marxist thinking (class conflicts, alienation of the workers by capitalism, the importance of correct actions for an understanding of an orthodoxy and its constant adjustments). Members are urged to fight for the justice that cannot be dissociated from faith in Jesus Christ and also to fight for freedom against any political domination, since no regime can appropriate the ultimate meaning of history which comes from God to humanity. The actions to be taken may be of a social nature (mutual aid, solidarity), but they are usually placed in context by an analysis of the structures that perpetuate misery, injustice, and oppression. The structures of the churches are not exempt from critical examination.[7]

This sharing of ideas, when allowance has been made for the wide variations in intellectual levels among those present, is notable for its lively concern with obtaining information, sometimes laboriously, from the best sources of exegesis or sociology. The discussions are usually a preparation for a celebratory sharing of bread and wine—a memorial to him in whom the promises live, inserted as well as possible among the impatient expectations, difficult discernments, and the differences and divisions which have found expression during the discussions.

Torn between messianic impatience and eschatological expectations, the climate of prayer is one of hope which the injustices of the world have brought to a ferment, to white heat, even, and to the verge of vehemence, indignation, and anger.

It is not surprising to find opposing viewpoints here, sometimes so violent as to challenge the celebration of the Eucharist. It would be more surprising to find the opposite. Does not each participant, according to the allegiance or militance of his background, bear the marks of a society divided by conflicts in which each feels and proclaims his solidarity? Here we have men or women, rich or poor, literate or illiterate, invested with power or relegated to the fringe, social classes and political parties, tactics and strategies adopted; we would be more inclined, *at least at the outset,* to mistrust a euphoric unanimity which might blind them to the struggles ahead, or a religious message with a spiritual emphasis in which the beatitude promised to "the poor in spirit" led them to forget the poor themselves.

At least at the outset, as we emphasized. For, as we shall see, there are certain reefs on the way which threaten the navigation and the very existence of groups not sufficiently unified, or whose Christian identity is too fuzzy to prevent them from breaking up.

The conduct of meetings

The prayer meetings in question consist in sharing the word and sharing the bread. Sharing the word begins with a time in which each one can have his say, usually about experiences outside the group but sometimes on a theme previously agreed upon together—possibly based on a Bible reading—after which the meaning it has for each one is shared. This time of free contributions to the general discussion perhaps constitutes the originality of this renewal of people gathering in the name of the Lord. For many of the participants these groups become a place where each one has the acknowledged right to express, however hesitantly, his uncertainties, doubts, and questions; in short, it is a place where each one has the right to speak at the risk of being wrong. The maintenance and development of these spaces and times of freedom, Christian because they are instigated and experienced in the name of the Lord, seems to many to offer a chance for Christians to live communally; it gives them a dimension that is essential to them.

It is obviously the wish of the majority, if not of all, that this should be followed by a time in which the difficulties or options presented can be worked out and taken up in the light of the gospel. But each one also understands that this long-term work cannot be piously wrapped up in a biblical text hastily linked to the situation. To silently weigh the shared difficulty is the best way, in certain cases, to provide the interval necessary if it is to be looked at from a Christian viewpoint, that is, on the basis of the breaking of bread, the indispensable memorial of the death and renewed life of the Lord.

Nowhere has the running of this type of meeting been better presented as a condition and actualization of a Christian prayer than in a chapter of *Vêpres politiques* by Dorothee Sölle and Fulbert Steffensky, in which, in our view, the *specifically Christian experience* of this renewal is clearly indicated. This text is especially interesting for its "doctrinal presuppositions."

Structure for prayer meetings[8]

A. Preliminaries

Decide together on a theme relevant to the establishment of the Kingdom of God today: Third or Fourth World; wars in Vietnam or the Middle East; strikes; unemployment; unjust or degrading treatment of prisoners; rights of immigrants; special forms of atheism, prophetism, conversion, etc.

Approach the theme by bringing together the documents describing or analyzing the situation, finding help in the Bible, prayer, meditation, singing, with a concern to find some possible action for the members of the group that is constructive for the future. All this *is* prayer.

B. Doctrinal Presuppositions

1. Christian prayer forgoes miracles.
2. Prayer prepares man to accept his responsibilities toward the world. His action will not be replaced by God's.
3. Man can only accept responsibility for the world as he sees it and can know it.

Therefore: *Information is the first stage of prayer.*

4. In a community free of authoritarianism, there can be no

question or information being given by one and received by the others. Within the limits of members' competence, exact knowledge of the situation is the result of common research, each one understanding and weighing the value of the others' arguments.

Therefore: *Presenting and discussing the facts is a second stage in prayer.*

5. Prayer makes us aware of what is not yet, but could come about through us.

Therefore: *Discussion of possible action figures as a third stage in prayer.*

6. In formulating a prayer, man adopts God's point of view. He expresses his *pain* that the Kingdom is not a reality, his hope of the Kingdom, and his responsibility in bringing it about. For man, praying is taking over his part in the Kingdom to come.

7. Even when man is powerless to act to help other men directly, prayer sustains and develops his *wish* for the Kingdom, makes him more human in his very dissatisfaction, and prevents him from abandoning himself by giving up hope of introducing into this world a Christian meaning.

Thus prayer of intercession, often rejected in its individual and solitary form, is restored in a communal form.

It is obviously impossible to know how many of the groups mentioned at the beginning of this chapter adopt and continue this line of conduct in their prayer meetings. Various observations by participants have shown that they frequently come close to it in practice without always being aware of the underlying theology or, as Dorothee Sölle wrote, "the doctrinal presuppositions." In comparison with charismatic groups, the prayer meetings of socio-political groups in Europe and North American have received much less help from the local or diocesan ecclesiastical authorities. They have regularly been the object of mistrust if not rejection by those authorities who are obviously sensitive to their tendency to question the liturgical practices of traditional parishes. So it is not surprising to discover that their practices are often psychologically superior to their theology. A certain reserve in Latin America toward liberation theology does not help matters. Several of these groups are almost beyond the fringe, verging on the clandestine ("Underground Church" in the United States). Nevertheless their rapid proliferation and their sociological composition[9] demand attention; they constitute places of prayer frequented by people who have been baptized but became nonbelievers or nonpracticing, either due to their social environment (the poor, workingmen) which tends to make them feel strangers in the churches, or from a critical attitude inherent in their professional training (university students, men of letters, scientists) which makes them allergic to religious teaching that is sometimes vaguely fundamentalist concerning the Scriptures and sometimes harshly moralizing concerning certain aspects of their private lives, the sexual area for example. Both are looking for *meanings* that this religious teaching, these scriptural texts, and these prayer meetings could have today. How can they be related to life's commitments, possible class struggles, choices demanded by events, conflicting ideologies, religious or atheistic thoughts?

These thousands of places where prayer is shared in the particular style just described offer a profoundly renewed Christian experience, if we are to believe those who frequent them. In the formulation proposed by Dorothee Sölle, these are some of their psychological characteristics.

An experience of active synthesis

The *human* experience, as lived in these groups, avoids various kinds of compartmentalizing in the meetings: a) The "outside" world is constantly being presented in the sharings (preoccupations, information, projects, decisions) and prevents the group from turning in on itself. b) The emotional feelings (joy and pain, love and hate, hope and discouragement, gentleness and vehemence) are all accepted. All, even aggressiveness, are considered to be of constructive value for the world to be built. But what is experienced must be accepted and understood. Awareness unites affectivity and reflection in the shared contribution. c) Divergences, differences, and even divisions are to be recognized insofar as they are spoken. Communication is a prerequisite, always possible; unanimity is a product, often contingent. When unity is impossible, union remains the value and task to be pursued. Consequently, the group is not a place of happiness but of conflict to be worked through with a goal in sight.

Religious experience, in the sense of the spontaneous religiosity or functional religion described in the first part of this book, is fairly suspect in these groups. The least we can say is that it is not encouraged: a) Miracles are renounced, at least as a more or less secret objective of prayer. To expect individual or collective favors from God that will modify the course of history is surely to attribute a potential role to him in make-believe that will allow people to drop their arms to their sides, if only temporarily, while appearing to raise them to God. If there is a miracle, it is in the mystery of the incarnation, death, and resurrection of Christ. This mystery, welcomed in the spirit of a constantly renewed Pentecost, returns Christians to their own actions. b) There is renunciation of the illusory cut-off limiting an action of God who, at least in certain cases and at certain moments of prayer, is seen as relieving man's responsibilities. But we have a world that can only be changed by knowing it and by applying enlightened, definite, competent actions to further the prospects of the kingdom founded by Jesus Christ. c) There is renunciation of the image of a God who satisfies man's wishes. On the contrary, man is stimulated to listen to and understand the calls of this God revealed in Jesus Christ. Consequently, the group does not pray that its wishes be fulfilled but that it may make itself more capable of shouldering its responsibilities in the advent of the Son of Man, always on his way. It cares nothing for being religious; it wants to be Christian.

Lastly, the *Christian* experience, as developed in these base communities, comprises *dynamic tensions* which are stimulated by prayer, *dangerous decisions* that are instigated by hope, and *conflictive paradoxes* which are symbolized in the shared faith.

a) *Dynamic tensions* between an evangelical message expressing the wishes of the God of the Christians and the disclosure of the sins of the world, the church, and the group itself, insofar as it is not loyal to the calls of that God. The poor are not evangelized, their rights are not respected; worse still, evangelizing them sometimes consists in making them give up their rights. Power is not exercised in a spirit of service, contributing to fraternal union an enlightenment in the faith, but in the power and wealth structures that the group has allocated itself as if it were seeking to parody Christ returning in glory. Communication between members of the group itself reveals not only differences and divisions but confrontations in which they do not listen to each other, power struggles and violent rivalries leading to fatal disintegration.

Dynamic tensions between efforts that are often powerless, actions that fail, the apparent senselessness of commitments that are soon refuted by the march of history (of the church as well as society) and that presence, always living yet always other, in the "Memorial"— situated historically in the Passion of Christ which the group prepares to celebrate in faith.

Dynamic tensions between Christ "already there," present among the members of the group gathered together in his name, and that Christ "not yet there" with his promise for the future.

These tensions must be kept dynamic. To maintain them consciously and actively *is* the Christian experience itself, that of hope in the conflict.

b) *Dangerous decisions,* because the situations and concrete events that the group examines do not have *one* hidden, religious sense, to be revealed by spiritual experts. Consider that earthquake that claimed twenty thousand victims in the Cordillera of the Andes. It would be too easy, and not really honest, to announce to the survivors that it was a punishment from God or a brutal expression of the destined order. Such vaguely "religious" meanings, which force intellects to bow to the unfathomable plans of Providence, put too much emphasis on the value of resignation to be acceptable after reading the gospels. In reality, of itself the earthquake makes no sense; it waits for the Christians concerned to give it a meaning on the basis of practical charity: material aid, the adoption of children, moving whole populations, improved building techniques, or better forecasting of seismic shocks. That can all result from shared information, from discernment that must at times be tactful (it is not possible for just anybody to adopt just any child, even out of generosity), from political combat that is sometimes dangerous.

That clearly political strike, called in a difficult economic situation—was it decided on so as to obtain greater justice? Is it right to take part in it, to encourage it, to oppose it, to break it? All these choices may be good on the basis of information discussed together. It may be that one makes a different choice from another. It may even be that, on the basis of the same political and evangelical inspiration, the options are different. In short, to come out on strike may have several meanings, even several Christian meanings.

These risks, these choices, these conflicting decisions are the concern of the prayer group, since this is what Christian experience *is*: It is the discernment of a historically situated commitment. In the majority of these cases, no one can predict the outcome. "We are going up to Jerusalem" (Mark 10:33), declares Jesus in spite of the fears and against the advice of Peter and the disciples.

c) *Conflictive paradoxes.* There is no lack of these, once the group celebrating the Eucharist accepts that these dynamic tensions and dangerous decisions must be expressed and lived.

Thus *nonviolence* generates conflict both in theory and practice.

Theoretically

Nonviolence is the synthesis of two historic Christian positions, namely: the thesis of just violence (that is to say, the moral doctrine which places violence at the service of justice) and the antithesis of an "escapist" spirituality (the Christian perfection that delays the establishment of justice until the next world and preaches reconciliation of hearts in this world). This synthesis can be reached by taking the will to engage in the struggle for justice on earth from the first attitude and the renunciation of all violence that gives rise to death or hatred from the second, while bringing a new surpassing element into play: faith in the temporal efficacy of love.[10]

Practically

The origin of the conflict engendered by the contact between nonviolent Christianity and the theology of revolution must be clearly understood. Both the revolutionary and the nonviolent theologians aspire to construct a new society in which more and more the cohesive force is love rather than constraint. But whereas it is precisely to constraint that the revolutionary resorts in order to establish a society without constraint, the nonviolent believes that a start must be made this very day on building that society from the foundations, while accepting the risk involved in a unilateral renunciation, with no *quid pro quo,* of the most extreme forms of constraint (cruel violence) and trying to use the force of love experimentally. . . . Very often, however, the apprentice of nonviolence discovers, for his consolation, that the revolutionaries who diverge from him doctrinally act like true nonviolents in practice and display more imagination and boldness than he does in their struggle for justice. "They charged them not to speak in the name of Jesus . . . and they left the presence of the council, rejoicing that they were counted worthy to suffer dishonor for his name" (Acts 5:40-41).[11]

Even *Christian political commitment* in the camp of the oppressed and exploited becomes conflictual once it is realized that the church is divided because the class struggle cuts across it. Concretely and in the experience of life

it is paradoxical that we should have this intuition about the liberating role of the church on the basis of experience acquired in Marxist political practice. . . . But, at the same time, we have observed how the church is impregnated with ideological influences completely opposed to the real interests of the most oppressed. . . . We say then that the church must be saved from a path that will take it daily further from the people to whom it should be devoting itself. It is precisely these oppressed and exploited people who must be the vehicle of liberation in which the church is involved. . . . Some people accuse us of "using" the church for our own political ends, whereas in effect our politics are the reverse of those practiced directly or indirectly. The "status quo" (in the countries to which we refer) favors the present situation. . . . Others accuse us of wanting to divide the church whereas we have simply become aware that the church *is* divided from the moment that the class struggle cuts across it. . . . We conceive only of a single church, whose authority is based, not on the reflected power of civil societies, but on active commitment alongside the poorest through dialogue, respect, understanding and love. . . . We are aware of many difficulties to be avoided. But we are not ready to give up everything that can help us to set the people free and consequently to construct a prophetic church which shares their journey. . . .

This position we have taken will allow *contradictions to be maintained;* as they are resolved, new ways will emerge leading to a church that will be ours in the Future of Hope, whither all men are called together.[12]

Some senior churchmen, more numerous, no doubt, in Latin America than elsewhere, are also finding the path that brings them closer to the people they should devote themselves to: "those poor people, the first object of the church's mission." In these terms forty bishops addressed their "brother" Archbishop Oscar Romero, whom they knew to be particularly threatened; their message (Puebla, February 1979) could not save him from death (San Salvador, 24 March 1980).

We know that the Lord placed the pastoral charge of the diocese of San Salvador on your shoulders at a moment when your church was subjected to a veritable persecution in words and deeds because of its work for the Christian liberation of many poor and oppressed Salvadorians who lack fraternal support and from whom the face of God our Father was thereby being hidden. Over these two years we have, in solidarity, followed the progress of your commitment to the poor. You have increasingly made your own the problems and struggles of the peasants and workers with whom a minority, clinging to wealth and power, refuse to share on a basis of equality. You have not merely spoken in their favor; you have defended their right to form their own communities and associations; you have fostered and encouraged them. . . .

We rejoice greatly that this liberating activity has borne fruit in your diocese . . . and are happy to know that these humble people have seen their decision not to accept attacks on their dignity with resignation reinforced in this way. Thus, oppressed but not crushed, neither life nor death will be able to separate them from the love of God revealed in Jesus Christ. . . .

"Some Pharisees said to Jesus: Master, rebuke your disciples. But He replied: I tell you, if they were to hold their peace, the very stones would cry out" (Luke 19:40).[13]

The fruit of seeking to become a liberator of the oppressed is that the church experiences internal and external tensions to the point of death. Archbishop Romero, like hundreds of other Christians each year, died not *for* Christ (as idealizing language would have it) but *like* Christ and *for* the poor. "I have often been threatened with death," he said a fortnight before his assassination. "As a Christian, I do not believe in death without resurrection. If I am killed, I shall be raised again in the Salvadorian people. I say this in all humility. As a pastor . . . I shall have given my life for those I love and that means *all* the Salvadorians, even those who want to assassinate me" (*Dial*, quoted in *Le Monde*, 21 March 1981).

Such is, for our purposes, the way of a *really symbolic experience*. It initiates or restores, on the basis of current realities, the meaning at the heart of a traditional but often ambiguous language: Christ "died for us, died in place of us . . . and he lives." What is its meaning? That was made brutally, realistically, and materially plain to those simple folk who, having run away and hidden for fear of the police who had just felled Father João Bosco, met together on 18 October 1976 at seven in the evening to celebrate "the Mass of the seventh day." A dossier containing the facts, the celebration, and the interpretation has been constructed by the bishop of Sao Felix (Matto Grosso), Pedro Casaldaliga.[14]

The Facts

Father João Bosco Penido Burnier, a Brazilian Jesuit, was on a coordinating committee among the Indians in the prelature of Diamantina. On 11 October, at Ribeirão Bonito, we had taken part together in a procession down to the river where the baptismal water was blessed ready for the baptisms the next day. . . . Shortly afterward a lad told me that two women, held in custody at the police station were being tortured. A contingent of the Barra police had come to Ribeirâo Bonito following the death of Police Officer Felix, who was notorious in the region for his brutalities and even homicides. . . . On the arrival of the police, the people had again scattered along the banks of the river. Some were seized, beaten, and tortured. . . . The young lad became more specific; these two women could be heard from the street, shouting "Don't hit me!" I felt obliged to go to the police and intercede for them. The lad wanted to go with me, but I wouldn't let him. Father João Bosco heard what we were saying and insisted on accompanying me. The courtyard of the police station is surrounded with barbed wire; two officers and two soldiers are waiting for us aggressively. They start insulting us. We try to start a dialogue. But when Father João Bosco declares that he might report their arbitrary behavior to their superiors, the soldier Ezy Ramalho Feitosa punches him and immediately fires the fatal shot. . . . A doctor attended to the Father in our dispensary, and we took him to Goiana. But it was no use, as the doctor had thought. It was an explosive bullet and it had burst in his brain. For two whole hours, Father João Bosco was able to go on talking to the people with him. He continually offered his life for the Indians, for the people. As he repeated several times the " Consummatum est" of our Lord, he said to me: "Dom Pedro we have completed our task. . . ."

The Celebration

When the police had gone away again, the population of Ribeirão Bonito came together to celebrate the Mass of the seventh day, to set up a great cross on the spot where the assassination had taken place, as is the Christian custom among these people, and lastly, in the presence of the two women who had been tortured, the people decided to open the doors of the prison and, in great anger, several started demolishing it. This all happened in a single collective gesture. Those who were not able to break anything gave their opinion: "That prison has not been used in the cause of justice. Better get rid of it at once." During the celebration of the Eucharist, a letter from the community of Ribeirao Bonito was read. It was addressed to all the Christians in the area and began with these words: "The passion and death of Christ have been present among us and have been renewed in Father João. . . . Like Jesus Christ, Father João died because he was defending truth, justice, and liberty. But death is not the end. This death comes to wake us up." After the readings, the celebrant invited the people to say what they thought about this event and about people's lives. Views like this were heard:

—"Father João died for us because he defended the liberty of two women of the people. We must not forget that, for the same reason, the bishop and all the people at the mission are treated as communists and subversives."

—"Father João died in our stead because we did not have the courage to all go there together. And if one of our brothers is arrested unjustly tomorrow, shall we all have the courage to come here, as we have today, to set him free?"

—"Father João is not dead. He is still living with us. The blood he shed for us will give us strength so that we do not falter."

—"This cross (that we are setting up) is our liberation. Between the prison and the cross, we had best choose to do away with the prison." "It is Easter here with us. The passion and death of Christ has been repeated in Father João, just as it happened to Jesus Christ. And we want you to know this in these days when a church of the people is being born in struggle and hope. This death and the threats will be a witness for others who are also struggling for a new Man."

The Interpretations

In this story, we have a genuine experience of resurrection by a rereading and truly Christian interpretation of the event. Intervening in the course of a celebration of the Eucharist, it is by faith in Christ that these Christian voices told the meaning of this death for those taking part. Conversely, the very harshness of this event on the human and secular level is effective in prompting the witnesses to grasp the meaning of the words they have learned in the catechism about Jesus Christ. Thus the *symbolic Christian experience* is born in an active synthesis.

At the end of an interesting discussion of these levels of interpretation, the theologian Ignace Berten was able to conclude:

> The community is living through an *experience of resurrection.* It is once again standing on its feet or, more precisely, it feels that it is being set on its feet, that it is being opened to a future of solidarity, courage, and striving for freedom: a hopeful future, even though the community seemed to have died of discouragement. This community perceives that it owes this strength to stand on its feet to João Bosco, and with the same insight it understands that João Bosco still lives. It proclaims this event and witnesses to it. João Bosco becomes a kind of symbol. And that symbol proves effective; it creates the people's unity, it stirs up the people like an irresistible force. . . . I would call this linking of events "a symbolization process. . . ." But does this process of symbolization lead to a "true" understanding of what, fundamentally (even if partially), the business of João Bosco is all about and of the reality of Jesus Christ in his death? We can only answer this question positively on a twofold condition. First that we share the Christian faith which is the giver of meaning here. . . . Next, that up to a point we are in communion with the situation and sufferings of the people and in one way or another share their revolt, their struggle, the perception of the injustice of the system. As Bishop Pedro said explicitly in his report, the judgment we

make on the gestures and the voice (of the people) depends on how closely or not we share in their suffering and their hope. It depends on the extent to which we live the Gospel, made flesh in one moment of a people and its history.[15]

This example is exceptional in several respects. But it shows that a Christian experience in a celebration becomes symbolic provided that an *interval* is maintained, so that the two components get into a state of tension: one pole supplying experienced reality centered affectively on a human wish and another pole that is invisible, not experienced psychically, present-yet-not-present beyond the perceptible and imaginary polarizing toward a founding wish made flesh in a "memory," in this case the memorial of the passion and resurrection of Christ.[16]

But because this example is exceptional (due to the death of the actual witness, Father Bosco) and obviously does not represent all Christian practice capable of being celebrated by symbolic and effective comparison with the gestures and words of the Lord, it must not hide *the basic psychological condition* that makes any symbolization possible: a state of *frustration,* of bereavement, of "pain and dissatisfaction" (D. Sölle), of "contradictions" (S. Gutierrez); in short, of impatience at the nonarrival of a Christian future. Conversely, religious language is often formulated in such a way that it gratifies the wish either in religious terms (God) or in evangelical terms taken literally (praying that the miraculous draught of fishes may be repeated today). But a celebration can lead to an effectively symbolizing Christian experience only if it intensifies the wish and so maintains the interval between the present wish and the future fulfillment of a piece of Good News—promised, but in such a way (in the Christian case) that it demands man's *active* cooperation: "I will make you to become fishers of men" (Mark 1:17). These conditions of constantly "active synthesis" are and will regularly be held in check in the groups by the latent wish to avoid a climate of frustration. Almost unconsciously, this wish throws up obstacles, sidetracks the group so that, if it is not careful, the element of frustration experienced in such meetings will ultimately be reduced or abolished.

> *To celebrate* is to live. But a celebration is not life, it is stepping outside the timescale of daily life to rejoice together in the meaning of that life. Without life there is nothing to celebrate. Without an experience of struggle and of hope in the future, there would soon be no cause to rejoice. To celebrate is to enclose an interval of time in order to enjoy together what was yesterday's battle (victory or defeat) whose meaning is asserted in renewing the wish for what will be tomorrow.

Obstacles:

a) Intellectualization

In many prayer groups it can be observed that the experience of prayer without unanimity is so frustrating that the end result is an intellectualization of the shared activity. Discussion based on divergent analyses of a situation goes on indefinitely as though each one dreaded having to bear the weight of these divergences in silence. Discussing conflicts intellectually may serve as a distraction. It has the same psychological function as a certain use of religious language which calmed them in an idealist mode, and that is just what these groups reject. Certainly a failure to recognize the existence and specific nature of the conflicts is to be deprived of the means of handling them reasonably. But Christian socio-political groups seem inclined to forget the warning of one of their leaders that "a theory of conflicts could be used to mask conflicts."[17] Dorothee Sölle in the text quoted at the beginning of this chapter suggested that in the final stages of a communal prayer meeting there should be an expression in prayer of *pain* that the kingdom of God is still so little realized and the transformation of that same dissatisfaction into a renewal of the desire for change. Observation shows that these affective moments are very much foreshortened in some meetings which spend a long time in intellectual exchanges and end in a climate of impatience verging on chaos. "Life must be lived in indignation," wrote Camus. No doubt we need to learn how to remain indignant.

b) Ideology

Sometimes, too, ideology and utopia occupy a disproportionately large place in the prevailing talk, in which case they are functioning as substitutes for religious beliefs. No doubt many Christians in this renewal are well able to avoid confusing ideology and belief, utopia and hope. They utterly reject that primary "horizontalism" which is sometimes thrust at them as a new heresy. However, the most enlightened of them recognize that they are caught, not to say stuck, in a permanent paradox: There is no belief without some ideology, no hope experienced without a utopia in the imagination. But the threat remains, and it is not fanciful, that groups may be invaded by utopianizing ideologies in their political struggles. This ideological or utopianizing talk then makes them partially blind to the practical conditions for discerning a creative action, in just the same way as certain fragments of the disputed idealist discourse does (for example, talk of a conversion of the heart as a preliminary to or source of political change). In this case, groups impoverish the open creativity demanded by the specific substructure of Christian messianism and by the need for constant adaptation to concrete historical conditions which can be traced to its roots in Judaism.

c) Activism

The activism of militant speech, indispensable as it is to collective and effective commitment, may so powerfully mobilize energy in the short term that it obscures that horizon of hope ("God coming from the future") so important for the constant regeneration of energy and the freedom to attend to new initiatives to which it is summoned by the Holy Spirit residing in them. This is followed by a disciplined, even militaristic march (are they not militant groups?) to ensure the effectiveness of an ethical will to *do* justice rather than to let it germinate by creating the most favorable political structures. Once again, the prayer group finds itself impoverished. Expulsions follow, on ever more petty and short-term grounds, in the name of a sacrosanct "orthopractice" which occasionally makes the Christian dimension superfluous in the long run. No doubt the march to the "promised Land" requires discipline. We cannot hold it against these Christians that at certain critical moments they identify themselves with the Israelites of the Exodus[18] to such an extent that they never enter the Promised Land. Who could confuse the promises of the Good News with their fulfillment in the present day? All the same, a Christian group is on the way to losing its specific inspiration once it becomes psychologically and totally absorbed in the works it performs through group discipline and by its own collective strength, as it were. It will easily die once it breaks up into tiny groups, each with more and more narrowly defined orthopractices. These tiny groups then function as micro-caricatures of the churches when they find themselves wanting to be saved, not by ever more generous inclusion but by their human reflex to exclude in order to protect themselves; they turn inward on to an identity that is more and more limited to instructions for action, more and more imposed in the name of unity of discipline. Sectarianization is a process at work even outside the religious sphere. The sociologist must say whether it is destructive in every case.

Internal paradoxes

The obstacles we have discussed can probably be avoided once they are known and the voyage can continue, thanks to leaders and presidents of assemblies who encourage the groups to become aware of them. But are there not also internal paradoxes in these groups, permanent conflictive, perhaps structural tensions? Psychological observation can detect at least two, which, like the pitching and rolling of the open sea, must be constantly born in mind and adjusted to by the navigators.

a) Aggression and communion

Psychologically, what means have we at our disposal to stimulate communion when communication (analysis of situations, strategies) shows disagreement, divergences, potential conflict? In fact, we have a considerable affective force: *aggression*. People united in anger or hatred—much more easily achieved than to unite them in love or respect, incidentally—have a strength which may indeed be fearsome but of which most political, professional, or religious groups have some experience;[19] they have attempted to develop it in order to obtain benefits, if only secondary or short-term ones. It assumes that the group, community, or church can achieve unanimity in relation to an "outsider" an "enemy of the people" or simply a rival group to be ousted. The pragmatic principle of class struggle (Marxist theory presents it as a practical rule) is remarkably efficient in mobilizing revolutionary energies in the political sphere. The concept of the "proletariat" may not be very consistent or scientifically rigorous on the plane of economic and social theories, but it contributes to *one* interpretation for the reconstruction of new societies which has an amazing power to mobilize on the affective plane. And for about a century now no one has found a better one for getting unjust or fossilized social structures on the move. This interpretation (by class struggle) associates solidarity in the present with a variable degree of aggressiveness or violence for the purpose of modifying what appear to be the most vested interests.

But when dealing with Christian people, gathered together in the name of the Father or even with Christian groups calling on the Spirit of charity on which they are based, can they possibly, without contradiction, describe that "enemy of the people" other than with abstractions borrowed from the vocabulary of the times (imperialism, property-owners, oppressors) or from the religious vocabulary of all times (pagans, infidels, apostates, possessed by the devil). In short, all those are "bad people"; they are "not us"! For want of scapegoats other than the Evil One or those who live in his spirit (this has been used to justify homicidal violence several times in history), Christian aggressiveness must obviously come to terms with love in order to harmonize militancies in the group with the Christian inspiration, namely, love for one's enemies. This concrete task is concerned first with the network of relationships between members, but here (unlike the charismatic groups) each one militates in a section of a fragmented world or a party-ridden society since this militancy is not debarred from contributing to group discussions. So we perceive, painfully or with difficulty, that the class (or any other) struggle cuts across groups or churches which would much prefer to do without it.[20]

How can we speak of a message of reconciliation, open to all in a real sense, and at the same time give aggression its rightful place, suspected or feared as it is by a certain idealistic spiritual tradition? And yet aggression is not suspect of itself. It does not always lead to death, to murder, especially when the conflict is verbal. And vehemence is often necessary to give a true expression to the aggressive impulse. This tension, which is probably structural and structuring for Christian groups, may give birth to a critical, and therefore suffering, community of sharing and celebration. It is more reminiscent of the Last Supper (when our Lord was anticipating his contact with the Gentiles or his death that would result from his faithfulness in proclaiming the often provocative message of the Father) than of Pentecost, if we think of it as a gathering in a closed chamber, ignoring the order to go out into a world religiously hostile to the Christian message. The fighting structure of the Christian inspiration is considerably devitalized once there is no room in it for aggressiveness and if aggressiveness is mistakenly interpreted as intrinsically bad. The groups under discussion in this chapter no longer fear it. They accept it, not merely as a condition of Christian life, as of all life, but as a tension in which each one must learn to live, to find joy, and to place his hope.

"The place of liberty must be not after the struggle for it, but *in* that struggle. If liberty (like love) is not *already* alive in it, it will never come" (J. Comblin).[21]

b) Division and celebration

But it is in prayer and eucharistic celebration that the tension inherent in the Christian experience pursued by these groups would be lived most fully. What and how can they celebrate in division?

Liturgically, is it possible to celebrate *in spite of* divisions? The answer to this question presents no difficulty: All Christians do it, either in their "separated" churches by appealing to the ecumenism of their vows and so already living it in hope, or even together, where the division is on a point not considered essential to the identity of their church. But their festive language in these celebrations might seem ambiguous or idealistic so long as it is content to refer to a hidden spiritual being, such as the allusion to "Christ who remains our reference *in spite of everything,* our common hope," or to "our Christian hope of reconciliation centered on the prospect of collaboration between classes in defense and promotion of the *common good.*" Such talk clearly erases the conflicts, battles, and divisions of today by referring to an abstraction (the "common good") or an expectation ("our common hope"). It does not lack grandeur or psychological effectiveness in laying conflicts temporarily to rest during the celebration, but it contributes nothing to their historical solution. We must go further.

Is it possible among Christians to celebrate *with and in* the divisions? It is certainly often done, especially after shared readings from the gospels which have revealed complementary if no contradictory aspects (miracles as wonders or as conveying a meaning to be grasped—beatitude of the "poor" or of the "poor in spirit," etc.). There is no doubt that the celebration can be eucharistic (giving thanks) and joyous: It is possible to rejoice in the divergence of opinions and interpretations, however important and painful, insofar as the conflict concerns meanings relating to the person of Christ. Is not the very diversity of views proof that each one refracts a color of the prism and none has a monopoly on the whole truth about Christ: white light, absolute, a synthesis operated by the diversity of the colors? That symbolism is particularly suggestive when preparing the sacramental presence of the sharing of the body of Christ between all these participants, each of whom will live only a small part of it. But when conflicts (especially class conflicts) bring active combatants together, will it be improper to celebrate together? According to Jean and Colette Guichard, "It is not the presence of class adversaries at the celebration that causes difficulties, but the symbolic language, if it implies a sacralization of class oppositions and situations of domination. . . . Neither the economic nor the political situation of the participants is decisive in making the celebration impossible. The difficulty begins when the awareness engendered has repercussions on the symbolic level, the level of liturgical consciousness, and clashes with the type of language used. That means assuming a contradiction at the level of the figures and symbolic language in operation."[22] According to the authors, various experiments they describe have shown that the liturgical form given to a ceremony implying some contrasts in faith is never neutral. "In the majority of cases, it has been noted that it is not militant workers who reject the presence of "the adversaries" at a celebration. Quite the reverse: practicing members who are conscious of belonging to the dominant classes never agree to take part for long in celebrations which, through a new symbolic language, take on a meaning of radical opposition to injustice; they squeal about "politics" and denounce it to their bishop or else change parishes."[23]

Would it be possible among Christians to *celebrate* (eucharistically) *the conflict itself?* That is the ultimate question. We have already seen that it refers in any case to the creation of new forms, new figures, a new language in the Eucharist itself. This continuous creativity in liturgical practice is now a fact. According to some, if there are battles (political or not), then there are things that must be said and inserted into a liturgical celebration. But the mystery of life and death, which is at the heart as well as the surface of Christianity and has been all through its history from the earliest beginning, must still be there. Internal conflict, external conflict: the two frequently overlap.

The first thing to say is that there are signs of death: *death is at work in the district.* There are physical deaths: houses fall down and kill people. Hundreds and thousands of people are pushed out to the outskirts. But there are also signs of resurrection and resurrection practices, for example when the district succeeded in preventing the departure of 1,000 persons from a *hacienda* because they were sufficiently loved and organized to oppose the police or because people were no longer afraid of the police or, again, because they managed to move on to some wasteland as a sign of their intention to stay in the district, come what may. *For us the liturgy is not possible if these two lines of talk are not present in the group.* Not on an abstract, but on a concrete level. If the group cannot tell itself what death it is living through and cannot tell itself what resurrection it is living through, the conditions are not there. Our liturgies are simply centered on that.[24]

As we have seen more than once, to celebrate the conflict in this way is to restore an effectiveness symbolic of the "commemoration" of the life, death, and resurrection of Christ. Psychologically it is an experience by active synthesis between two realities (death-life) which actually signify the mystery of Christ. Sacramentally, it maintains or restores the possibility of celebrating the conflict itself. An internal conflict between Christians, where the wish to possess Christ exclusively as one's own from an objectively unique point of view, succumbs in the exchange of views to the reality in which the tension exists. An external conflict, where discernment of the commitments to be taken with or without violence depending on each situation, involves the risk that some die so that others may live. For, "here we have the saying verified: 'One man sows; another reaps' " (John 4:37).

If Christians had to give up celebrations structured in this way, if the celebration of their militant hope could no longer be centered on this tension and battle, if the Last Supper could no longer be shared in terms of a more or less remote departure (to go to the heathen) at the risk of a mortal Passion, then it would never be celebrated in the fullness of its symbols and in the diversity of the gospels which have carried the written record down to our own day—never again. So it is fitting that we should seek to celebrate it in this way, to remake it in ever new synthe-ses. It is undoubtedly a most uniting experience, linking and bringing to life socio-political renewal groups, whose prayer meetings we have just been analyzing in their functioning, their obstacles and their dramatic tensions.

CONCLUSION

Although there are ideological differences, theological diver-gences, and distinct forms of celebration in prayer meetings be-tween the socio-politically oriented base communities, they all agree that they share a Christian experience with a number of common characteristics in active synthesis:

1. The Christian faith is inseparable from a *fight for justice* which calls on all men without distinction. By asserting that Jesus Christ is God and Savior, it accepts and maintains a state of conflict, possibly a battle to the death, in the human condition. This conflict, which is present in the history of man, is not suppressed by the faith but accentuated and determined on the basis of the appeal made by this God-among-men: the announce-ment of good news to the poor, the oppressed, the outcasts and sinners. This conflict takes on the aggressiveness inseparable from love.

2. Christian hope is nourished by *dissatisfaction:* dissatisfaction that the Sun of Justice is not yet here, dissatisfaction that launches hope once more on an action to bring that sun to the societies in which men and women organize their existence and relationships. By proclaiming that Jesus, who died, has risen again, and entered as Savior into the glory of the Father, it accepts the commitment to make him keep rising again in his second coming. The frustrations of the present day are not soothed by a vision of future times but are made more acute by the wish of the Spirit who "groans" and toils in the interval between promises and their realization.

3. Christian prayer *starts from a happening,* any happening, and tries to discern its meaning and how to bend it so that it takes on

the value of a "sign" of the judgment of God, of that God who revealed himself in Jesus Christ in certain events and conflicts of his time. It also *starts from a person,* from any person, in order to decide in what sense these different persons, strangers or enemies, can become a "neighbor" in a relationship that is always new. It is not enough to bring down images or words from the gospels and superimpose them on the facts or persons of the present day. Such a parallel, enlightening as it might be, would constitute an imaginary connection, more dream than reality. The *Christian experience* becomes a "eucharist" when the events acquire meaning through a practice inspired by that of Christ. It is then that events and persons become transforming for those who pray according to the wishes of the Spirit. Only then do the words and gestures of eucharistic prayer (sharing of the Word, sharing of the Bread and Wine) according to sacramental rites acquire the fullness of their efficacious and transforming symbolism and free us to give thanks for the mystery of the death and resurrection of Christ, made real once more.

Such then are the main components of this Christian experience according to those who practice and interpret it. It restores messianic fervor ("if the seed does not die") and buries it in the historic reality of events and persons so that it may bear fruit. It maintains a frustrating tension between present prayer and a future willingly tinged with a touch of eschatology: Things are bad and will get worse still, but you are not alone, even in your solidarity.

Despite the amazing vitality of base communities in Latin America, despite the depth and relevance of the theological renewal instigated by them (particularly in their socio-political dimension), no one can predict how the encounter, always conflictive, between Christian maturity and adult practices in social life on the one hand and between communal renewal and church institutions on the other will work out. Psychologically, the Christian experience renewed by these groups is broadly "dysfunctional" if we compare it with the functional religious experiences described in the first chapter of this book. So there will be a very strong temptation to attenuate this psychologically frustrating functioning, either by investing all the affectivity of the participants in their political projects, so that their link with the church or even with the gospel gradually becomes less interesting or fades away completely, or else by accepting a spiritualist theology in contrast with their practices and inferior to their fundamental aspirations. These dangers are the less fanciful as the return to the gospel is inevitably accompanied by a critical, not to say hostile attitude toward certain aspects of the church as institution, especially to the extent that the church would reimpose a liturgical rigidity and a language marked by obsolete symbolisms.[25]

Yet most groups seek to achieve and maintain the double encounter mentioned above. Their enterprise may be crucial, even more than it would seem, once the question is asked about a truth *of God* to be reached *in* the experience. This will be the subject of the two chapters in the third part of this book.

Notes

1. Vincent Cosmao, O.P., "Charismatiques et politiques: vers de nouveaux clivages entre chrétiens," in *Foi et développement,* 26 June 1975.

2. A good sociological approach, often with theological discussion, is given by Danièle Léger, *Etudes* (February, 1976), pp. 283-94, and in the special numbers of *Lumière et Vie* 99 (1970), and 109 (1975), and of *Concilium* 104 (April) and 109 (November) 1975. Here again, *Pro Mundi Vita* 62 (September, 1976) has an exceptionally good international survey showing successes, failures, and trends in the base communities. Also recommended is the remarkably well-informed presentation of Bruno Secondin "Communità (cristiane) di base," in *Dizionario di Spiritualità degli Laici,* (Milan: ed. O.R., 1981), vol. I, pp. 131-146; the information is presented continent by continent.

3. Quoted from *Noticias Aliadas* (Peru, 6 September 1979), reprinted in the special number of *La Lettre 157* (March, 1980), "Les communautés en question," p. 10.

4. J. P. Deconchy, "L'image des communautés de base comme support

cognitif pour des croyances menacées dans leurs fondements rationnels: étude expérimentale d'un phénomène de contre-emprise," *Actes de la Conférence Internationale de Sociologie Religieuse* (Lille: Secrétariat du C.I.S.R., 1975), pp. 285-307.

5. The paragraphs that follow are the result of observations made in prayer groups (Belgium, France, Italy), confirmed by the publications of certain leaders or founders of these groups (free parishes, Christian collectives, communes or communions, Christians for socialism, alternative groups). Thus Philippe Warnier, *Le phénomène des communautés de base* (Paris: Desclée De Brouwer, 1973); Xavier Godts, *Alternatives d'Eglise* (Brussels: Recherche et Vie, Cahiers du Cefa, no. 16, 1978); numerous other articles in *Communauté chrétienne* (Montreal), *La Lettre* (Paris), *COM-Nuovi Tempi* (Rome) by leaders discussing the pitfalls, crises, and resurgences of these groups.

6. The socio-political prayer groups found their exegetical renewal in Fernando Belo, *Lecture matérialiste de l'Evangile de Marc* (Paris: Cerf, 1978, 3rd edition) and its popularizers (Clévenot, Girardet). This exegetic approach continues with greater precision, information, and subtlety with Emile Morin (and the teaching teams), *L'événement Jésus dans les structures de la société juive* (Paris: Cerf, 1978), G. Theissen, *Le Christianisme de Jésus* (His social origins in Palestine) (Paris-Tournai: Desclée et Cie, 1978), and A. Nolan, *Jésus avant le christianisme* (Paris: Editions Ouvrières, 1979). The collective use of *realist* (nonspiritual) readings from the Bible has been described for several French and foreign groups in *La Lettre*, no. 237 (1978).

7. Among the theologians who were an inspiration to socio-political groups, we would single out particularly J. B. Metz, *Pour une théologie du monde* (Paris: Cerf, 1971), and the critical comments on it by M. Xhauffelaire, *La "théologie politique"* (Paris: Cerf, 1972), André Dumas, *Théologies politiques et vie de l'Eglise* (Lyon: Chalet, 1977), and also the "liberation" theologians such as J. Moltmann, *Conversions à l'avenir* (Paris: Seuil, 1975) and G. Gutiérrez, *A Theology of Liberation* (Maryknoll, N.Y.: Orbis Books, 1973). On recent developments of three tendencies in this theology by base communities in Latin America, a reading of Segundo Galilea, "The Theology of Liberation," in *Lumen Vitae* 33, 3 (1978), pp. 331-54, is recommended. Unfortunately he gives no backup references.

8. This text is translated from *Politisches Nachtgebet in Köln*, by Dorothee Sölle and Fulbert Steffensky (Stuttgart: Kreus Verlag, 1971), Vol. I, pp. 24-25. The two volumes present many plans for and reports of celebrations. In Germany, the inspiration of these "Vêpres Politiques" groups has had a strong influence on the "Christians for socialism" groups.

9. While noting that the great diversity of these groups raises prob-

lems in producing statistics, Danièle Léger, *Etudes*, (February, 1976), pp. 283-94), estimated that since 1972 about a hundred groups (4,000 members?) were calling themselves "base communities" in Paris and the Paris region. For France, using B. Besret and B. Schreiner (*Les Communautés de base*, Paris, Grasset, 1973 and some numbers of the monthly *Courrier Communautaire*, they were estimated (in 1975) at 400 meeting places for about 16,000 persons. The November, 1977 number of the monthly *Incroyance-Foi* reckoned at 400 the number of "catechumenal communities" with 56 percent of working class members. In these communities, the ratio of men to women was about equal. In Italy the offical directory of "local communities" spoke of 300 groups offering a meeting place to "at least 10,000 people" (active members of permanent cells) but probably many more (*Pro Mundi Vita 62*, November, 1976, p. 23), with working class men in the majority. In Canada, Guy Paiement ("Voies d'avenir des communautés de base," *Relations*, April, 1976, p. 98) counted 75 French-speaking groups in Montreal, Quebec, and Hull, "recruiting largely from the various sections of the lower middle class." In the Netherlands, 80 communities took part in the second national conference (1200 participants). One ecumenical community alone, like that at Ijmond, has 600 to 700 members, 238 of whom pool some of their resources (according to the *Bulletin européen des communautés de base*, no. 1, 1980, quoted in *La Lettre* no. 257, March, 1980). It is estimated that more than 20 percent of Catholics have taken part in celebrations in a style modeled on the lines described. The Netherlands is probably the only country in Europe where the movement is already influencing the future of the church. Hence the institutional reactions to block it. In the United States, Father Edgar Beltran (Secretariat for Spanish-speaking Catholics) numbers base communities at 4,000 with the active participation of 50,000 persons (*National Catholic Reporter*, May 16, 1980, p. 20). Their success is attributed to "the inability of the (parish) church to meet the aspirations of the (poor, often recently immigrated) people" especially when the liturgy has remained rigidly traditional. In Latin America the base communities are becoming cells with a decisive part in the evangelization and transmission of the faith among the very poor. Taking this continent (half of Christendom) into account, the importance of the renewal emanating from the base communities is already statistically far greater than that of the charismatic renewal which, because it is more unified, easily gives the opposite impression, especially in view of the spectacular effect of its mass meetings.

10. Gonzalo Arias, "Le caractère conflictuel de la non-violence," in *Concilium 109, Vie chrétienne et conflits* (November, 1975), pp. 121-25.

11. Ibid, p. 122.

12. Susanna Gutierrez, "Témoignage d'une militante révolutionnaire sur l'assomption des conflits," *Concilium 109* (November, 1975), pp. 115-19. The passages quoted amount to an abridged version of the article.

13. The *Lettre à Mgr Romero* is quoted from *Informations catholiques internationales*, no. 549 (15 April 1980), p. 60, which presented extracts in homage to the bishop who was shot down while he was celebrating Mass in a hospital chapel in his diocese in the capital of El Salvador (Central America). The text appeared in full in *Documentation Catholique*, no. 1762 (April, 1979), p. 365. It had been signed by forty bishops (out of 187) at Puebla meeting together during the Third General Conference of the Latin American Episcopate. The lines from Archbishop Romero quoted subsequently are taken from an interview in the Mexican newspaper *El Excelsior.*

14. The *Dossier de Ribeirão Bonito*, compiled by Bishop Pedro Casaldaliga, was circulated in French by D.I.A.L. (Diffusion de l'information sur l'Amérique Latine), Paris, D335 of 21 October 1976 and D 338 of 11 November 1976. It was presented with an analysis of the various possible readings and interpretations of this death by Ignace Berten *opus citatum),* "He died for us . . . he lives!" in *Lumen Vitae*, 33, 4 (1978), pp. 403-34. The quotations in the text cover the greater part of the article but obviously leave out many details and finer points. Nor do they reproduce an important theological reflection on the question: if João Bosco becomes a symbol through the efficacy of that other symbol, Jesus, where does this symbolic efficacy of Jesus for most Christians come from? In short, why does Jesus make tradition in Christianity, in a fundamental and original sense, unlike any other saint? Psychologically, we need only show by this exceptional situation *how* the Christian experience develops in a symbolic process of this nature. We need not show what makes the resurrection of Jesus still credible today, as it has been throughout a long tradition.

15. I. Berten, article quoted; these quotations are taken from pp. 422-27.

16. These conditions for symbolization in eucharistic celebration have been explored and analyzed in a remarkable article by Herman Lombaerts, "Religious Symbolization in a Youth Mass," in *Lumen Vitae*, 35, 3 (1980), pp. 291-316. The subject is a piece of empirical research, on the basis of experiments lasting six years, in a group which finally, from very complex motives, broke up. Further details on this research are supplied in the articles by H. Lombaerts published in *Temps et Paroles*, nos. 17 to 21 (February to November, 1978).

17. G. Girardi, "Un théologien dans la lutte des classes," in *Concilium 109* (1975), p. 108, note 1.

18. F. Denantes makes this accusation in "Une logique influente," in

Etudes (October, 1976), p. 303. He even feels obliged to add that "their socialism (that of these Christians) becomes too idealized, so that they do not fear its coming to pass." But is that a reproach? Might it not rather be an indication that, for these (Marxist) Christians, Christian hope relativizes, without altogether suppressing, the fascination with the Marxist utopia or prevents it, in the last resort, from exercising an "idealizing" function?

19. On this paradox (aggression-communion), not as a pitfall, but as a meeting place for emotions to be kept in tension, there are some contributions by psychologists like J. Claude Sagne, "L'alternative communautaire," in *Le Supplément 106* (September, 1973), pp. 261-82, or Guy Paiement, "Communication et conflits dans les communautés de base," in *Concilium 104* (April, 1975), pp. 123-30, and some others by sociologists, occasionally involved in base communities, who have contributed to the collective works *Politique et foi* (Strasbourg: Cerdic, 1972), and *Eclatements dans l'Eglise* (Paris: Cerf, 1972).

20. Receiving sixteen Jesuit worker-priests in Rome on 9 February 1980 Father Arrupe, the General of the Order, said he had noticed that "the worker mission (some sixty Jesuits throughout the world) had been neglected or else had unleashed passionate reactions. . . . Complete cultural involvement in intellectual or welfare circles is readily allowed while the same involvement in the working proletariat is disapproved. Might this not be the remains of class prejudice?" (*La Croix,* 2 May 1980, p. 8).

21. Joseph Comblin, *Théologie de la révolution* and *Théologie de la pratique révolutionnaire* (Paris: Ed. Universitaires, 1970 and 1974), quotation p. 173. In a rather different sense, the theologian Alain Durand discusses the renewal of hope, on the basis of class struggle, in terms of discernment (which camp am I in?) rather than of experience to be lived and celebrated, notably in *Pour une Eglise partisane* (Paris: Cerf, 1974), and in a short but penetrating article, "Lutte des classes et perspectives chrétiennes de la réconciliation," in *Concilium 109* (November, 1975), pp. 27-36.

22. Jean and Colette Guichard, *Liturgie et lutte des classes: symbolisme et politique* (Paris: Idoc-France, L'Harmattan, 1976). Also of interest are C. Duquoc and J. Guichard, *Politique et vocabulaire liturgique* (Paris: Cerf, 1975) and H. Bausch-Hug, *Neue Gemeinde-Wachsende Gemeinde: Gruppen Dynamik und Liturgie* (Lucerne and Munich: Rex Verlag, 1974). Sociologists have tried to set the liturgical renewal and the creativity manifest in it in the broader framework of an "impact of the social symbolics that underly or develop in them" (J. Remy, E. Servais and J. P. Hiernaux, "Formes liturgiques et symboliques sociales," in *Social Compass* 22, 1975 (2), pp. 175-92). More striking, because of its rigorous method, is Felice

Dassetto's analysis *Production liturgique et Judaisme* (Louvain: Centre de Recherches socio-religieuses, 1975). On the basis of sermons broadcast over a six-month period in Belgium, France, and French Switzerland (210,000 words), of commentaries on these Sunday Masses in two daily papers representing traditional and institutional Catholicism (*La Libre Belgique* and *La Croix,* with 17,500 words), and of two collections currently distributed to the faithful (19,380 words), amounting to 157 communications containing one of the key words chosen as indicators, we find that 156 focused on religious ideology and only one had a sociopolitical thrust. Analysis of the content reveals a wholesale application of Judaic texts in the liturgical commentary. On the other hand, the situation in the state of Israel and the Palestinian question are not mentioned. The difference is the more disturbing in that numerous social or ethico-religious implications are drawn in these texts when dealing with so-called "Lenten" sermons or those relating to poverty. The level of tension between a factual pole (what is accomplished) and an ahistorical pole (what is not accomplished) varies widely in the three types of text under consideration; it is almost nonexistent in the liturgical type, comes to light in the sermons, and is developed in the journalistic type. So in 1973 there was far from being a language of celebration which took to itself events discerned from an evangelical point of view as "signs of the times," a term that has become, since the Vatican Council (*Pacem in Terris, Gaudium et Spes, Ecclesiam suam*) "not only a theological category but one that is constituent for the study of the conditions of evangelization" (M.D. Chenu, "Les signes des temps: réflexion théologique," *L'Eglise dans le monde de ce temps,* Paris, Cerf, 1967, p. 225). The same theologian has presented the liturgical dimension called for by Christian celebration of the events of history in "Anthropologie de la liturgie," *La liturgie d'après Vatican II* (Paris: Cerf, 1967), pp. 159-77, and in "Orthodoxie-Orthopraxie," *Le service théologique dans l'Eglise* (Paris, Cerf, 1974), pp. 51-63.

23. J. and C. Guichard, *opus citatum,* 1976, p. 63.

24. René Coulomb, "Pratiques symboliques et liturgiques dans la lutte des classes," in *La Lettre 224* (April, 1974), p. 15. Note that this death-life pairing, introduced in this way into a community, endows it with a dynamism, the effects of which are unpredictable. Witness this comment: "Our point of view is that it is not important that a community live forever. Of course, we are not thinking of killing it, but what is an immortality principle if not the law of institution? The law of the gospel is of resurrection after passing through death. The concern that 'if we do so-and-so we are endangering the survival of the church' seems to us to be contrary to the law of the gospel. We must be concerned not with immortality but with dying in the path which the gospel tells us is full of

the promise of resurrection. At least, that must be the concern of a base community." (J. B. Franzoni, "Une vraie communauté chrétienne," in *Etudes et Dialogues 137*, May, 1980, p. 8.)

25. In contrast with the very broad welcome given by the church authorities to the charismatic movement (which poses no liturgical problem since the specifically charismatic exchanges are followed by entirely classic eucharistic celebrations in these groups) there has been increasing reserve and even disapproval toward the base communities. In order that they might be "a hope for the universal church," the apostolic exhortation *Evangelii nuntiandi* (Documentation catholique, 4 January 1976) laid down conditions so that very little difference would remain between these communities, when finally recognized as "ecclesial," and traditional parish meetings. At the conference in Puebla (January, 1979) these conditions were nevertheless discussed again and considered to be "important but not exclusive" for those "nuclei of a church born of the people under the impulse of the Spirit" (Jacques Van Nieuwenhove, "Puebla and the Grass-Roots Communities," in *Lumen Vitae 34*, (4) (1979), pp. 311-30). The imbalance between the understanding and help given to these two types of renewal, while perfectly understandable on the part of a centralizing institution, causes an awkward increase in tensions between these groups whose Christian experience and ecclesiology are largely contradictory. Cardinal Suenens has insisted several times on the importance and urgency of "attempting to overcome a tension which polarizes two types of Christians: those who stress the spiritual and those whose priority is temporal commitment" ("La double approche," in *Magnificat* III (1), January 1976, p. 7). On the fringe of the ecclesiological debate, which is obviously important, psychological analysis of both types of Christian experience in these two chapters and the following one will no doubt help the reader, not to solve the question, but to see it in another light.

III

Experience of Self or
Transforming Experience in Faith

Oak and cypress trees do not grow in each other's shade.

Let there be spaces in your communion that the winds of Heaven may dance between you.

For the pillars of the temple are erected at a distance.

KAHLIL GIBRAN

Introduction

From the Critique of Illusions to the Transformation of Wishes

God: illusion or reality?

Have I encountered God or myself?

To accept the hard reality of life and death, is that not to set aside the imaginary projections of our wishes?

Three expressions of the same dilemma.

This is how many of our contemporaries formulate the religious question, query their own religious experience, endeavor to face up to fate, to change the world, to live more authentically in human solidarity by setting religious faith aside.

Cultural Freudianism with its woolly expressions is their hand-me-down philosophy. A rationalism stamped with suspicion, typical in current speech, suggests that this dilemma is the correct viewpoint for evaluating the future chances of an illusion, if not of its truth.

Objective beliefs or the projection of our wishes: This simplification is far removed from the Freudian spirit and from that of Marx or Feuerbach too, no doubt, though they are often invoked on the basis of quotations taken out of context. But this dilemma comes in handy to serve wishes in two opposite directions. Nonbelievers want the freedom and courage to live by eliminating various unconscious emotions of a religious nature. Believers wish to avoid critical reflection on the dynamism unconsciously at work in their tranquil convictions, their ritual practices, or their experiences of faith.

By thus posing the religious question *as a dilemma,* the unconscious can be ruled out in both cases by trusting "once and for all" (at least that is to be hoped) either in rational evidence or in the lively awareness of moral or spiritual experiences: courage and freedom for the first, tranquillity and trust for the second. But even when ruled out the unconscious is never quite asleep. It watches and wakes us for the length of a sigh, a dream, a doubt, as the case may be: supposing it is true? supposing it is wrong? I know perfectly well, and yet . . .

The unconscious components of wishes

I know perfectly well, and yet . . . Freud's atheism was indisputably sincere and loudly proclaimed. By what secret paths was he led to a passionate interest in religion? He makes clear that he asked himself the question by speaking of "an order I receive from my unconscious connections." He followed that order by working for two years on *Totem and Taboo*, then on his more philosophical than psychological works on the meaning of monotheism after Moses and of its transformation after Christ. His clinical work with a clientele consisting largely of believers revealed to him in an exceptionally powerful light what the Christian religion is not; or, more precisely, what it can no longer be for adults who are informed and critical, and rallying to the banner of the "reality principle." It is a mishap in Freud's story that neither in the Judaism of his childhood nor in Christianity (in the Moravia of his time where the Christians persecuted the Jews) had Freud encountered the presentation of a God who was on the side of that "reality principle." It remains true that in proposing to understand human evolution toward maturity as a slow transition, always uncompleted, from "the pleasure principle" dominating the younger years to a preponderance of the "reality principle," he went beyond the false dilemma that opposes reality to illusion and correctly located the psychological problem of religious faith, with all its components including the slow maturation of affectivity, in its unconscious sources and structures.

I believe, I trust, and yet . . . By what complex pathways, psychic, social, cultural, does doubt mingle with the religious beliefs of millions of Christians who have been told the Good News since childhood and throw them back into the realm of illusions? This is an inviting question for psychology, to be examined from the point of view of the evolving mental and affective structures. The resort to religion *as an experience,* described in its richness and variety in the first two parts of this work, demands that it be examined up to that point. Does the God (the gods) concerned resist the application of the Freudian criterion to the various forms of experience described? Or, even though we challenge them, must we declare the Freudian claims insuperable at least in their application to these experiences?

To challenge them is easily said. It would not of itself get rid of the element of disbelief mixed up in all belief. "The gnawing, irrefutable worm is not for you who sleep beneath the slab; he lives *on death* and never lets me go" (Paul Valéry, *Le cimetière marin*).

Note

1. "The psychology of religious faith and attachments . . . I know I have embarked on a tortuous route in relation to my (medical) work, but it is an order I receive from my unconscious connections" (August 1911), quoted by E. Jones, *The Life and Work of Sigmund Freud,* 3 volumes (New York: Basic Books, 1957), vol. II, p. 373. These "unconscious connections" have been analyzed by Louis Beirnaert, "Introduction à la psychanalyse freudienne de la religion," in *Etudes* (February, 1968), pp. 200-10. Facts which help toward an understanding of the permanent battle fought by Freud on the subject of religion can be found in G. Zilboorg, *Freud and Religion* (Westminster, Maryland: Newman Press, 1958). The works of old age alluded to in the text are *Civilization and Its Discontents* (1930), *Revue française de psychanalyse* (1934); no. 4, *Moses and monotheism* (1939), (Paris: Gallimard, 1967). They had been preceded by *The Future of an Illusion* (1927), (Paris: Denoel et Steele, 1932). Freud styled them "the works of an old man returning to humanity's taste for philosophy."

6

The Critique of Illusions

The psychological critique of illusions has neither the first nor the last word in religion any more than in love. But if religious conduct and experiences claim, as is the case in fulfilled love, to take us beyond ourselves and establish a transforming union for the *ego* and its relational network, it is incumbent upon them to confirm the points at which they are anchored in a reality which is *other* than the personal needs of the subject. They call for progressive understanding and awareness, confrontations through mutual communication, transformations in the drive structures of the unconscious.*

The psycho-spiritual discernment of positive religious experiences, those that open up to someone other than the self, involves examining how illusions are rooted in conscious wishes and how projections operate unconsciously.

Belief-illusion according to Freud

Not all illusion is belief, neither is all belief illusion.

A belief is an illusion when its motivation is predominantly the realization of a wish and so no heed is paid to the links of

---

* As far a possible in this chapter, technical terms will be avoided, but there is a limit. Certain terms will be found designating reactions, movements, or products of the *unconscious,* such as: phantasm, ideal of the ego, narcissism, impulse, superego. For these words that have passed into current speech, but not without misunderstandings, the reader is referred to the second section of the thematic glossary at the end of the volume.

that belief with reality, just as illusion itself does not seek confirmation in the real.[1]

In interpersonal relationships it is through language that the "link with reality" is maintained and developed.

So, Barbara, beautiful, unknown, only glimpsed: illusion *or* reality? Did I meet Barbara or myself, in my easily roused sexuality? Trapped in this false dilemma, there is every chance that the questioner will never meet Barbara, either in her own reality or in the truth of the burgeoning relationship. If he waits till he has removed his imaginary projections before approaching her, he will probably never speak to her. But that won't prevent him from holding forth on the subject of "woman." Courtly love came from that source (see Denis de Rougemont).[2] Condemned by the dilemma, Barbara will float for a long while between reality and illusion without much chance of being recognized as *the* woman she is with her actual wishes. She may become a myth, too. It is known that certain women (and certain men) are not averse to it.

But with the help of language, this false dilemma can be broken. And then we have: "Barbara, dear illusion, do you know that I love and desire you? Barbara, since I first saw you and spoke your name, I don't know whether it is you I met or only myself." If Barbara starts to talk— and that is no more sure than in the case of God (the gods)—she takes the risk that she may be rejected or still desired, neither more nor less than the word of God (or the gods, if they speak). Speaking from her own wishes, she transforms the dream relationship (illusion) into an awakening to reality. She is in danger of arousing a defensive aggressiveness (unconscious or partially conscious) in her interlocutor and so "losing her erotic power, at least temporarily."[3] Confusedly desired, will she be loved?

But there is no other way. Through the demand made to Barbara, the total sexual urge toward her becomes confronted with what she will say, revealing her wishes and, hopefully, her own demand for love. So, from demand to wish and wish to demand the interpersonal link does not suppress the aggressiveness each feels on discovering the "otherness" of the other, but bends it to serve a mutual recognition that becomes more and more genuine. A certain amount of vehement self-assertion has never harmed true lovers strong enough to accept the insuperable narcissistic basis that thrusts them together in the primitive sexual urge. By first exchanging words, then gestures, of tenderness, they pave the way for a deep transformation in the unconscious: libidinal and aggressive impulses, disjoined from time immemorial, are about to combine to produce and maintain at the optimal distance recognition of the "other" in the joy of being "together." Happiness in love is maintained, not by the illusory fulfillment of desire, but by the constant deepening of the other's wishes in each one; these are recognized and diversified more and more up to the waning phases of a duration necessarily limited by death. The discontinuous time of the impulses is transformed into the duration of a constructed love.

The failure of the sexual drive to produce an encounter of love in the experience of "the other" may obviously have many causes. The most frequent is probably immediate satisfaction of desire, either when the partner as "other" is radically ignored in a wordless coitus, or when he is recognized only in an objectified demand, such as the demand for money in prostitution.

But many other failures on the way to an opening to "the other" in dialogue can be attributed to more subtle illusions due to the unconscious mechanism of projection.

Projection and projections

In the strict psychoanalytical sense, projection is an unconscious operation by which a person or a group, failing to recognize its own wishes or fears, tends to locate in others the qualities, intentions, or powers he rejects in himself. The *Vocabulary of Psychoanalysis* adds to that definition: "This is a very ancient defense, seen at work in paranoia (persecution mania) but also in normal modes of thought like superstition."[4]

Barbara, the object of sexual desire, easily becomes endowed with a host of qualities and charms that are instigated and sustained mentally by the person desiring her. These are undoubtedly projections, the most general of all being her imaginary submission to all the wishes of the one accosting her. Here we are dealing with conscious imaginings.

But things can get more complicated, especially when, by keeping her distance, Barbara frustrates the partner's wishes, producing an aggressiveness that quickly spreads confusion. The attitude of the interlocutor becomes ambivalent in this very precise sense: failing to recognize his own hostility, for example, he attributes it to her, suspecting her of spiteful intentions toward him. Or again, failing to recognize in himself certain inclinations to leave her for another girl, he attributes them to her and falls victim to a jealousy that gradually consumes the first links established. The suspect intentions attributed to Barbara are obviously conscious since her interlocutor never stops talking about them and seeks to justify them by observed "facts," duly interpreted to that end. But the dynamism of the projection remains unconscious and manages to hide his own aggressive movements from the subject. In the end, this defensive and repressive operation forms a protection against any opening toward the other by contaminating the dialogues that are henceforth devoted to self-justification.

The more an object of a wish is vague, distant, idealized, mysterious, or silent, the more likely it is to be invested with subjective expectations and imaginary features; the more capable it becomes of mobilizing individual and collective energies without modifying their egocentric or sociocentric character, the more ready it is to close the breaches in an affective system, especially if it functions in an anxious, defensive, infantile (regressive) mode. God (or the gods), as a term designating a transcendence, offers a prop peculiarly suited to focus this kind of expectation, wish, or fear. So does the devil, of course. But so too do certain nonreligious unrealistic objectives like changing metals into gold.

For several centuries in Europe the idea of alchemy and the hopes it engendered provoked considerable investments of effort, time, and human lives, out of all proportion to the results obtained.

In the history of Christianity there have been millions of women and tens of thousands of men, all convinced they had made a pact with the devil, to meet him in somber Sabbath orgies. The inquisitorial reaction, as we know, achieved record-breaking abominations of repression and stupidity in its procedures. The promise that their lives would be saved if they admitted having met the devil and entered into a compact with him brought millions of supplementary confessions from people who were clearly convinced of the contrary. Thus the courts engaged in witch hunting continually reinforced the collective impression that the object or stake of the hunt was real. In the sixteenth and seventeenth centuries, the only fight they were engaged in was to justify their existence. Social and cultural conditions having changed, they were presiding over nothing but a void. These courts disappeared. Witchcraft, for its part, continued.

So we must get used to the idea that the intensity of an experience, the commotion it causes in communities, the institutional way in which it consolidates itself in society are no guarantee of its value or of the reality of its goal. Contrary to the popular adage, there is much imaginary smoke without real fire, except that kindled by men. In order to dispel illusions, therefore, it would be better to endeavor to understand their affective ties and social conditioning.

Three sources of spontaneous religiosity

According to Freud, this is how religions speak to human wishes. The psychoanalytical study of religion, "that of the common man, the only religion which ought to bear that name"[5] reveals its affective ties according to whether it is studied in its practices, its beliefs, or its mysticism.

1) *Ritual practices* actualize the stories and promises that are the subject of beliefs. But for the magical mentality they also offer their services in the granting of certain out of reach wishes, the fulfillment of certain expectations by entrusting them to the all-powerful, in quelling revolts, and especially in lightening the burden of guilt.

In the parallel he drew in 1907 between "obsessive acts and religious practices,"[6] Freud pointed out in these types of behavior an impulse to accomplish certain stereotyped practices and an uneasy feeling of guilt once those practices are omitted. Such conduct is motivated, at least partially, by the fear of yielding to repressed, and thus unconscious, tendencies. But, he wrote, whereas in obsessional neuroses we are dealing fundamentally with sexual tendencies, religious observances are related more to the repression of aggressive or antisocial impulses. So religious practice would be particularly suited, not to the sublimation of aggressiveness, but to keeping it repressed by calming the co-existing sense of guilt. Sacrificial and penitential practices would have that meaning psychologically—at least for a great number of "ordinary believers"—despite the symbolic import studied by academic theology.

In the Christian myth the original sin was against God the Father. If, however, Christ redeemed mankind from the burden of original sin by the sacrifice of his own life, we are driven to conclude that the sin was a murder. And if this sacrifice of his life brought about atonement with God the Father, the crime to be expiated can only have been the murder of the father. In the Christian doctrine, therefore, men were acknowledging in the most undisguised manner the guilty primeval deed, since they found the fullest atonement for it in the sacrifice of this one son. . . .[7] But the murder was not remembered (in the Scriptures); instead there was a fantasy of its atonement and for that reason this fantasy could be hailed as a message of redemption (evangelium). . . .[8] And a son-religion displaced the father-religion. Communion was instituted in which the company of brothers consumed the flesh and blood of the son—no longer of the father—obtained sanctity thereby, and identified themselves with him. . . . [In effecting this shift] Christian communion is essentially a repetition of the guilty deed.[9]

By assuaging the guilt, the common lot of mankind, this ritual keeps the aggressiveness (of fathers against sons and vice versa), which is its origin, repressed.

For Freud, at the time of his study of obsessive acts and rituals (1907), guilt provided an explanation for the creation and use of religious rites rather than a foundation for the idea or image of God. But the use of rites can be replaced in the broader framework of his subsequent writings, relating to beliefs imbued with the magnified image of the father and/or mother, all-powerful and all-gratifying. This throws light psychologically on another function of devotional ritual: a system of magic fulfillment of wishes that clash with harsh reality ("illusory" aspect) and the maintenance in the unconscious of a childish wish (unchanged) for omnipotence ("projection" aspect).

2) *Religious beliefs,* contained for the most part on mythical tales and promises, are incapable of proof or verification by reality. The dominant factor in their motivation is obvious: an intense wish for consolation, for compensation in the renunciations imposed by life in society, for security and immortality. "It is a very striking fact that all this is exactly as we are bound to wish it to be."[10] Religious beliefs, like the history of religions, are precious as a "psychological inventory of civilization." In them we are revealed, right down to the unconscious dynamism of our impulses.

A large portion of the mythological conception of the world, which reaches far into most modern religions, is nothing but psychology projected into the outer world. . . . We venture to explain in this way the myths about paradise and the fall of man, of God, of good and evil, of immortality and the like.[11]

These ideas which are given out as teachings are not precipitates of experience or end-results of thinking: They are illusions, fulfillments of the oldest, strongest, and most urgent wishes of mankind. The secret of their strength is the strength of those wishes. . . .[12]

The gods retain their threefold task: They must exorcise the terrors of nature, they must reconcile men to the cruelty of fate particularly as it is shown in death, and they must compensate them for the sufferings and privations which a civilized life in common has imposed on them. . . .[13] Thus the benevolent rule of a divine Providence allays our fear of the dangers of life; the establishment of a *moral world order* ensures the fulfillment of the demands of justice, which have so often remained unfulfilled in human civilization; and the prolongation of earthly existence in a *future life* provides the local and temporal framework in which these wish-fulfillments shall take place.[14]

The common man cannot imagine this *Providence* otherwise than in the figure of an enormously exalted father. Only such a being can understand the needs of the children of men and be softened by their prayers and placated by the signs of their remorse.[15]

When the growing individual finds that he is destined to remain a child forever and that he can never do without protection against strange, superior powers, he lends those powers the features belonging to the figure of his father; he creates for himself the gods whom he dreads, whom he seeks to propitiate and whom he nevertheless entrusts with his own protection. . . . The defense against childish helplessness is what lends its characteristic features to the adult's reaction to the helplessness which he has to acknowledge—a reaction which is precisely the formation of religion.[16]

As can be seen from a reading of these texts, religious beliefs appeared to Freud as mental formations on the level of wishful thinking, that is, as thoughts based on illusory compensation. Writing of *The Future of an Illusion* a few days before it came out, he stated frankly: "This booklet deals with my attitude in the matter of all forms of religion, even the most degraded, which is one of total rejection" (Letter to Pastor Pfister, 16 October

1927); and a week later: "The text already seems to me childish; the analysis is weak and as a personal confession it is inadequate" (Letter to Ferenczi, 23 October 1927). This dissatisfaction drove him to shelve the whole problem during the next ten years, but without any fundamental modification in his approach and interpretation, as can be seen from other texts quoted from his later works.

Meanwhile, analysis of motivations in the genesis of beliefs provided him with a few landmarks for the classification of religious experiences: polytheism, animism, monotheism, spiritualism.

When human beings began to think, they were obviously compelled to explain the outer world in an anthropomorphic sense by a multitude of personalities in their own image; the accidents which they explained superstitiously were thus actions and expressions of persons. In that regard they behaved just like paranoiacs, who draw conclusions from insignificant signs which others give them, and like all normal persons who justly take the unintentional actions of their fellow beings as a basis for the estimation of their characters.[17]

We too believe that the pious solution contains the truth but the *historical* and not the *material* truth. We believe that in primeval times there was a single person who was bound to appear huge at that time and who afterwards returned in men's memory, elevated to divinity. And we assume the right to correct a certain distortion to which this truth has been subjected on its return.[18]

The *animistic* phase would correspond to narcissism both chronologically and in its content; the *religious* phase would correspond to the stage of object-choice of which the characteristic is the child's attachment to his parents; while the scientific phase would have an exact counterpart in the stage at which an individual has reached maturity, has renounced the pleasure principle, adjusted himself to reality and turned to the external world for the object of his wishes.[19]

Two sorts of elements will be recognized in religious doctrines and rituals: on the one hand *fixations* to the ancient history of the family and survivals of it; on the other hand, revivals of the past and *returns* after long intervals of what had been forgotten. . . . All this may encourage us to inquire whether the religion of Moses brought the people nothing else besides enhancement of their self-esteem owing to their consciousness of having been chosen. And indeed another factor can easily be found: that religion also brought the Jews a far grander conception of God or, as we might put it more modestly, the conception of a grander God. Anyone who believed in this God had some kind of share in his greatness, might feel himself exalted. . . . The prohibition against making an image of God certainly had profound effects, for sensory perception took second place to what may be called an abstract idea, a triumph of intellectuality over sensuality or, strictly speaking, an instinctual renunciation with all its necessary psychological consequences. . . . That was unquestionably one of the most important stages on the path to hominization.[20]

These descriptions of the religious shift in its progressive mutations, interesting as they may be, must not make us lose sight of the main thread: Born of a defensive reaction against agonizing situations in his destiny, religions fail to lead man toward a life organized under the banner of the "reality principle" or to resolve his aggressiveness by turning it to the service of love in an opening toward another. They merely repeat in various guises conflicting drives (eros-thanatos) whose components they repress by obscuring them. This reproach applies too to religious mysticism, as we shall see.

3) *The mystical element* in religion and *the wish for the absolute* evident in certain religious experiences did not escape Freud's attention. He drew them together by putting their affective source in the primary and total affectivity which establishes the child originally in a "fusion" relationship with the world and other people, represented at this first stage of narcissism by the mother, not yet perceived in her personal differentiation. Faith, as distinct from the content of belief, has its source there, in his view: "It happens that intellectuality itself is overpowered by the

very puzzling emotional phenomenon of faith . . . and no believer will let himself be led astray from his faith by these or similar arguments. A believer is bound to the teachings of his religion by certain ties of affection."[21] How is this primary affectivity to be understood, thanks to which religion may bring certain men happiness in love compensating for any renunciations that may be made?

Here is Freud's crucial description of it. Some words have been italicized with a view to the conclusions reached in this chapter.

> A small minority are enabled by their constitution to find happiness in spite of everything along the path of love. But far-reaching mental changes in the function of love are necessary before this can happen. These people *make themselves independent* of the object's acquiescence by displacing what they mainly value from being loved on to loving. They *protect themselves* against the loss of the object by directing their love, not to single objects but to all men alike. They *avoid* the uncertainties and disappointments of genital love by turning away from its sexual aims and *transforming* the instinct into an "impulse with an inhibited aim." What they bring about in themselves in this way is a state of evenly suspended, steadfast, affectionate feeling which has little external resemblance any more to the stormy agitations of genital love, from which it is nevertheless derived. Perhaps St. Francis of Assisi went furthest in this exploiting love for the benefit of an inner feeling of happiness.[22]

Freud immediately raised certain objections to this view of love as a source of happiness: It is far from being within the grasp of all men; it does not discriminate and "seems to lose some of its value by doing injustice to its objects"; in the end it is transformed into a commandment, "Love thy neighbor as thyself," which becomes "at once the strongest defense against human aggressiveness and an excellent example of the unpsychological proceedings of the cultural superego."[23] In these "vast modifications of a psychic order," he omits any consideration of the factor of identification with Christ, which he had singled out some years before (1921) as essential to Christians (see further on).

Remember for the moment that the "impulse with an inhibited goal" could also apply to the contemplation that precedes artistic creation, to the state of availability in readiness for the great choices or commitments in life. To the irresolute and then verbalized transfer that, in psychotherapy, permits psychic modifications in the process of elaboration. In the best cases, *the way is paved* for inner liberation. This awakening of the inner life, or reawakening of unconsciously jammed narcissistic feelings, must not be confused with their *fulfillment* in reality without which wishes turn in on themselves. This nonachievement is masked by various kinds of ethical or spiritual discourse, but their healthy issue is compromised. When "the Ego Ideal" is objectified, for example in a moral principle, in a "commandment," it mobilizes an affectivity which is thereafter bound by a collective superego and ends by filling the original breach. By thus repressing the fundamental aggressive component, it has a way of sealing off in a feeling of heroic pride any possibility of being open to the wishes of the "other," of the neighbor in his material reality.

The absolutization of principles, duties, good works, or good attitudes is a late intellectual formation responding to the demands of life in society. In the unconscious, it is based on an "ideal ego" impervious to the new solicitations of wishes but favoring the religious humility that proclaims "God alone is good."[24]

> It is easy to show that the ego ideal answers to everything that is expected of the higher nature *of man*. As a substitute for a longing for the father, it contains the germ from which all religions have evolved. The self-judgment which declares that the ego falls short of its ideal produces the religious sense of humility to which the believer appeals in his longing.[25]

With this impetus, even mystical religious man meets not God but only himself.

Identification must complete love

From an examination of these texts, the psychological study of the affective ties of religion no doubt appears to be narrowly confined within the movements that either favor or hinder maturity of love between two persons who talk to each other and attempt to evolve together. The little fable of Barbara, the abortive object of desire for her interlocutor, was certainly not irrelevant from this point of view.

But Christian experience does not compare on all points with this interpersonal relationship made up of immediately concrete interactions. Its reference to Jesus Christ, dead and risen again, occurs on the one hand through the Scriptures and on the other in living communities throughout history and in churches. Freud encountered this collective dimension only once in his analysis of the ego. This text closely resembles those produced by traditional theology and deserves careful reading, the more so as it is rarely quoted.

The equal love of Christ for all the faithful without exception or distinction is expressly enunciated in these words: "Inasmuch as you have done it unto one of the least of these my brethren, you have done it unto me." To the individual members of the group of believers he stands in the relation of a kind of elder brother. . . . All the demands that are made upon the individual are derived from this love of Christ's. . . . It is not without a deep reason that the analogy of a family is invoked and that the believers call themselves brothers *through the love which Christ has for them.* There is no doubt that the tie which unites each individual with Christ is also the *cause* of the tie which unites them with one another.[26]

Freud then points out that this affective ("libidinal") link exists too in the constitution and continuance of hierarchical groups which, like the army, stimulate a team spirit centered on the person of the chief. He adds, however: "A similar hierarchy has been constructed in the church, but it does not play the same part in it economically (from the point of view of the distribution of affective energies), for more knowledge and care about individuals may be attributed to Christ than to a human Commander-in-Chief."[27]

But that is not the main difference. Here it is, spelled out in "Some Supplementary Considerations" added at the end of the study.

> It is obvious that a soldier takes . . . the leader of the army as an ideal (thus offering a common object to the ego ideal, allowing the soldiers to identify with each other in a spirit of comradeship and mutual help); . . . a soldier would make himself ridiculous if he tried to identify himself with the general. . . . It is otherwise in the Catholic Church. Certainly every Christian loves Christ as his ideal and feels himself united with all other Christians by the tie of identification. But the church *requires* more of him. He *must* also identify himself with Christ and love other Christians as Christ loved them. Identification *must* be added where object-choice has taken place and object-love where there is identification. This addition evidently goes beyond the constitution of the group. One can be a good Christian and yet be far from putting oneself in Christ's place and of having like him an *all-embracing love* for mankind. One need not think oneself capable, weak mortal that one is, of the Savior's largeness of soul and strength of love. But this further development in the distribution of the libido in the group is probably the factor upon which Christianity bases its claim to have reached *a higher ethical level.*[28]

In the two main passages just quoted, a theologian has no difficulty in recognizing a major statement of the Christian message: It is on the basis of love *received* from Christ that all Christian communities are founded (brotherhood of the faithful), but it is on the basis of identification with Christ loving *all men* that a community remains faithful to him. The first component (love received) is pursued in the psychism under the sign of "pleasure principle." The second component (active identification) introduces an attitude consonant with the "reality principle" if it opens on to a neighbor selected as significant.

Yet the words underlined in these texts show that this was not how Freud understood the dynamic structure of the Christian message established by Jesus Christ. He presents it as a "demand" by the church, a "claim" and three times as a duty, a law. It then fits in to the affectivity like the "collective superego" which he had already criticized in Judaism. Furthermore, the aim of this law (love for all men) would be to obtain a "higher moral level." No mention is made of the "forgiveness of sins" or of loving one's enemies (significant persons: whom do you call your neighbor?) leading to "forgiveness of those who persecute you." In other terms, perhaps because of his Jewish background, Freud is presenting a moralizing and intellectual interpretation of a *message*. He has not examined the dynamic of love and identification as *experience*, still less as a condition of a religiously credible experience.

Freudian challenge to religion

If the Freudian critique of illusions and religious projection applies mainly and usefully in the four directions discussed (practices, beliefs, mysticism, community identification) his challenge is supported on a single reproach: Religions are not capable of contributing to man's maturity by directing him toward the dominance of the "reality principle." The sublimation expected of them is not achieved.

The belief in immortality can be taken as an example. It will be noticed that it is approached from the angle of a moral recompense.

A doctrine of reward in the afterlife for the—voluntary or enforced—renunciation of earthly pleasures is nothing other than a mythical projection of this revolution in the mind: the substitution of the reality principle for the pleasure principle. Following consistently along these lines, religions have been able to effect absolute *renunciation* of pleasure in this life by means of a promise of compensation in a future existence. But they have not by this means conquered the pleasure principle.[29]

If religion fails to achieve an opening to the reality principle, whereas science or art come "much closer" to it, it is because religion proceeds by constant idealization of the object. Thus it makes a harmonization of the impulses (libidinal and aggressive) more and more impossible, aggression being repressed inside a more and more inflated ego-ideal on the basis of its primitive and undifferentiated narcissism.

Art brings about a reconciliation between the two principles (pleasure and reality) in a peculiar way. . . . The artist finds the way back to reality from his world of fantasy by making use of special gifts to mold his fantasies into truths of a new kind which are valued by men as precious reflections of reality. . . . He can only achieve this because other men feel the same dissatisfaction as he does with the renunciation demanded by reality and because that dissatisfaction, which results from the replacement of the pleasure principle by the reality principle, is itself part of reality.[30]

Sublimation is a process that concerns object-libido and consists in the instinct's directing itself toward an aim other than, and remote from that of sexual satisfaction; in this process the accent falls upon deflection from sexuality. *Idealization* is a process that concerns the object; by it that object, without any alteration in its nature, is aggrandized and exalted in the subject's mind. . . . These two concepts are to be distinguished from each other. The formation of an ego ideal is often confused with the sublimation of instinct, to the 'detriment of our understanding of the facts. A man who has exchanged his narcissism for homage to a high ego ideal has not necessarily on that account succeeded in sublimating his libidinal instincts. It is true that the ego ideal demands such sublimation, but it cannot enforce it. . . . As we have learned, the formation of an ideal heightens the demands of the ego and is the most powerful factor favoring repression. Sublimation is a way out, a way by which those demands can be met without involving repression.[31]

In the last analysis, the Freudian critique of religious illusions ends in dispute and rejection. From its standpoint, religious practices, beliefs, and sentiments do not obtain what religions seem to promise: a transforming sublimation of the affectivity in its opening up to reality.

Summary: the contribution of Freud

Freud, an atheist passionately interested in religion, has put religious and nonreligious men equally in his debt. While the discoveries that allow a better understanding of the psychic conditionings of the unconscious in the development and wishes of man were being clarified, he situated the religious question in its proper place: on the side of reality, not as a fulfillment of compensatory desires; on the side of stimulation to reach maturity in opening out to the Other, not consolation or the avoidance of subjective ordeals; on the side of active symbolism in the interval created by a word that may be transcendent, not the imaginary bridging of that interval.

If the founder of psychoanalysis had not been interested in religion and inclined through his Jewish ancestry to situate it in this way, it might have taken fifty years[32] for believers in all religions to begin to ask the religious question in this form: If God (or the gods) exists and manifests himself, it must be by words and wishes discernable by the wishes and requests that men address spontaneously to God (the gods). There might have been a long period of philosophical, indeed theoretical efforts to accredit and justify the most "religious" of unconscious motivations, to demonstrate that God (even as revealed in Jesus Christ) coincides with an ego ideal in search of the absolute, with the wish for love in search of fulfillment. Moreover Jung, by introducing archetypes, presented a "religious" interpretation of the unconscious that opens directly on to a gnosis[33] not lacking in fascination for certain religious, even Christian, thinkers.

Let us agree, however, to ask the question as Freud did, that is, in terms of a belief which does not avoid the reality of either conflict or death; in terms of a wish possibly originating in the Other and not as a simple projection of the wish itself; in terms of a nonidealizing identification—terms that are essential if the "reality principle" is to predominate.

It is clear that everything described in the first chapter of this book as manifestations of functional religion does not satisfy these terms of Freud's; that means that it is shaken, to say the least, by his critique of illusions. Functional religion is all perfectly comprehensible as a projection or organization or inhibition ("deferred satisfaction") of human wishes, whether of individuals or groups. So must it all be untrue? *No.* Doomed to disappear? *Not necessarily.* Blameworthy when functional religion, as is always the case, comes to terms with religious teachings centered more firmly on the gospel? Not so, and *it is not for the psychologist to be the judge.* Let us look at these three questions and answers in the light of two examples.

Madame Marie Leplancher is a fifty-eight-year-old French-speaking Canadian. Since her husband's death she has had money problems and is behind with her rent. On the advice of a neighbor, she decided to gamble in the parish bingo games.[34] She equips herself with a medallion of the Virgin, obligingly lent by the neighbor, which will allow her to pray and concentrate when the winning numbers are being drawn.

Is this prayer wrong? No. It is a quite genuine expression of Marie Leplancher's wish to pay her debts. It also reveals indirectly a certain latent image she has of the Virgin as an intervening power capable of influencing luck in her favor. More profoundly perhaps, if it is true that "every request is at bottom a request for love" (Lacan), she is linking her request for love to the ever-helpful divine Mother.

Is this type of prayer doomed to disappear? Not very likely. First because it has always existed and plays an important part in most religions. Then, if a socially dominant religion were to attempt to reduce the expressions of it (perhaps by abolishing parish bingos, or again by removing the collection boxes for "favors requested"), this wish would probably reappear in a secularized form (state lotteries), perhaps accompanied by progressively private or clandestine prayer practices.[35] These would then officially be "superstitions."

Will it be said that such a prayer is undesirable because it does not fit in with a Christianity that announces the good news of God's wishes for men? This is not for the psychologist to decide, any more than the continuance in church crypts of games of chance that have long been prohibited. It all depends on the objectives and strategies of a Catholic pastorate and on its view of the relationship between some expressions of functional religion and the core of Christian religion, between the prayer-cry and the Word of God.

Psychologically we note that if she obtains repeated satisfaction, due strictly to chance, Marie Leplancher will see it as confirmation of practices to which her neighbor introduced her. If she has exceptional wins, she acquires "a social prestige and a new image as well; this is seen picturesquely by Louis Painchaud (p. 68) as "the Epiphany function of bingo" at work. Repeated wins show "the superiority of the player who guessed right after praying."

So it is nonsatisfaction, particularly repeated nonsatisfaction, that would bring Marie Leplancher back to the harsh reality of her debt, symbolic here of her want. Moreover, for believers one prayer, at least, will always fail to be satisfied, the one asking to avoid their own death or the death of others. So nonsatisfaction is the ordeal and, as it were, the test of a prayer for favors. Such a prayer constantly satisfied would merely produce a frenzied system of illusions, a religious psychosis that not even death would interrupt. Unsatisfied, it can produce a lively awareness of noncoincidence, of the interval between the religious wish and its object.

All the manifestations of functional religion could be questioned in this way: What about the wishes they express and how are they met by the teachings of institutional religion? For there is nothing to stop religious teaching from presenting itself as the fulfillment of man's wishes, pure and simple. Even the central mystery of Christianity, the revelation of a God as a union of three Persons, can be treated in this way.

Look! even from a distance their heads can be seen leaning toward each other as if to share an embrace that nothing will ever be able to separate. It is as if they wanted to bury themselves in each other. Each of them is there for the Other: too much love for it not to overflow into the Other. . . .

Tell me, listener, have you ever dreamed of being totally present to the one you love, of being identified with him and so becoming what you are? Dreamed of a transparency that no shadow could obscure, of a communion that no disagreement could mar? Have you ever dreamed of a love that is all fire? Of a kiss that burns and is never healed?

Look at this mad dream. Look it in the face. It exists. It is in front of you. It is waiting for you![36]

Rarely has a Christian mystery been so well presented with the help of a latent ideology (that of uniting love without distance or words). Rarely too will it seem more vulnerable to the psychological critique of projective illusions born of wishes. It is impossible for the psychologist to assert that such an account is not true for it has all the truth and consistency of human wishes: absolute love, transparent and immediate. How far removed is such an account from the revelation of the Father and the Spirit given by the Son incarnate, dying for our sins? It is not for the psychologist to judge.

These two examples have been chosen to illustrate the kind of reflection, based on the problematics of desire and the meeting of wishes, that is called for if we are to take account of the Freudian critique of illusions. Obviously it can be dispensed with or considered too weighty for beliefs which are no more than that. "The human spirit," wrote T. S. Eliot, "cannot stand a strong dose of reality." But if we adopt that view, we should not be surprised by the recurrence of persistent doubts, the aversion

to admitting so-called "modern" problematics, the practical difficulty of conducting so-called "spiritual" discernments while ignoring the slow progress of dynamisms moving from the unconscious toward consciousness.

If we want to cut out the problematics of desire in the religious
field, how are we to situate the gospel message in its relationship
to the manifestations of so-called popular religiosity or of functional religion? "Religion is the sigh of the creature overwhelmed, the soul of a heartless world. . . . Religion in its wretchedness is at once the expression of real wretchedness and a
protest against it."[37] If Christians do not accept that their religion is no more than that, they would do better not to burn the
books that take that view but to show how Christianity *can* in fact
be something else.

The last chapter will try to make a contribution in that direction by underlining certain components of Christian *experience* in
accordance with the critical purpose of this book.

Notes

1. Sigmund Freud, *The Future of an Illusion,* in *The Complete Psychological Works of Sigmund Freud,* Vol. XXI (London: Hogarth Press, 1961), p.
31.

2. Denis de Rougemont, *L'amour et l'occident* (Paris: Plon, 1939).

3. These words are taken from Francois Duyckaerts who has described better than anyone else how aggressiveness is aroused in the
dynamism of *The Sexual Bond* (New York: Delacort-Dell., 1970), (French
ed. Paris: Dessart, 1964), p. 119. For a more detailed look at how
sexuality is related to verbal contributions see André Alsteens, *Dialogue
et sexualité* (Paris and Tournai: Casterman, 1969).

4. "Projection" in *Vocabulaire de la psychanalyse,* by J. LaPlanche and
J. B. Pontalis (Paris: Presses Univ. de France, 1967), p. 344.

5. *Civilization and Its Discontents,* p. 74. Freud did not always refer to
the study of the unconscious in "ordinary believers" (does he mean his
clients? the people he mixed with in Vienna?) Several times he mentioned "Paul who was a religious being in every sense of the word" and
spoke of "St. Francis of Assisi . . . the man who probably went the
farthest along this road (internalization of love)." As for Moses, in most
of the writings he is the oedipean pivot of the whole of Judeo-Christian

history. The main texts of Freud in matters of religion are collected with commentaries in A. Plé, *Freud et la religion* (Paris: Cerf, 1968). Emile Granger has published *Le croyant à l'épreuve de la psychanalyse* (Paris: Cerf, 1980), which is more concerned with Lacan than with Freud. It is a short but clear *vade mecum* which is purely theoretical and omits all consideration of the identifications in the Ideal of the Ego, to which Freud, as we shall see, attributes a decisive role in his objections to religion.

6. "Obsessive Acts and Religious Practices," 1907. This article contains the famous and generally misunderstood statement that "religion can be called a generalized obsessional neurosis." This is so, he explains immediately in the following lines, in the sense that obsessional neurosis is a *pathological counterpart*, the tragi-comic *caricature* of a private religion: "Die Zwangneurose als *pathologisches Gegenstück* zur Religionsbildung . . . ein halb komisches, halb trauriges *Zerrbild eines Privatreligion*" (Freud, *Ges. Werke*, Band VII, pp. 138-39).

7. *Totem and Taboo* (1912), in Vol. XIII, 1955,. p. 154.

8. *Moses and Monotheism,* in Vol. XXIII, 1964, p. 86.

9. *Totem and Taboo*, p. 154. Certainly the interpretation of the death of Jesus as a sacrificial debt in which the Son takes the place of humanity before the offended Father and so obtains satisfaction by substitution is a theology that is completely outmoded today: a "primitive theology of blood" (R. Bultmann). And it is not enough "to obstruct this idea by asserting that it was for love that God delivered up his son to be an obligatory sacrifice. There can hardly be a more obsessional phantasm than that of a God who demands that his son be tortured to death to assuage his anger", as A. Vergote wrote very pertinently (*Dette et désir,* Paris, Seuil, 1978, p. 161). And yet, would it have been possible to establish such a theology as a respectable system of interpretation without some complicity with the probably unconscious affective ties? And do we not see the latter reappearing under the schemas of expiatory suffering and renunciation of pleasure that mark a certain woebegone Christianity that is denounced and yet endlessly renewed? Psychological analysis leads to a better understanding of certain resistances encountered by a Christianity in which "the sacrifice, a symbolic gift, is not self-mutilation in order to pay a bankruptcy debt. It does not seek to pay a debt but to assert that the debt is not to be paid" (A. Vergote, p. 162). For if that is the intention and the word of God, it is at odds with the human religious wish (untransformed by the Other): to pay through suffering.

10. *The Future of an Illusion,* p. 33.

11. *Psychopathology of everyday Life* (1901) (London: T. Fisher Unwin Ltd., 1914), p. 309.

12. *The Future of an Illusion,* p. 30.

13. Ibid., p. 18.

14. Ibid., p. 30.

15. *Civilization and its Discontents,* pp. 101-2

16. *The Future of an Illusion,* p. 24. Three words underlined by us in the text demand attention. Why is Freud's supposed projection in terms of a *father* figure? Undoubtedly because at that time Freud had not yet tackled the role of the mother phantasm in the unconscious genesis of beliefs. The research mentioned in our first part obliges us these days to replace *father* by *parent* (father and/or mother, depending on individuals and cultures). Then it is the *defensive* aspect of the reaction, remaining unconscious in the projection, on which Freud bases his criticism and final rejection of a religion invoking love in appearance and, as it were, superficially. In any case that reaction is presented as *"engendering religion."* This genetic view does not close the door on subsequent mutations, even if Freud himself never encountered or analyzed them.

17. *Psychopathology of Everyday Life,* p. 310.

18. *Moses and Monotheism* (1937), p. 129.

19. *Totem and Taboo,* p. 90.

20. *Moses and Monotheism,* pp. 84, 112-3.

21. Ibid., p. 118 and *Future of an Illusion,* p. 47.

22. *Civilization and its Discontents,* pp. 101-2.

23. Ibid., p. 143. The expressions used by Freud in connection with the declaration of the law are of interest: "To love . . . all human beings equally" then "To love one's neighbor as oneself." The gospel which proposes that we should "love our enemies" avoids that generalization. The enemy, like the friend, belongs among the psychologically significant beings. Both the one and the other become "the neighbor." Remember that Jesus did not answer the question "Who *is* my neighbor?" except by a parable in which the terms are reversed: "Whom *do you make* your neighbor?" This distinction is an experience each time in which the term is concrete and the inspiration an attitude and not a law. This attitude is clearly not spontaneous and the conduct it inspires consists of choice resulting from Christian discernment, not from laws, thus from internalizing Jesus's attitudes.

24. "To love anyone, regardless," writes Jean Le Du, "reminds me of the play by Gabriel Marcel *Un homme de Dieu.* The hero declares one day to his wife: 'Tell yourself that, whatever you do, I shall always love you and nothing will change for me!' Can there be a more elaborate form of contempt? If you make an absolute of the principle 'To love anyone, regardless,' you can only do it by deploying your efforts around an image, that of yourself-capable-of-loving-absolutely-anybody" (*L'idéal en*

procès, Paris, Cerf, 1975, p. 46). This is exactly Freud's psychological objection.

25. Freud, "The Ego and the Id" (1923), in Vol. XIX, p. 37. Father A. Plé completes this quotation with this note, found on Freud's desk after his death: "Mysticism: obscure autoperception of the realm external to the Ego, that of the Id" (*Freud et la religion*, Cerf, 1968, p. 40; this posthumous note figures in the standard English edition of Freud's works, vol. 23, p. 300). In reductionist terms, taken to the ultimate limit the secret of "the realm external to the Ego" is returned to the "Id," that is to say, to the primordial urge in its initial state of undifferentiated impulse: a silence prior to any cry.

26. *Group Psychology and the Analysis of the Ego* (1921), in Vol. XVIII, p. 94.

27. Ibid., p. 94.

28. Ibid., p. 134. In these "additional considerations," Freud returns to the regressive process by which a leader (the head of a group, community, or church) substitutes himself for the ego-ideal of each person by trapping him on an idealized (hero) figure common to all, typical of the constitution of any organized group set-up. Identification, on the other hand, constitutes and enriches the ego, as during the Oedipus phase when the total investments in the parents are abandoned and replaced by partial identifications. From passively received parental affections the child moves on to active identification with the parent of his sex, but not without internal conflict (or affective ambivalence).

29. Freud, "Formulations on the Two Principles of Mental Functioning" (1911), Standard English Edition, Vol, 12, p. 223.

30. Ibid., p. 224.

31. Freud, "On Narcissism: an introduction" (1914), Vol. 14, pp. 94-95. The article ends with the observation that the ego-ideal concentrates largely on the homosexual libido, arising from fear of losing parental love; it uses the process of idealization combined with a rough sublimation in various object-directions and it warns of the "involution of sublimations and the possible transformation of ideals in paraphrenic (psychotic) disorders" (Ibid., p. 102). Interesting presentations of false sublimations, or dangerous but sometimes successful desublimations can be found in the second part of A. Vergote's studies, *Dette et désir* (Paris: Seuil, 1978).

32. It took fifty years before Pope Pius XII uttered words of "warm sympathy" to Catholic psychotherapists and psychoanalysts in congress at Rome in 1953. He attempted thus to fill in the gap of ignorance and prejudice which yet another defensive reflex had dug between Freud's discoveries and the Catholic world. He was also alluding to the dangers

of a Freudian "pansexualism," an expression derived from a collective myth rather than a study of the texts. The works of the philosopher Roland Dalbiez (*La méthode psychanalytique et la doctrine freudienne*, Paris, Desclée De Brouwer, 1936) and the Swiss psychoanalyst Charles Odier (*Les deux sources conscientes et inconscientes de la vie morale*, Neuchâtel, Baconnière, 1943-1947) had prepared the way. From 1951 to 1953, Leo Bartemeier (an American Catholic) was president of the International Psychoanalytical Association and as such had met Pius XII in 1951. However, Freud's approach to the religious question was not studied seriously until a little later by G. Zilboorg (various articles collected together in *Psychoanalysis and Religion*, New York, Farrar, 1962) and by Louis Beirnaert (papers given at annual meetings of the Catholic Center of French Intellectuals and in Cahier 21, *Problèmes de psychanalyse*, Paris, Fayard, 1957 and articles reprinted in *Expérience chrétienne et psychologie*, Paris, Epi, 1964). So, gradually, the central psychological question came to be asked: How do religions speak to human wishes? And how can they reinforce in that way the ideologies of the most diverse groups? This last question is handled well by the sociologist Jacques Maître, "Psychanalyse et sociologie religieuse," in *Archives de Sociologie des Religions 33* (1972), pp. 111-34.

33. The irresistible drift of Carl G. Jung toward gnostic speculation, in spite of certain personal protestations, has been highlighted by the most complete study of his texts and countertexts (according to the various editions of the same work) published by Raymond Hostie, *Du mythe à la religion* (Paris: Desclée De Brouwer, 1955).

34. This example is a free production, consisting of observations from the very original research of Louis Painchaud, *Jeu, argent et religion: les bingos paroissiaux*, thesis for a theology degree. Quebec, Université Laval, 1975. Excellent summary published as: "Le jeu et le sens," in *Cahiers du C.R.S.R.*, vol. 1, 1977, Québec, Université Laval, Centre de Recherches en Sociologie Religieuse, pp. 7-76 (bibliography: 57 titles). Bingo is a game of chance played in groups and institutionalized in many parishes. In 1975 there were thirty games weekly in the town of Quebec alone. Women account for 95 percent of those attending and two out of three of them are over forty. The Archbishop of Quebec has made a not too successful move to stop these games gradually and make other financial provision for poor parishes (1980-1983).

35. This more or less clandestine privatization can be found in the history of French parishes when authority has kept aloof, to varying degrees, from the conviviality of devotions invoking healing saints or processions planned to include visits at miraculous springs. This often very picturesque history has been carefully collected and described for the Charente region by Marc LeProux, *Médecine, magie et sorcellerie* and

Dévotions et saints guérisseurs (Paris: Presses Univ. de France, 1954 and 1957).

36. Daniel-Ange, *L'étreinte de feu: Icône de la Trinité de Roublev* (Paris: Desclée De Brouwer, 1980). This quotation is the more amazing in that, in Roublev's work, the three angels are largely isolated by the *interval* of a table on which are represented the breaking of bread and wine, a rectangular sealed stone, their stools separated by a triangle of earth toward which Mambre's oak is descending—we might say by the diversity of their *historical* operations, to which the divine persons owe their names. The text quoted is on pages 125-26. Needless to say this is not enough for a judgment to be made on the whole work of an author inspired by "unarmed gentleness."

37. ". . . it is the opium of the people." Karl Marx, *Introduction à la philosophie hégélienne du droit* (1844). An interesting discussion on the real and imaginary status of Christianity and socialism in Michele Bertrand, *Le statut de la religion chez Marx et Engels* (Paris: Ed. Sociales, 1979).

7

The Christian Experience

What has the Christian religion to say to human wishes? How do spiritual experience in the faith and certain other activities born of faith become open to God's wish which is discernible as different from our own wishes?

It is time to take advantage of the psychological criteria of discernment, mentioned briefly in the preceding chapter and to examine how the Christian faith *can* be other than an illusion, a projection of wishes; how Christian experience *can* bear the mark of listening to Jesus Christ and the prophets (ancient and modern) so as to be drawn "to the side of reality" and even of harsh reality.

The purpose of this chapter, as we shall see, is not apologetic. It does not seek to demonstrate that the act of faith has an ontologically true referent and consequently that faith is obligatory. How could any psychologist talk in such a generalizing manner when all he is acquainted with is believing or nonbelieving subjects revealing the structure of their beliefs or convictions and of their experiences according to their actual motivations? So the reflections in this chapter are not normative in the way that theological work is, taking the Word of God as its starting point and ultimate reference. These reflections are presented by a Christian psychologist, familiar on a cognitive level with the Christian experiences described in the Scriptures or observable in our own day; they will simply bring out *the way in which* some specific psychological components of those experiences make them credible, even after the empirical critique of illusions, of which the method and some observations were recalled in the preceding chapter. It matters little here that these components are constituents of the faith, that they are normative or central in the teachings of the ecclesiastical Magisterium or of qualified theologians. It is enough for my purpose that they are present and allow the Christian to discover their importance if he should happen to be psychoanalyzed or is himself a psychoanalyst or is familiar with psychology or if he simply wants a better understanding of God's wish for him and to respond to it in more flexible and personal ways than those of the institutional church.

It is obviously my hope that these psychological components of Christian experience might, in addition, be useful in making personal or pastoral religious choices, but of that the reader must be the judge.

Stages in this reflection

With this in view, the Christian experience will be examined in four stages: A. As a transforming experience, as seen in some New Testament texts. B. As an active-synthesis-experience, then and now. C. As a resistance in faith to divine words introducing wishes other than purely religious (functional) ones, a resistance which may be repressed. D. As an experience of identification which comes as a fulfillment of love.

The too superficial distinction between the active and the contemplative life in Christian experience will be dealt with briefly at the end.

A. Transforming Experience (The New Testament)

Experience of God is never chronologically a primary one—not only because every child is born into a culture and raised either in an institutional religion or outside religion (tolerant secularism or a more or less reactionary atheism), but also because the adult, raised as a Christian in the faith of his church, cannot be content with a "religious" life of beliefs, ritual practices, values or ideals derived from Jesus Christ and referring almost nominally or second-hand to his message. Obviously many Christians do live like that;[1] their Christianity responds to an ego ideal that is not without grandeur or sacrifice but does not transform their personality on the basis of a specific wish of God encountered in an experience. So they live, sometimes heroically, a Christian faith according to the letter but not to the Word made actual and alive in the risen Christ.

Saul of Tarsus

As he went up to Damascus, his heart full of aggressiveness toward the new Christians, Saul of Tarsus embodied Jewish traditions that had received a severe shock from the new attitudes of people won over by a style of prophet opposed to the Temple: a Jesus baptized by John. Since he was persecuting them to the point of wanting to "bring them bound to Jerusalem" and had procured "letters from the High Priest" to that end (Acts 9:1-2), Saul was feeling concerned and even vaguely threatened, in his Judaism, by this God who was the talk of the Christian communities.

So his conversion did not spring out of nothing. The shock of reality came to him in a single word: "Why do you persecute *me?*" (9:4). A God identifying himself with the persecuted: This shock was enough to throw down the (Jewish) horse which tradition says he was riding. Saul became blind for three days. When Ananias of Damascus reopened his eyes, the Other* in his wish had been revealed, reversing his religious tendency, as a Jew of the Temple, to maintain a high barrier between Jews and the heathen. After this conversion, he in turn came up against members of Christian communities who hesitated to carry the word to the heathen unconditionally and without demanding circumcision.

---

* The use of the capital (the Other) does not designate God but any personal, even partial, referent of a concretely founded relationship (on this subject, see the definitions in the glossary, section B, at the end of the book).

Such a reversal is not of itself incompatible with the dynamics of a wish, however; to burn what one has adored (but with the same flame), to adore what one has burned (but in the same absolute intolerance) is not unknown and can be explained without any real sublimation of aggression. The absolutization in the new Ideal of the pursued Ego is maintained without any effective mutation of inner impulses: Only the content, or, as here, the people being hunted have changed. Such a conversion is astonishing because it is so spectacular. Yet it would remain "religious" if it were not possible to locate another transformation.

In Saul of Tarsus, now Paul, the remarkable *psychological* transformation is to be found elsewhere. Whereas the early Christian groups could psychologically have organized themselves and prospered in a profound hostility to the tenets of traditional Judaism, whereas they could have reinforced their identity by an aggressive projection of guilt on to the Jews, held responsible for Jesus' death, Paul will have no truck with this reversal of aggressiveness, this humanly valuable asset for cementing the unity of new communities: the existence of a scapegoat, an enemy number one. Paul will devote three whole chapters of his Epistle to the Romans (Romans 9 to 11) to a *laborious* demonstration of how, despite the rejection of Christ, Jews can still be saved. Such an effort can certainly not be explained by a process of aggressive projection, of reversed absolutization. It is a struggle to assimilate an "other" wish.

This is an admission of the Other's wish, a movement indispensable to a genuine experience of God in a Christian context. This can be seen from the great trouble Paul takes to accomplish this demonstration intellectually, a real squaring of the circle: giving up the praxis of a "chosen people," officiating at the birth of one religion from another and proclaiming a Word that changes a certain image one had of God. Reading these laborious chapters of Paul's letter has always put me in mind of a man battling with himself: He accepts the Other but, as in love, he has to go on accepting him afresh. Paul is trying to demonstrate to himself what it is that he loves and that has taken possession of him, but not entirely. In short, he is battling with his *resistance* to the Other and, in so doing, *experiencing* it.

"*Truly, my heart's desire is that the Jews might be saved* (Romans 10:1). . . . *And I say the truth in Christ, I have great sorrow and unceasing anguish in my heart*" (9:1).

It is not simply a question of discovering a moral principle, "Love your enemies" or "Love all men like yourself," in Freud's view, nor even of pronouncing a beatitude, "Blessed are you when men persecute you." Saul could have heard all that among the early Christians in Jerusalem. It is a matter of a terrible discovery, made in the actual experience of active persecution: God is on the side of the persecuted. While Paul is persecuting in the name of Yahweh and with the mandate of the Sanhedrin, the Word is forced upon him: "Why are you persecuting *me*?" While his Ideal of the Ego, duly sanctioned by the High Priest, is mobilizing his persecuting aggressiveness, the word expressive of Christ's wish takes hold of Saul "against the pricks" of his own wish. Thus the identification by which the God of Jesus Christ is found in the persecuted and not the persecutor, be he even the High Priest, sounds like an "other" wish in the religious experience of Saul. He is blinded by it and with reason.

And then it is with that wish that he must try to live. To maintain a shared identity with him who will exclude no one, especially sinners, is neither natural nor spontaneously dominant in the wishes of religious persons. Neither is renunciation of the use of an affective appeal to an "excluded third party" in order to reinforce the identity of a community by condemnation and persecution of the "others," those who are not the elect of God.[2] This fight, this battle between two wishes gave birth to the first Christian theologian, Paul. It is to this inner struggle that Christianity will owe the most fundamental pages of its specific thought: those on the Law that exists and yet does not save; those on works that are good but out of proportion with the world of the promises; those on Gods' love *and* wish. This masterly interpretation of what the Apostles lived through has come

down to present-day Christians through no less masterly interpretations by Augustine, Thomas Aquinas, and some great Re-
formers. The psychological cost of these pages must not be forgotten: being torn between two conflicting wishes, giving up the
ego-ideal as a seat of the absolute, acceptance that God is abased
to the human condition and, consequently, rejection of the practice of the "excluded third party."

Whoever proclaims anew the implications of this experience
will not be above the Master. Denounced in Jerusalem by the
Jews of Asia, Paul appealed and was taken to Rome. He who had
not known Jesus finally died identified with him. Between Saul
of Tarsus and Paul of Rome stretched the interval that separates
two wishes: there was true love but also death.

Jesus' disciples

Experience of God is never immediate. Recognition of the
other requires dialogue, awareness of his wishes, and very often
an action undertaken in the common agreement of a project,
contract, or alliance.

Witnesses in Galilee had *seen* the man Jesus, had heard a
prophet speaking of God and partially echoing their own wishes
in expectation of the Messiah, had occasionally followed him and
adopted his practices. *In the long run* and *communally* they had
been able to *believe* in the Lord, the Christ.

In the long run, because they had to understand and accept him
in his strangeness. The gospels show clearly that the surprises
went on for a long time for these disciples. Neither an Essene of
the desert, nor a political zealot, nor a disciple of that John who
had nevertheless baptized him, this Son of Man (as he called
himself) had new practices. Without repudiating the Law, he
spoke "with authority," solved thorny questions, healed the sick,
and announced even to the poor, the sinners, and the religious
outcasts (the lepers) the new image of a paradoxical and slightly
shocking Father.[3] That the words, parables, and practices of
Jesus were not always in line with their wishes but often opposed

them and sought to modify them, this much is clear from all the gospels and from the commentaries of the experts in exegesis. Does this image of the Father mean that we must forgive "up to seven times"? Who will be seated next to God in the kingdom soon to be established? Peter himself, after his confession of faith ("To whom should we turn? You have the words of eternal life"), is unwilling to risk going to Jerusalem where the people in the Temple will undoubtedly show no mercy for this new prophet. But Jesus, while showing plainly that he is tempted not to go ("Get behind me: you are a real Satan!") will take them all with him. To be silent or run away from the opportunity to proclaim the image of God that filled him ("my Father and your Father") was unthinkable for him. Filled with that wish, he died of it. A mystery of love and death.

Communally because the shock of the events, the condemnation and death of Jesus almost dispersed them. The paschal meaning of the last meal together was only assured at Pentecost and is inseparable from the mission to the world ("Baptize them in the name of the Father, of the Son, and of the Holy Spirit"), from an action resolutely embarked on in history ("The Spirit will guide you toward the whole truth. . . . He will take back what you have not the strength to bear now so that you may know it). The death of the Messiah, desired and awaited in glory, finds meaning in the early communities by the action of the Holy Spirit: that Other of their wish. The action was gradual and slow if it is true that after the Lord had appeared (Acts 1:6) the disciples were still asking: "Is it now, Lord, that you will restore the kingdom to Israel?" Nostalgia of a dream, and mourning process.

So the first experience of faith in the mystery of the trinity of God was made certain in an interval in tension, resulting psychologically from two wishes, a distance necessary for co-presences to be established in the symbolism of signs.

"Show us the Father," begs the wish. The Father is made manifest in the Son, his Word (Matthew 11:27, Luke 10:22).
"Show us the risen Son," begs the wish once more. "Until he

comes," the Son puts into the hands of the disciples the signs that are distinguishable in the Spirit. This risen Son is so different from what they expected that two disciples walk with him discussing the Scriptures as with a stranger until the Spirit gives meaning to the sign of sharing: "As he broke the bread they recognized him and he vanished out of their sight" (Luke 24:30-31).

The upper room was still a place of refuge ("for fear of the Jews"), a place of regrets for something imagined, born of human wishes. The inn at Emmaus is the end of mourning, the resumption of preaching ("Do this in remembrance of me") hereafter actively celebrated according to the other's wish: breaking of bread, the sign of forgiveness for an unforgivable death; sharing of bread, the sign, indefinitely prolonged, of a new covenant with the men with whom his Spirit has chosen henceforward to be identified: the hungry, the destitute, the oppressed, the prisoners, the sick, the sinners ("you will have done it unto me").

From Mount Tabor to Calvary there was the interval between two nonconverging wishes, there was death. Christian hope, by celebrating the resurrection of the Lord communally in the church in accordance with his Spirit, does not separate eternity and history: it links them, not by gratifying in imagination the religious wish of man, but by sending him back to the harsh realities which he must transform by the sharing and the forgiveness. Pentecost is not consolation in bereavement. It transforms a wish wounded by death into the urgency of action arising from new wishes. Jesus died once for all time, committing his last breath to the Father. The time of the second breath has begun, a time to preach again in order to change the world.

B. Experience: Active Synthesis

The psychological movement of faith, in the early Christian experiences just recalled, highlights their structure of active synthesis between a fact or event located on the side of reality— possibly of harsh reality—and its meaning as a manifestation of God's wish.

In the case of the Apostles, the gift of God was both outside in the man Jesus, whose words they heard and in whose actions they participated, and inside in their Jewish religious expectation of a liberating messiah. But what they saw or heard outside was far from matching their indwelling wish in terms of the ego-ideal derived from their Jewish education. So their affirmation of faith could be only gradually transforming, as many episodes in the gospels indicate. At Pentecost they managed to establish communally and without changing anything in their living perception of Jesus, including his revolting death, an actively revealing synthesis between the historical reality of these events and the meaning they acquired (that of forgiveness of sins, for example) once they were willingly prolonged by rereading the Scriptures in the Spirit, that is, as a new expression of God's wish.

Active synthesis of presence and interpretation: This structure remains for every Christian, today and tomorrow, a constituent of his *experiences* in terms of faith. Please note that I am not saying that this structure is a constituent of faith. It is for the theologian and, in the last resort, for the Magisterium to decide how the Augustinian adage ("To see the man (Jesus) and believe the God (the Word)") applies normatively to the faith of every Christian, not just to that of the Apostles.[4] But when it comes to psychological and spiritually Christian experiences, or again psychologically observable spiritual experiences, it seems to me that only "active synthesis" experiences (conforming rigorously to the structure of the faith seen in the Augustinian adage) can withstand the critique of illusions which we have sketched in outline. They alone can lay claim to the title of "sublimation," not the false one denounced by Freud, but the genuine one ("way out").

We must further examine how Christian experience can be an active synthesis once Jesus the Christ is no longer there in person but is offered or assimilated as a component of the Ideal of the ego by the churches and their catechesis from childhood on.

Already for St. Paul, as we saw, the presence of Jesus no longer existed, except through those witnesses, the early Christians, who repeated certain of his words but whom Saul of Tarsus hated and persecuted. If the wish for Jesus Christ became the subject of experience for him (leading at once to faith in his meeting with Ananias of Damascus), it was by a word that transformed the meaning of his persecuting attitude into an *act* and in its *concrete* object: *I* am the one *you* are persecuting.

Active synthesis, as a structure of specifically Christian experience, is established in a twofold linking movement: first between *nonidentical wishes,* wishes of spontaneously religious man and wishes of Jesus the Christ reaching man through his living words and actions—and then between those wishes that reveal the God incarnate in Jesus and his decision to identify himself preferentially with the poor, the persecuted, the outcasts, wherever they may exist *concretely* in history.

Where this twofold linking movement operates in active synthesis, there is not only Christian faith but experience in terms of faith. That the Christian life, in order to remain faithful to its inspiration, should *move perpetually from the sign to what is signified,* is a classic requirement in the interpretation of fundamental Christian activities and of the attitudes (faith, hope, charity) which inspire them.

The Eucharist. "To recognize him in the breaking of bread" is a symbolic practice (effective sign, sacrament) for every Christian taking part in the Eucharist: a memorial of death, a token of resurrection. If he is more familiar with the Judeo-Christian history of the old and the new covenant (the well-instructed Christian), the sign is enriched with all its symbolic resonances: the wandering in the desert, the covenant, the forgiveness of sins, the action of festive grace, the expectation of a banquet still to come. This better acquaintance with the eucharistic sign is merely the content of spiritual experience which gives thanks in the faith and surrenders to the invisible reality signified: participation in the mystery of the Trinity. It is an active synthesis and so is asserted rather than seen, confessed rather than felt. Is it therefore a psychologically transforming experience in the sense we have said? My opinion is that it only becomes so in relation to a real and concrete sharing: a sharing of words, perhaps, among those who are celebrating—a sharing of bread and of all kind of goods with the Christ who is present in the poor of today.[5] Thus the sacrament becomes experience. And the least instructed Christian can live it in this way: a sharing celebrated, inspired by God; a sharing made real, provoked by the poor man who has become a "neighbor" on the basis of God's wish.

The remission of sins. "Repentance preached in his name among all nations with a view to the forgiveness of sins" (Luke 24:47) is the way of salvation that no Christian church has ever ceased to proclaim, even if the church organization of forgiveness has had varied fortunes.[6] In the Christian hope of salvation, good works obviously figure as well as repentance for misdeeds; the latter finds expression in confessions made in expectation of signs of forgiveness. But this conduct and these psychological dispositions are only the moral aspect of a spiritual movement which looks, in hope, for a promised justification outstripping any merit on the part of man. "Lord, forgive me for I am a sinful man," said the publican, unable to pay his debt. Any additional expectation would have brought him closer to the Pharisee who had no knowledge of the hope proclaimed in Jesus Christ. This is an active and very paradoxical synthesis. If Christian penance made us aware only of our guilt, it would no doubt appear human, very human and even vulnerable to the morbid drives of self-accusing egocentrism. If, on the other hand, Christian confession and the gesture of absolution opened the door to psychological liberation alone, they would have to be examined as illusions, even institutionalized. No. The richness and strength of hope in Christian penance lies in maintaining the two poles of the paradox: guilt and renunciation of payment of what cannot be a debt. The unconditional love of God, revealed in Jesus Christ, always comes first in time and so cannot be paid. This is again an active synthesis, maintained in the wish rather than coming from the wish. Is it thus a transforming psychological experience? I think it only becomes so in relation to real forgiveness, given or at least offered to some person we or others have offended or to another rendered guilty by his faults or frustrated by the unconditional love that others have always refused him, perhaps since childhood. Thus penance received in faith becomes experience. A Christian, even if he is unlettered, *can* live it in this way—having divinely inspired hope in man; receiving remission of faults or debts, actively proposed in favor of the offender or the poor man, the sinner, who is now his "neighbor" on the basis of God's wish.

We could go on analyzing the main situations of faith and Christian experience in this way. Affirmation and investigation of what is *signified* in and through the *sign.* That is what all *the sacraments* are: human rites and words, studied and understood better through anthropology and psychology, placed in the faith as signifying the efficacy of God's gestures which are in no way proportionate to man's dispositions. That is what the *Bible* is: read, analyzed, situated in its socio-historical context, actively comprehended in the faith as Scripture expressing the divine wish whose meaning must be revived today in different contexts and cultural environments. This work must constantly be done afresh in syntheses that are always incomplete, not only because the present context calls for pastoral commentaries but also because the progress of history and exegesis specifies ever more precisely what Jesus' original reactions were in relation to the human and religious problems of his time. That is what the *church* is too, in its role as institution and power system: situated sociologically, imperfect, capable of improvement, listened to loyally in faith and actively supported in the burden its authorities bear in the Spirit of the Lord. "Those who exercise authority among the nations are called benefactors . . . but you shall not be so: let him that is greatest among you be as the younger and him who governs as he that serves" (Luke 22, 25, and 26). Admirable church in its dream of power (Christianity resting on civil power) which is its weakness; astonishing church in its weakness which gives rise to resurgences of its authority all through history and in the revealing compromises of the conflict of wishes: bride (very human) of Christ! A covenant to be constantly renewed in unpredictable syntheses that are upheld by charity, that love which must come to complete identification with its Founder. Church, is mother of Christians insofar as it speaks to them of the Son.[7]

Every *prayer* ultimately reproduces that structure once it becomes a Christian experience, inseparable from a *discernment*. For anything can find a place in Christian prayer: friendship and love, wish, doubt, failure, emotion, events, leisure, thought, plan, revolt, work, life or death. There is nothing that cannot be related to the words of God revealed in Jesus Christ; nothing that cannot become, in prayer, the occasion of confrontation between our wishes (human and religious) and the Spirit, that "other" of the wish.

Let us consider just the case of the *event* that calls for a decision.

The event must first be understood with all the resources at our disposal before we decide how we fit into it. Earthquake or rumors of war, unemployment or strike, class war or generation gap, professional practice or payment of taxes, betrothals, marriages, children hoped for or unwanted, infidelity or divorce, "vocation" or doubt about vocation, illnesses, accidents, bereavements: none of these situations is simple. No one can say, in another's place, what meaning a particular situation will acquire in a Christian discernment. That significance and the action it calls for is not laid down in the event as if all that was needed was to unveil it in faith or through recourse to an expert in interpretation. Most of the situations we have mentioned are ambiguous and are open to several options. Recourse to the pastor, supposedly an expert in these matters, is merely an appeal to one counselor among many: his advice, wise as it may be, should not replace either prayer or action. In prayer prior to decision, the Christian endeavors to see the situation or the problem on the basis of what the Spirit of the Lord wishes, possibly by comparison with a gospel story or by decoding a parable; and he will be impatient to transform the situation, however slightly, into a Christian event. The raw facts of history are, according to Pascal, "masters given us by the hand of God." It is for us to work on them so as to bring them in line with God's design the incarnation of which in history is prolonged by each Christian. We should add that it is often in the action itself, in the commitment reexamined later, that the Christian meaning of a historically situated event or choice becomes clear, sometimes communally, and always in the long run. The truth of an option is not entirely independent of the march of history. And Christian discernments are no exception.

As we see, the Christian's experience in prayer of discernment occurs in an actively maintained psychological and spiritual synthesis. On the one hand, the situation provokes and stimulates the confrontation of his own wishes (according to a moral and religious system that is often latent) with words revealing the wishes of the God of the gospels. Prayer is thus the place of twisting for his wishes as they intertwine with "other" wishes; a twisting not without resistance as we shall soon see. On the other hand, if the mystery of salvation, as transmitted in the gospels and at work in the traditions of the church, moves the Christian from within (in the same way as the ego ideal), it moves him to an encounter with realities that are often confused and harsh and which demand all his intelligence, all his heart, if they are to become Christian events. For it is not just a question of enduring them like spiritually stimulating ordeals or occasions of sanctification. Rather it is a question of giving them significance by transforming or fitting in to them. The ineluctable situation born of chance, conditionings, or human egoism then *becomes* a Christian event.

Prayer of discernment includes everything necessary to be a *Christian experience* (active synthesis: *Erfahrung*) that is perfectly capable of responding to the psychological exigencies of the critique of illusions. Think back to the examples given at the beginning of the second part of this book in order to spell out the meaning of the word when the French language alludes to a man "of great experience." Take the example of the surgeon called to a difficult case. For his diagnosis he mobilizes everything he has acquired so far (scientific, conceptual, and practical training, reading to keep up-to-date, operations performed in the course of his career). This inner wealth is used in the first place to *perceive* (he looks, listens, palpates, studies the results of biochemical tests) a bundle of realities which *become* signs, no pun intended, operative signs: indications of an operation to be performed by himself or by others. For, in the opinion of all clinicians, his diagnosis cannot be totally separated from the action to be taken. And it is the action taken that will supply the full truth in an *experience* which is either healing or doomed to failure.

It is the same with Christian discernment. In the prayer preceding decision, the believer is the bearer, not only of human information that throws light on various aspects of the situation, but also of tendencies or attitudes reflecting both his own wishes, including religious ones, and certain wishes of the God revealed in Jesus Christ as they seem to him to emerge from the gospel and the traditions perceived through his life in the church. So he perceives the situation in a more complex way. It would be his dream to end this social conflict with a general reconciliation in the name, for example, of brotherly love, *the ego ideal* given him by his Christian education: that at least is his own wish. However, reality forces him to be part of a society that is historically, here and now, not reconciled. At this moment a discernment intervenes which takes account of his identification with the Christ of the gospel and of his wish, uttered many times, to identify himself with the poorest, the unjustly oppressed. The truth of the ensuing commitment will come to this Christian only from the *experience* he will have of it in his concrete action and from subsequent modifications he always can, and sometimes should, bring to it.

Discerning prayer is of such capital importance in the *Christian* experience, both personal and communal, that it would be a grave matter to see it impoverished by reducing discernment to mere obedience and the prayer to a contemplation not centered on a knowledge of Jesus Christ. A *religious* wish alone can easily so restrict itself, as is the case in Buddhist monasteries and Hindu ashrams. But the Christian tradition has always wished discernment, the gift of the Spirit made real in communal study of the gospels in depth, to be more and more widespread among Christian people of all kinds. We have seen in chapters IV and V why the spiritual family known as "charismatic" ends up by reserving it for a few, in spite of its declared intentions. Prayer meetings in the base communities, on the contrary, encourage its dissemination, even among the least educated.

The Christian experience is an active synthesis between inner attitudes and an action that can transform the world; it is also a synthesis between the wishes originating in man, even religious man, and those derived from the God revealed in the gospels. It is a center of conflict and an interval opened up not merely for spiritual, but for psychological combat. Thus it is a place for resistance. Let us examine some aspects of the resistance, in relation to the first chapter on spontaneous religiosity and functional religion.

C. Christian Experience as Resistance

What have religions to say to human wishes?

To answer that question would involve a comparative description of religions, not as systems of rites or beliefs, but of their effective teachings: institutional language and implicit languages.

How can the gospel (Jesus of Nazareth) speak to the human wish today, other than by illusions gratifying that wish?

In this book, we have investigated whether the gospel and the tradition that continues it tell man of a wish that is different from his own, that is, from one which gives rise continuously to functional religion.

"The general structure of the *question* of God, stated as a *question* of the Other," write Georges Morel, "comes up at once against the fact that, under the pretext of paying homage to God, religion has managed to feed all the anthropocentric passions, particularly in periods of belief. . . . We need only scan briefly the almost universal world literature to realize the vast amount of talk about hunger, thirst, and eros it contains. . . .

Now, the relationship of man to God cannot be rooted in a need any more than the relationship of God to man. Only *a wish* is fit to qualify such a relationship."[8]

Many contemporaries, even those brought up as Christians, speak of God as if he were there to grant their requests, to rally them round a demanding moral code, to give them peace despite surrounding turmoil, to help them avoid the psychological rupture of death, to set their guilty consciences at rest through his ritualized forgiveness, in short and fundamentally to fulfill their needs. True, by making the "sign of the cross," they inscribe the central badge of the Christian mystery on themselves, a shorthand for the salvation being offered, the landmark of a god who is "other": he took on flesh and lost it but rose "in the glory of the Father" in a way most disconcerting to any imagination of survival. Historically, he comes back to life through his Spirit at work in the community of those who open the door to his inspiration. But, as the late pastor Georges Crespy used to say, we "Christians are so prompt to embalm the risen Lord, wrapping him like a mummy in the bandages of our own wounds!"[9] that we must conclude that our wishes do not always coincide with the words or practices of Jesus the Christ. Some examples as a reminder:

The religious wish for a *powerful and interventionist God,* arising from the needs of our human condition, is not answered by a Father who will not send his legions of angels, who will go on making the sun rise on both the just and the unjust, and will let the wheat and tares grow together. What is the use of such a God?

The religious wish for a *just and moralizing Father* who renders to each according to the measure of his works and for whom we pine, is not satisfied by a Father whose patrimony is already divided into two parts and who awaits the return of the prodigal son in order to reinstate him as heir to all his possessions, to the apparent detriment of his brother. Is not such a Father somewhat scandalous?

Membership in a religious society with a strong *identity*

which is recognizable once and for all *by the exclusion* of other pagan nations does not correspond with a community of those who proclaim in the Spirit salvation for all, including even sinners. Is not that utopia at odds with the sociological conditions of functioning that make a church viable?

A religious organization has always functioned, say the historians, on the basis of a clearly defined frontier (in the rites and the myths on which they are founded) between *the sacred and the profane*. Can it adjust to a prophetism that cheerfully transgresses the limits of the "pure" and the "impure" and proclaims that "the Sabbath is made for man"?

It is common knowledge that on this last point the Jewish authorities soon understood that such a prophet was profoundly subversive and that if he continued to take his disciples—and worse still, the multitudes!—down that road in the name of a God called "Father," he must be gotten rid of at any price. Subversive, this prophet undoubtedly was. In one sense the guardians of the Law were doing no more than their duty in terms of a fundamental option: They were refusing to be that religion of the open door announced by certain of the last well-known prophets (Jonah, for example). But as we know, a sacred text can be sacralized, by encasing it in illuminations and incense, to such an extent that it is no longer read.[10]

What is less apparent is the psychological *resistance* that is bound to follow in the train of a message and practice corresponding to *those wishes*. Not only did they clash head-on with an ego-ideal carrying certain Jewish traditions, but they turned the general economy of spontaneous religious wishes topsy-turvy. To assimilate *those words* and perhaps recognize them as divine meant admitting that they do not speak to religious wishes in terms of needs satisfied, of consolations to be received, of rights recognized, of gratification guaranteed, or even of love offered in such a way as to satisfy the wish for love.

The gospel stories, our Lord's answers, the parables in particular[11] frequently introduce an ungratified request for something that is lacking, a consolation, a right in justice, as the opportunity to enter into a relationship of love with the presumed giver rather than with his gifts. The living water and soon the miraculous water which removes all thirst are the concrete opportunity and then the illusory and metaphorical utopia which will introduce, on the one hand, the forbidden relationship ("Jews have no dealings with Samaritans") and, on the other hand, the announcement of the Messiah ("I that speak to you am he"), marking the end of exclusive temples (on Mount Garizim as well as at Jerusalem) and a worship in spirit and in truth ("worshipers according to the will of the Father," John 4:1-42).

Far from satisfying thirst, a metaphor for the wish for love, the Word of the Lord intensifies it. If love is announced everywhere, it is mixed, even in John the Evangelist, with words indicating the divine wishes of which that love is the bearer: those of the Father whose conduct and words are expressed in the Son. In Freud's words "identification must come to complete love here." And what is identification in this case if not love confronted by a different wish?

Just as love between a man and a woman is not established in the complementary nature of their sexual attractions but in the gradual recognition of their persons in their *difference* and, up to a point, in the *discordance* of their masculine or feminine wishes, with the added variation introduced by their own individual histories, so the love the gospel is speaking of is not the result of God's satisfying our religious desires but the revelation of wishes peculiar to him: unconditional forgiveness of sins and offenses; personal identification with the poor, the prisoners, the persecuted; power exerted in the manner of a servant and the inevitable persecution accompanying the expression of such wishes of the Father. All these frequently run counter to the wishes of men, not as some super moral code but as an offer of love mixed with wishes of another sort. "Woe unto you when all men speak well of you for so did their fathers treat the false prophets" (Luke 6:26). One might as well say that in the Christian system the sacred union is not for tomorrow as long as there are prophets, men and women speaking of the wishes of the Spirit of the Lord to the people of their time and culture. Those wishes, even recognized in the joy of sharing, bring not peace but the sword.

In short, the word of God, presented and addressed to us in Jesus Christ, is an *embarrassment*. It invites us in love and discerning prayer to wish on the basis of God's wish, in the last resort to allow God gradually to wish in us. Many perfectly understandable resistances oppose the conversion of our wishes and can be located psychologically. The use of "sacred" texts provides some examples.

Resistances that are almost consciously accepted come to light, for example, in the *recurring selection* of certain texts from the gospels or quotations out of context to "prove" or reinforce what goes along with our wishes. The spiritual family known as "charismatic" repeats and sings its fill of a few passages inviting us to celebrate the presence of "salvation now" in a vaguely fusional joy and peace. The militancy of the socio-political family delights in stories and parables announcing salvation in a critical, frankly subversive fashion. Thus each one makes his choice in terms of the project that seems to him desirable and readily corroborates it, while sidestepping the embarrassing confrontation of examining the plan itself on the screen of other texts or of the context. This is a resistance we could all acknowledge without false shame: is not science itself partisan?[12]

A resistance that is assuredly very popular confines interest in the miracles almost exclusively to the *factual* narrative, isolated from the *meaning* which is often indicated in the text itself (the healing of the sick of the palsy as an image of the remission of sins; the miracle of the loaves as a foreshadowing of the eucharistic sharing, etc.). Do we not often see a sort of scandalized amazement if a priest, strong on exegesis, confesses that he is not keen to linger over the miraculous draught of fishes, but is inclined to turn his attention and interpretative effort to the meaning which is often given: "So will you be fishers of men," a declaration of capital importance in the disciples' vocation. Now this fixing of attention on the miraculous aspect of a catch that is unlikely to be repeated today averts us from the Lord's wish which, in prayer, should be the object of a meditation and discernment that always refer to the present. So this resistance weights the scales almost exclusively on the side of the human religious wish and not on that of its transformation suggested in the text.

A much more subtle resistance consists in honoring certain texts only in a sung version (formerly in Latin). This was the case with the Magnificat, that hymn that is almost revolutionary in several of its verses and which Luke (1:40-55) courageously places on Mary's lips (paraphrasing it from 1 Samuel 2:1-10). I can remember that, from childhood and for many more years, the admirable Magnificat, whose unintelligible words were triumphantly punctuated by the parish organ, assured me of the order that reigned thanks to the mighty, installed on their throne (before me: the clergy in all their glorious vestments), threatening only those who came late and empty-handed (far behind me at the back of the church).[13] It was not really serious because, after all, the text was in my missal. I confess that I am more perplexed on discovering in Bossuet (or rather one of his disciples) this astonishing countertext: "God has ordained that the poor man should honor supreme authority by his submission; he ordained that the rich man should imitate infinite mercy by his generosity; he wanted to give the one the *merit* of patience and the other the *merit* of charity."[14] Here, I fear, the resistance to Christ's wishes becomes totally unconscious, covered up by a cunning intellectual arrangement. May the Lord forgive those who know not what they are saying when they think they are speaking of his love, if that is indeed the case.

The subjective appropriation of fragments of text is presently held in check by the structural approach to the reading of the Scriptures and also by the recurrent attempt to achieve a prayer of petition "purified" of any "favors" to gratify wishes. It remains to be seen whether there is not a great risk of thus repressing the wish-words of man by reducing the feeling of embarrassment or resistance provoked by the psychological cohabitation of two partially divergent systems of wishes.

Here are a few hypothetical observations on these topics.

Resistance and repression?

a) *The structural reading of texts of Scripture* (the **Bible**) is being rapidly introduced into the training of teachers and is beginning to have a place in the catechesis in schools. At an opportune moment it is replacing the classic problematics of the *substance* sought behind the *form,* or of the *meaning* recaptured by placing the words of the text against the *external reality* (socio-political, for example), which occasioned them. A structurally analyzed text provides an abundance of significant relationships, to the discovery of which there can be no end and between which the reader is spurred to choose, perhaps on the basis of his current life situation.

Psychologically we might fear that the resistance arising from interference between the wishes (religious, for example) of the reader and certain challenges made by Jesus of Nazareth to his listeners could easily be masked by the connotations of the text. Structural analysis is often presented as a useful tool for getting rid of subjectivism or partisanship in the use of certain texts. By making the reader abandon mastery of the text it could contribute to a repression of certain wishes in the reader who would no longer be aware of them in himself and would be able to discuss them in their relationship with the interpellation which was the occasion of the words.

By using various exercises of receptive reaction to complete the structural analysis and an inventive proliferation of new "writings" produced by the readers (students, future teachers) to extend the reading, André Fossion and some other practioners of this method[15] are engaged in constantly evading the risk which they do not fail to recognize. They manage first to restore joy in the reading of texts that are too hackneyed. Their approach is a very effective exercise to counter idealizing rereadings which hide the conflicts in prematurely spiritual, generalizing interpretations. Finally, "the readers are invited to do battle with the analyzed texts and with other texts from their culture: stories, narratives, articles, cartoon strips, audio-visual presentations, mime, bodily expression. . . . This stage of production opens a space in which a new word can be born, a word acknowledging the Scriptures as law" (A. Fossion, p. 73-74).

Will the risk of repression and evading conflictual wishes thus be avoided? In the absence of publications referring to the words or reactions of the listeners in a productive period, it is difficult to form an opinion. Is "the overwhelming wish to taste of meaning immediately" (A. Fossion) "outstripped," sublimated, or merely by-passed? By making "the text appear in its otherness and not as one would wish it to be," is the wish being "educated" or simply ignored?

Whether a letter conveys love or hate, there is no method of rereading that can reasonably dispense with a reaction to it in the awkward interval it *reveals* between the intentions behind the writer's choice of words and the conflictual wishes working in the reader and becoming conscious as he reads. Reading/replying to such a letter involves investigating the intentions of the speaking subject (henceforth frozen in a text) and discovering *oneself* anew as a reading subject. Such an encounter is only possible given an interval (a lack) in which the word—letter or reply—is to be heard as that of a subject *asserting* his wish by a perhaps unconscious choice of words without being taken in by words. It is not so much the written text of the letter as what is not written that *reveals* to the recipient what could be only a fantasm of his own wish for love or hate . . . or merely indifference.

The same goes for the human and religious wishes of any man about to read a founding Scripture like the New Testament. Neither the believer nor the nonbeliever can get away from the intentions and wishes of the Lord when he *chooses* certain words from his religious heritage (body, water, spirit, son, poor, sin, father . . .) to be the bearers of shattering new meanings. Thus he initiates new conduct not generally permitted in his religious environment.

So, in order to break the imaginary appropriation of the text in fantasm-readings (mirror-readings) of the Scriptures, we must combine structural reading with information from socio-historical exegesis—A. Fossion states this with some reservations—but, psychologically too, we must allow resistances to speak for as long as they can be heard in a reaction or question.

In catechesis, writes André Fossion, "we must be able to accept this kind of question, answer it or suggest lines of research in the socio-historical context." But he also adds that in this way "new illusions must be foiled. . . . since what has really happened has been lost and wiped out to make way for the text. So the Scriptures rise up on a foundation of irremediable absence. And the elusive past constantly refers us to the texts, to our act of reading, to our responsibility as readers."

Fine. But by what right, or rather from what source does he declare certain questions to be inadmissible? In catechesis, he writes, "it is important to *denounce boobytrapped* questions, about whether the tomb was really empty or whether Christ really appeared to the disciples" (A. Fossion, p. 159).

I was more interested than André Fossion in the wish that prompted the questioner, personally or in a group, as it is revealed in his question. For, as long as it remains unconscious, that wish (or system of wishes), which may be religious, will perhaps go on operating as a *repressed* resistance to that "other" rebirth, which is exactly what the Scripture suggests in the passages mentioned.

It is the interplay of wishes made conscious that can reduce illusory fantasms. To sustain in love the interval necessary for that interplay, that battle, is for the believer to have a Christian experience not only of the "joy of the text" or of "battling" with the text, but of the resistance felt by his wish to the words speaking in it.

"Happy the child who, faced with the order to Peter to put up his sword, can take home from school, along with his dream of love, a secret resistance to that extraordinary sacrifice and yet an idea that it is there that truth is to be found" (Etienne De Greeff).

b) *A prayer of petition that does not ask for "favors,"* by allowing God to wish in us, could equally produce psychological peace by avoiding a conflict of wishes.

Once it is recognized that our spontaneous cries in the midst of our misery summon God (or the gods) to satisfy our needs with his gifts, once the inefficacy of these appeals to heaven to change the earth is accepted, some feel led to reject all prayer (practical atheism). But others endeavor to develop a "purified" prayer in which precise requests relating to present wishes give way to a movement toward unity with the divine will present in events and things on the one hand, and with the wishes of our Lord relating to the coming of the Promises on the other. Requests are still admissible provided they are in line with the general intentions of the Kingdom. And that kind of prayer, almost mystical in its aim, would lie at the heart of every Christian prayer worthy of the name: offering praise, asking forgiveness, opening the heart to the gift of salvation.

"Prayer," wrote Jean Claude Sagne in an article already quoted and well-constructed psychologically, "must clarify our wish so as to make us quite simply *desire God. . . .* This centering of our wish on a wish for God implies, in one sense, *a state of non-wish* on our part."[16]

I have had occasion to declare myself against this position which seeks too imperatively to purify our prayer-cries.[17] When I was preparing an article about a book on prayer, my mother (eighty-three years old) was wasting her last strength in the approach to inevitable death. That was the opinion of the doctors, at least. But can we ever rely on medical opinion in such cases?

How should one pray in such circumstances? Certain Christians abandon the idea of asking for anything. They prefer to put the life and death of their loved one in God's hands. Their wish to keep their mother alive no longer enters the language of their prayer in the form of a request. Their prayer is in line with their wish to be united with the divine will, expressed in the reality of the imminent death. Since they cannot change the order of things, they change themselves by modifying their wish to agree with and even anticipate the divine plan.

This prayer is not without grandeur; it stimulates research into the meaning of an event which is ineluctable anyway. After much hesitation I feel reluctant to adopt a position which would claim for such a prayer a place of privilege in Christian *experience*. Let us try to clear up the point of the argument.

"Elitist" prayer would be the reproach made by some pastors prompt to see the danger of devaluing the prayer-cry by depriving it of any immediate or even ultimate significance; it would be merely the starting point for a religiosity to be purified by being outstripped. Perhaps. But is it not traditional for prayers of petition, essential in any Christian order (we can only prepare for the Father's free gifts by asking for them), to move *gradually* upward from temporal favors to the gift of himself, made by the Giver in person? Is it conceivable that a Christian pastoral attitude should cease to be "elitist," at least in its prompting? So this objection is too shallow.

But can a prayer conceived in this way really claim to be a "conversion of the wish"? Or at least to prepare for such a conversion, however slight? It seems doubtful. This "state of non-wish" (Sagne) deserves further examination.

A baby cries, as they say, "for milk." If he stopped crying for good, so as not to have to endure waiting for his mother, he would build for himself neither a time structure nor an image of the person whose love is the ultimate thing he is waiting for. If the child stopped demanding, protesting, shouting his anger, he would not discover the harsh laws of the world and of men. If he was a good little boy and wanted to conform to all his parents' wishes, he would perpetuate the wish to remain with them always. Psychologically he would stop growing. He might never know what it is to want in terms of his own wishes, still less in terms of an "other" who is not a parent or their surrogate. These child-adults do exist. They may suffer very little, rarely be frustrated, but they have not learned how to hope or love. They no longer expect anything from the world or from any person. They are not even aware of most of their wishes, repressed because they are unspoken.

Can a Christian go down that road? Can he first forget the lesson of Job, the man who protests to his God? If all his prayer did was to unite him to the divine plan reflected in the universe of harsh realities, if it was nothing but a renunciation in the face of death, without protest, without asking to live, it would lead him to imagine a Father who spares him the supreme ordeal only through a survival after death which is more of a hallucination than a hope in faith. That was not the attitude of the Lord, of the Son. He accepted that he must die, but he still *asked* to live "if it be possible." And so he glorified the name of the Father and continued, without compromising, to reveal his wishes. For that, as we have already seen, he died on the cross: not stoned like a heretic but like one of his slaves in chains with whom he constantly identified himself in order to proclaim to them their freedom. And his disciples, accepting his death as a bereavement and presence, also *asked* that their hopes might live; thus they obtained, not the immortality of philosophy, but the Spirit which, on the first Pentecost, sent them straight out to the ends of the earth.

The conversion of a wish in the Christian experience of prayer requires a constant confrontation between the words announcing the wishes of the Father and all the wishes of the one who prays. So a Christian can usefully find in prayer a time and a place for expressing all his wishes, from the greatest to the smallest: to have fine weather for the next day's excursion, to pass his exam, to see an end to this flood or that famine, to have a child, that his father might be cured. For it is only then that this Christian faces up, on the one hand, to the harsh realities of the outside world and, on the other, to the words of our Lord which steal slowly in among his own wishes as a measure of the love that keeps them in a perpetually difficult symbiosis. If it is true that "renunciation is the pivot of the movement that converts need into wish" in terms of the Other,[18] that movement only begins and continues in a gradual transformation of requests (both human and religious) as they meet the words of the gospels. Mutation of the attitudes, when requesting in prayer, rather than suppression of the requests.

In prayer activities, just as in human relationships, two uses of language must be distinguished: a language for self-expression and communication with others (with a *unifying* aim) and a language that seeks to influence others, to put pressure on them (with a *modifying* aim). Between two adults bound by friendship or love, these two aims of language are kept in a stimulating state of tension. The expressive aim quite naturally takes precedence over the modifying, even manipulatory, aim. The same goes too for exchanges between persons linked together by team spirit or in a sharing community. We might even wonder whether the most religious beings have not learned, from their relationship with the words of a God whose wishes they have no thought of modifying, how to approach their own kind with a greater respect for their liberty and at the same time an ability to express themselves fully in their presence. But the reverse can be true in the case of someone who has never really loved, who has never really learned to *ask*, not on the level of his needs, but in terms of wishes that have no modifying aim and are not transformed into orders in the other's ears. In that case the image of God is consequently exceedingly faint, speaking from a Christian viewpoint. The intention of our Lord "not to call you servants but friends" (John 15:15) may be repeated in faith but it is not brought right down into the *experience of the conflict of wishes.* The spiritual battle in a case like this is fought in terms of an ego-ideal. In order not to stray into illusion, it often becomes absorbed in moral activism or mere obedience in execution. Then it brings effort, perhaps peace but rarely joy.

Prayer in terms of the Spirit of our Lord, prayer which continues to ask "to pray as we ought" (Epistle to the Romans 8:26) would thus link up with certain postulates of depth psychology by placing itself on the side of the "reality principle." By formulating requests, it maintains a consciousness (without repression) of the distance between the Father and the sons, of the resistance of the latter's requests when confronted with the words of the Son and lastly of the interplay of wishes where identification comes to *complete* love.

D. Christian Experience:
Identification as a Complement of Love

What does the Christian religion have to say to human wishes? The developments just discussed have emphasized that it speaks of love but also of an "other," different, wish.

The Christian message becomes insipid as soon as it is content to name God as love, an expression of love, a wish for love; and the use of capital letters (God=Love; God=Tenderness) does not disguise the woolliness of the illusions, the confusion always associated with linking this message with man's spontaneous religious wishes. The Christian message then takes on the nature of election oratory: the more vague and less specific it is, the greater its success. It addresses itself to all but no longer has any precise appeal.

Catechesis itself loses one of its most precious criteria for verifying *what* has happened to the announcement it wants to spread abroad of the new covenant offered to men, and also for verifying *how* it happened. It recovers that criterion as soon as it is prepared to take an interest in the reaction of the children or adults to biblical texts. Which character did they identify with during the story? Which animal, perhaps?[19] Some current research is very relevant here.[20]

Parable and identifications

Some eight- to ten-year olds are listening to the parable of the Good Shepherd in a standard version. They are then asked to draw a parallel with a present-day situation, if possible from their own lives or else with one they make up. The answers are collected or recorded.

Identification, as a key to classification, emerges from a straightforward comparison of these two responses.

Type A: "That reminds me how Mommy was worried because one of my brothers hadn't come home. She didn't bother about us any more until she had phoned around and made sure he wasn't lost." A rich and pertinent reaction, assuredly.

Type B: "It is like my building blocks. When I can't find one in my box, I go crazy; I can't go on playing till I have found it." At first sight this seems a rather silly reaction. We laugh at it, but then we realize it is just as pertinent, though in a different way.

In the responses classifiable as *type A*, the identification is not with the lost sheep (that would be a *type C*), but with the group of children temporarily deprived of their mother's attention. Undoubtedly it is a question of love, and the message is not completely overlooked since it could happen to any of the children to be late coming home, without necessarily being lost. But it will be noted that the reference is to *love received*, protective, if not possessive. It does not put the child in the position of an actor, quite the reverse. But it does situate him in his family.

Response B, on the other hand, shows that the child has immediately adopted the point of view of the owner in his anxiety ("my blocks . . . my box"). But in so doing, he finds himself on the side of *actively committed love*. He identifies himself profoundly with the worry and wish of our Lord and, in particular, has this charming phrase, "I go crazy (about it)." However imperfect the love in question may be (it is really more attachment to a possession), it is a matter of his wish and a wish which, in its own way, is in touch with that of the shepherd: none must be lost! Obviously in that form there is nothing that is specific to Jesus the Savior. A prudent man would have done the same, just like the child with his box of building blocks.

In this way the catechist pinpoints *how* the parable worked when these young children heard the story. He does not verify *what* was assimilated of the ultimate message of the parable: the suggestion of greater collective joy for one sinner who repents than for the ninety and nine who had no need of repentance. He only discovers the spontaneous aptitude of certain children to identify with *the metaphorical actor* of the story and indirectly (without thinking) with the storyteller, insofar as Jesus has already been presented to them as an object of love.

There is every chance that the message when fully explained—its meaning will only become clear to the child much later on—will be blocked on the level of Christian experience (even if it passes as "belief") for those who cannot put themselves in the place of the actor (and the storyteller) in the parable. This is an essential prerequisite if the parable is to work ("Which of you would not abandon the others to go and look for the one that is lost?"). When they are grown up, many people will retain from Jesus' invitation to rejoice collectively in an unconditional forgiveness only the gratifying announcement of forgiveness *to be received* by themselves (identification with the lost sheep . . . but repentant?) or the frustrating and vaguely subversive prospect of living with an authority more concerned with those who waste their substance than with those who stay at home and make no demands. Like the elder brother in the next parable (that of the paradoxical Father), they cannot get off the moral or religious level of justice and good works; they have a blockage once they are asked to enter into the joy of themselves forgiving those who have offended them. If we are to share in the joy of the Father, it is not enough to believe that he is a loving father, we must be able to identify with him in *that wish.* For it is *that* that makes him a different kind of Father, a God unlike the gods of the functional religions, an Other of our wish.

Attachment and identification

From this point of view, identification comes to complete love. Traditional concepts (imitation of Jesus Christ, *Nachfolge Christi,* the following or the practices of Christ) become psychologically operative. Not that identification can be induced (in catechesis, for example): Identification flows from attachment and completes love. But identification can be pinpointed as a jammed or a turning pivot in the transition from spontaneous religiosity to a Christian experience. A brief reminder of the meaning of identification in the most familiar situation of active life (the oedipean phase) will help us to understand.

Identification is part of the process by which the child, already attached to his parents by various links of passive dependence, accepts the wish and law of his father which regulates his affective growth: "You will not grow up in an exclusive union with your mother" and "You will not kill your father or your mother." In other words, "You will recognize that you are the son of an earlier loving relationship from which you received your twofold name." This *law*, which is latent during growth, only becomes effective, psychologically efficacious, if the wishes of the father and the mother conform to it and are perceptible to the child. It is by a break in his affective relationship with his mother on the functional basis of needs and then by a cleavage in his archaic wishes that the child brings about this structured opening under the sign of reality: renunciation of a mode of one-dimensional attachment, identification with the wish-law of the father (for the boy), with the wish-word of the mother (for the girl).[21] At this (oedipean) stage the psychic forces of aggressiveness and attraction become set. It is in these forces that the ego is formed in a responsible (it "responds" in accordance with the parents' wishes) and differentiated relationship; differentiated because the "response" based on sustained attachment differs according to sex. By this identification with the father's position, enshrined in the parental model, the child goes through a profound mutation of his affectivity: the affectivity of both girls and boys breaks away from a one-to-one relationship, a mirror dependency, and opens the door to the promise of a motherhood or fatherhood that is simply deferred. This mutation is the emergence of a capacity for *active* love, by free and personal choice, and it only operates on a foundation of permanent attachment which guarantees its fundamental continuity until the parents die and long after, in an internalized form. It is a laborious transformation and may be compromised insofar as the affectivity has been weighed down at some previous stage by an abnormal burden of anxiety, frustration, anxious aggression, or devouring or destructive counter-dependence. Then the attachment, indispensable as it is, will tolerate no distance, separation, or interval: it is imperative that the deficiency be made good immediately or rapidly if possible. Any object of a wish becomes functional as a mirror just as any investment becomes possession. Identification occurs on the have mode (approval of the mother, power of the father) not on a being relationship. It is blocked on the imaginary level without some opening to the other. In an extreme case, the mutation of affectivity is not brought off. The loving encounter, which may be passionate in its aim for possession or in the dominance conflict it instigates, will not know the joy of identification with wishes shared in their difference, an identification that is always only partial.

The identification in the situation that has just been described was basic for the human subject. But the personality is enriched and differentiated by a series of other identifications through which it is transformed by assimilating an aspect, an attribute, a behavior or a wish of the real, idealized, or even imaginary other (a hero in literature, for example). A subject's identifications as a whole do not form a coherent or stable system. This concept of identification that Freud used to further his studies of hypnosis, of passionate love, of artistic production, of group psychology, can also be used to understand one aspect of the difference between religious experiences and Christian experience.

Religious need and wishes, as described in the first chapter of this book, produce religious experiences which may be intense, in which God (the gods) does not figure as a subject with wishes. If the absolutizing or divine referent whose operations are expected or feared can indeed have intentions, they can only be explained in terms of the wishes and fears of man or in terms of faults in the social functioning whose authority and continuity are thereby reinforced (e.g., the "perennial" nature of the power of the pharaohs in ancient Egypt). In all the cases studied, man invests the divine referent with wishes that he himself needs. He does not identify with any "other" wish. Psychologically, the other is there to fill his own need.

If such a misapprehension infiltrates the use made of the beliefs or rites of Christianity, it is a regression comparable to that of the child's attachment to its mother for the sake of the gratifications she gives it, or to its mother and father for the sake of the orders-prohibitions-rewards which establish the child in a passive, submissive dependence for its own good. Even when assimilated, these gratifications and constraints only constitute a pre-moral code (the superego) whose functioning internalizes a bond of guilt with no responsibility other than to reproduce the image of the perfect child, an image which the child receives from its parents' decisions and from infinitely variable socio-cultural influences. That is indeed what happens in many religions whose orthodoxies and orthopraxies regulate the *moral* thoughts and behavior and no more, without referring their members to the One who should be their inspiration in his founding words and works. In Christianity, it will be said, this reference is constantly being made in the writings and intentions of the Magisterium. And nobody would dream of denying that the Christian identity is found wholly by referring the believer to a church that is itself regulated on the words of the New Covenant. Nevertheless, many Christians stop there and obey in faith without ever having thought, as Freud put it, of "putting themselves in Christ's place," of identifying with the One they wish to love (and do love in theological charity) in terms of his wish or wishes. These Christians then live out religious experiences in Christian faith and obedience. But their Christian experiences are rare or nonexistent. Beyond the ordinances of the church, or even within them, they have no knowledge of discerning prayer, for example, as it was described earlier in this chapter.

So, attachment to religion, to God, is not enough. Attachment to the personalities of the religion (saints, the Virgin Mary, even Jesus) is not enough when no mutation intervenes to transform it into a love that is perpetually seeking to know to which wish of the other it can respond. Only then would there be the beginnings of a specifically Christian experience.

We have already said that catechesis cannot produce this identification any more than education can produce to order identification of the son with his father, when there are blockages in the affectivity which was badly structured at an earlier stage. But it can at least work to avoid reinforcing manifestations of spontaneous religiosity in the Christianity of young children, as if those manifestations carried in them the wishes of our Lord or of a saint or the Virgin Mary. To reinforce them would amount to increasing the chances of a subsequent blockage, preparing the way for the very legitimate psychological doubt: Did I encounter God or myself? Catechesis can pinpoint these blockages too, reveal misapprehensions or resistances, and attempt to find a way around them. It will only succeed if the catechists themselves are clear in their minds about their own religious wishes, faced with those of the Spirit of the Lord. They are exactly like parents who only manage to foster the affective mutation in question if they are themselves, not a perfect couple, but united sexually and emotionally on a healthy foundation.

Identification, successful or otherwise, is a fundamental category in religious psychology for understanding what words mean. This has been highlighted by a piece of Swedish research on "God's guidance." It does not step outside functional religious language.

Twenty-seven believers between sixty-eight and eighty years of age were interviewed on their feeling of "being or having been led by God" in the course of their lives. Owe Wikström was interested in the relationship between that feeling and certain stories from the written tradition (Bible, lives of saints). He discovered a key for classifying their responses in "two different ways of linking the written story with the structure of the religious experience." By superimposing traditional stories on certain situations in their lives, some of them fastened their attention on an *intervention* by God which might, for their benefit, *repeat* a modification of the situation in which the hero of the story found himself. In that way they obtained a restructured view of their own situation. They were able to *expect* that God would play his part as he had done in history. But others (he does not say how many, and in any case it is of no consequence in such a small sample) in fact proceeded differently. They identified themselves to a greater extent with the character who *received* through God's intervention the means of *modifying* the chain of events *himself.* It is only in that case, if I understand the author's conclusion aright, that it is possible to speak of an "experience of God's guidance."[22]

In both cases, meditation on a traditional religious text acts *functionally* either to encourage patience or to stimulate the possibility of action "in a situation of extreme necessity." God's guidance would thus consist in providing strength through the distance that comes from meditation on a story from the past. There is no sign of a specific wish that is uniquely God's, but only of his timely interventions or inspirations.

The propensity to identify with Jesus when reading the gospels could usefully be the subject of various kinds of psychological research. Is it, for example, linked with the relational modes (dominance, dependence, animosity, altruism, mistrust, confidence) that prevail or seem desirable in social life? One study has made some progress in this direction.

Approaching belief as a system of lived relations, Dirk Hutsebaut[23] sees two groups emerge, whose socially negative relations (revolt, animosity, with religious guilt) are weak. These two groups, which are quite close in the high rate of their positive human relations, real and/or desired, and in their tendency to seek God in conviviality with their neighbor, show quite profound differences. One, much more numerous in the socio-economically weak group, shows strong signs of "dependence"; the other shows a significant accentuation of the "identification" described as that of the "person who identifies with Jesus Christ as an ideal man and an example" (p. 35).

These results confirm and illustrate with quotations a certain opposition between religious, functional "dependence" and "identification" (at least on the level of the ego-ideal). There is never any question of identification with the wish of Jesus Christ (nor, indeed, of love—a word no doubt considered very vague, and with reason). The author reckons that the study "recalls certain basic conditions for learning to identify: notably prior establishment of a positive contact with the model" (p. 38). He seems to be alluding to altruistic relations already established with other persons. But then, what has identification with Jesus Christ as an ideal personage to add? In short, where can a wish peculiar to him be made concrete in actual or desirable human relations?

But it can also happen that everything seems ready for identification in terms of the gospel spirit: correct information about the personage, the impulse of fervent prayer, socially normal and (perhaps) even emotionally rich human relations. And suddenly the anguish of an unbearable situation makes it all regress, in appearance at least, to a relationship of pure functional dependence. The following observation illustrates a movement of religious regression accompanied by repression.

"We mothers understand each other . . ."

Madame Pélerin, a Catholic with a lively, confident, richly spontaneous faith, is going through one of the most painful ordeals possible for a mother. One of her two sons has been mortally injured by a blow in a scuffle during a student demonstration he was taking part in supporting immigrants in Belgium. The twenty-three-year-old victim is in hospital and the doctors despair of his life. Madame Pélerin discusses with her husband and younger son an idea that came to her when praying: Suppose they joined the trainload of sick people due to leave for Lourdes in a week's time. The younger son is not very keen, the husband is more than unwilling: He objects that the doctors advise against a journey in the course of which their son might die.

Desperately worried, Madame Pélerin tells me all this. "And your son?" I ask her, "What does he want?" He is not against it. In fact, she adds, he is too weak to decide. My comment makes her think that her husband's opinion has some weight. She gets up and decides that, under these circumstances, her husband and son will remain at the hospital while she herself will go to Lourdes to implore the Virgin. As she leaves, she utters this magnificent and surprising statement: "You see, *we mothers* understand each other better!"

I get a card from Lourdes asking me to pray with her. Shortly after her return, the elder son dies. Six months later Madame Pélerin comes to see me again. She is slowly getting over her bereavement. But fortunately, she says, there is faith in the resurrection. And then, there is her other son. I talk about the dead son again and recall the circumstances in which he received the fatal blow. She says she has often thought about it and, as a Christian, she feels proud of her son. The journey to Lourdes is mentioned. "Yes," I say, "mothers understand each other." She asks me why I say that. I remind her that those were her own words. "Did I really say that?" she asks. There is a long silence and she seems upset, almost distressed. Then suddenly she gets up as abruptly as the previous time: "How awful!" she says with a faint smile "How could I have prayed like that? Never mind. I shall go there again."

Another card reached me from Lourdes, signed this time by her husband as well, with these words: "We are here together. This time the Virgin has really helped us."

All this shows: 1) That distress brings us back to spontaneous religion, to the prayer that tries to enlist the services of the Virgin for our wish, to *have* her for our own ends. 2) That in this case there was genuine repression of something that was well known: The Mother to whom the prayer is addressed lost her son too. "We mothers understand one another" can only lead to confusion in these conditions. The imagined Mother has lost a part of her past true story. 3) That spontaneous religious *attachment* ensures continuity in the transition (here a return of what was repressed) to the most complete identification. 4) That a roughly analogous *concrete* circumstance (the son's wish to be identified with the immigrants, by at least marching alongside them) intervenes effectively in the identification achieved during the second journey to Lourdes (accompanied by the dead boy's father). 5) Finally, that this mutation of attachment into love, with identification with the wish of Jesus, the indirect cause of his death, is not totally dysfunctional since this time "prayer has really helped us." Thus prayer has become (again?) a Christian *experience.* But at what cost!

To identify actively in love is to hear perpetually the voice of a wish originating from the other. In Christian experience, it is to hear the voice arising from the impotence in which the Son of God found himself as a result of his own wish and the identification *which he chose.* What kind of love was his?

"You did it to me"

Is it possible to speak of identification, a psychological process of human development, in connection with Christ?

There will be no lack of theologians to remind us, if it were necessary, that the *identity* of the Son is perfect, like that of the Father, in the mystery of the Trinity. And his incarnation, a mystery of love, in no way puts that in question. He loved men with the same love that unites him with the Father. "As the Father has loved me, so have I loved you. . . . If you keep my commandments you will abide in my love. . . . He who believes in me will also do the works that I do; and greater works than these will he do. . . . If the world hates you . . . remember the word that I said to you, A servant is not greater than his master" (John 15:9; 14:12 and 23; 15:20). What then is that wish-word that provokes hatred?

The love of that Father is made manifest in the human condition of the Son. This son has known growth and the psychological mechanisms of growth have operated in him: attachment, identification with the father, ideal of the ego, participation in the Jewish religion. But, in the absence of any precise information, the psychological study of Jesus (sometimes recklessly attempted) has no relevance, at least from the genetic angle.

The identification in question is of the kind an adult man is induced to make; it is reflected in his acts and he talks about it when he is conscious of it. *With this exception: there was not even an ideal model here.* There was decision and a *choice.* Jesus made his decision in favor of the underprivileged, the religious outcasts.

Not only did he turn to the weak, the sick, the friendless: that would not have caused scandal. Not only did he live with the poor, the women, those on the fringes of the society of his day (publicans, public sinners): that might have been surprising. But he attacked the barriers that the Law and its official commentaries increasingly raised between men: lepers, cast out as impure according to the Law, the possessed as being untouchable, prostitutes as worthy to be stoned, slaves as crucifiable. It was the choice of a neighbor as significant the moment he was poor, a sinner, an enemy, banished or religiously excluded, that made Jesus a stranger to the religious ideal of the people in the Temple and which still makes him an embarrassing prophet, even for the religious love of men and churches today and no doubt for all time. The fact that he wanted to "rank among the accursed of the Law" (Galatians 3:13) does not make the exercise of power easy in the churches that appeal to him in the service of Christians. Any measure of exclusion or condemnation runs the risk of an embarrassing repetition of the procedures acceptable to the ideal of the Temple.

By taking up the cause of these outcasts, Jesus rattled the juridically established frontiers of the sacred with both his words and his deeds, perhaps even the frontiers of every sacred thing originating in man's wishes. By announcing that he was doing it in the name of a Father God, by remitting sins himself, he became a blasphemer, abandoned by God according to the religious belief of his milieu and according to all illusion-belief (born of man's wish) everywhere. By asserting that his wish was to be identified with the poor, the persecuted, prisoners, the sick, he was formulating a *founding word* for a new hope for men: "For I was hungry and you gave me food; I was naked and you clothed me; I was sick and you visited me, I was in prison and you came to me" (Matthew 25:35-36).[24]

It is a literally unbelievable founding word ("When did we see you like that?" Matthew 25:37), and psychologically bewildering for the economy of even a loving wish: Whatever you did to one of these poor, you did it to me. Psychologically and sociologically, there can be nothing but conflict and battle for Christ's followers (loving identification with that wish).[25] The "reality" of a different wish is attested by the psychological resistance that it produces, by the counterpositions it provokes, not only in the emotions and the individual unconscious (ready to seize on any rationalizations that would eliminate that wish), but also in the will for power that accompanies the exercise of power in societies like the churches, incompletely converted to that spirit and to such an awkward love.

A non-Christian may well see in them *nothing more* than the proclamations of a prophet, and they are effectively that for whoever hears them. But he finds no cause to impugn them on the score of Freud's "illusion-belief." Jesus performed what he was saying, and what he was introducing into the Jewish society of his day became historically true when he himself was persecuted and regarded as abandoned by God. That was no utopia in the normal sense of the word.[26] For Christ's followers, imagination is neither constituent nor regulatory. The founding word is a decision involving a continuous connection between a certain wish for love, and work in the interval thus created by a love never satisfied by works. It is a new prophetism, indeed, and one which happily has never ceased to be proclaimed, if not practiced, in the Christian churches.[27]

The lowering of all barriers between men, *even those religiously justified*, by this identification with every outcast, every prisoner, every man condemned as legally abandoned by God, that is the "inclusive" and open wish. An ego-ideal operating in love in terms of such a wish keeps that "way out" open that Freud demanded if there were to be effective sublimation. There is not just a shift of affectivity toward another object nor idealization of the object with "goal-inhibited sentiment" (although that could be an obstacle to it or a caricature of it). The love proposed calls for a mutation, at least partial, of the wish itself. This identification and mutation are always evolving when it comes to their

historical accomplishment by men and in the churches. For the
believer who recognizes the Son in that prophet or the divine
origin of that prophetism, it was originally a case of *expressing* an
unchanging *identity* (that of the first-born Son) *through* that identification with the most deprived, the most rejected among men.
Once he is participating in (or "descending" into) the human
condition, he participates in the most radical way by "descending" equally within it through his wish to be identified with the
poorest and those most excluded by reason of sacralized barriers, now out of date. His "kenosis" through psychological identification, we might say, is the coherent expression of the theological "kenosis" (or "abasement") pointed out by Paul and analyzed
by subsequent Councils.

However faithfully the Christian identifies with our Lord's
wish, he will never develop it except on the basis of his fundamental deficiency (a deficiency that he thus gives up all idea of
filling "religiously") and a sufficiently adult capacity for love.
Perhaps the two go hand in hand if it is true that the coexistence
of two systems of wishes, not completely superimposable and
partially divergent, is only possible in the loving union and mutual transformation that it constructs. The founding word and the
identification it gives to human wishes are thus misunderstood if
they are interpreted as a moral precept, an obligation in the
strict sense, or as the means of "obtaining a loftier moral code"
(Freud). They are betrayed if they are presented as a promise
that the thirst for love will be assuaged or as a gratification of a
wish. The Christian *experience*, however, continues to live by it as
it can equally well die by it.

SUMMARY AND CONCLUSION

How does the Jewish religion speak to human wishes? In terms
of a covenant, of love, of the privileged position of a chosen
people.

How does the Christian religion speak to human wishes? In
terms of an offer of love and of wishes (the founding words)

distinct from simple human wishes at work in functional religiosity.

Among those wishes, that of identification with the most deprived of men has been singled out as particularly suitable for structuring Christian experience and letting it escape from the Freudian critique of illusions by keeping it on the side of the "reality principle" and making it undertake "the conquest of the pleasure principle." On the way, it was even possible to indicate, sketchily at least, how Christian experience is an active synthesis, gradually transforming an attachment to various images of a God or of interventionist powers, modifying the realities of the world (an attachment that is nourished by countless metaphors, some well and some ill used, signifying the Covenant in the Old Testament). This attachment, on the imaginary plain, is the affective base which psychologically sustains the varied manifestations of functional religion, exposes them to the doubt resulting from critical thought in a scientific culture but brings them back in cases of anguish and personal or collective crisis. Religious attachment, archaic or primary, remains fundamental in the religious wish whose conflictive mutation *can* be achieved in the Christian experience of following Christ as far as identification in terms of *his* wish for love.

The experience, an active synthesis as analyzed, develops thanks to a twofold anchoring in reality: an anchoring in events or situations that are historically determined but often ambiguous in meaning, and an anchoring in the wish for love felt as a constraint or resistance introduced by that "quite other" wish for identification with the most deprived, in faithfulness to that love.

It is not just a question of a commandment to love these most deprived people. Christian experience structured in this way does not consist in wanting the wishes of another and accomplishing them because he loves us: That could be done out of generosity. "Believing is not just wanting divine truth, but hearing the voice that issues precisely from the weakness of God."[28] What the theologian is asserting for the faith, the Christian psychologist is observing in his own way for experience. To love this very special God who find expression, lives and dies in Jesus Christ, to meet him as a presence-absence according to the wish for love with identification with the weakest, whereby he glorified the Father, is to experience the other-of-the-wish as a constraint and resistance in which the self is moved off-center more radically than by the difference of the sexes in love.

It is important to grasp the full significance of this observation. There is obviously no question of suggesting that this revelation of the Father by the weakness of the Son and the discreet invitation of the Spirit is acceptable *because* it is a constraint upon us, still less of thus proving that it is divine. That idea would be as strange as that of marrying a girl (or boy) for whom love was beginning to dawn because she (he) is a constraint or upsets us! No. But in the case of the difference of the sexes ("the other of sexual desire") as in the case of the god who constrains ("the other of religious desire"), one certainty at least seems to be emerging: This other-of-desire cannot be entirely reduced to an illusion. It can be misunderstood, rejected, repressed as in the homosexual whose desire in the end goes from the same to the same; it cannot be reduced psychologically to the product of a projection in the Freudian sense of the word. And this is even less so in that this constraint activates a fundamental narcissism, whether we are talking of the irreducibility of the sexes or of recognizing as God the one who has known the death in reality and is present in the breaking and sharing of bread. We are dealing here with relations that are not sustained on the imaginary level. They knit together in the depth of that interval where words bring about the encounter of wishes, possibly the symbolic pact through the promise of faithfulness. Wishes for identification in love remain partially disjoined. One must be a little "like the other" but not "have the other." The distance and the deficiency cannot be filled.

Other modalities of the Christian experience are obviously possible and the psychologist can only observe them. Certain Christians, experiencing the reverse, testify that their religious consciousness feels it is being seized by God, overwhelmed by

God, in terms of one or other vivid emotion experienced individually or collectively. But if they make this choice and stick to it, they can hardly expect psychology to comfort them in any possible doubts they may experience concerning the "reality" of what they have encountered: themselves or the Other? their wish accomplished in the joy of a fusional group? their Christian identity by mimetism, incorporating the leader of the group, the community, or the church? a renunciation of existence or of making themselves heard so that the group might live? For all that may correspond to *their wish,* with or without love.[29]

Psychologically, resistances are proof that the word of love and the wish spoken by Jesus Christ as a call and invitation do embarrass us. They upset our wishes, even the religious ones, to the point where the most lucid Christian admits at times that he never finishes accepting them. Like the mutual and joyful promise of human love in which each *asks* the other to receive from him the happiness of remaining faithful to him, the Christian experience can only be kept in active synthesis by prayer, by the expectation of a continuously sustained gift of presence. Thus it is registered in time not as a thirst assuaged but as an insatiable search for the source—at times a passionate struggle to free it from the stones obstructing it or preventing access for a greater number, at times a quivering contemplation, inhaling its freshness and urging us onward ever further in the light and shade of the night.

> Have you seen the source?
> I know the source, it flows, it runs
> but it is of the night.
> This living source of my wish
> I see it in this bread of life
> but it is of the night.
>
> —St. John of the Cross

Like the wind that is visible only when it swells the sail, the Christian experience of God is actively revealing rather than psychologically manifest. As St. Bernard wrote, "The face of the Word is never formed before our eyes but it is formative; it gives joy in the gift but not by the appearance of love."[30]

ACTION AND CONTEMPLATION

And what about Mary in all this? Mary of Bethany, the sister of Lazarus and Martha, who will never cease to delight Christian contemplatives? Did not she, and with her the whole contemplative way, find a definitive defender since she "has chosen the better portion, which shall not be taken away from her" (Luke 10:42)?

But who is talking of taking it away from her? No psychologist would dream of doing so, that is certain: For is she not the one who keeps silent in order to listen more closely to the words of her guest? Should she not on that score be the patron saint of all Christian psychologists?

If the reader had thought to find in this book on religious experience and Christian experience the smallest paragraph expressing suspicion of the strictly contemplative experience, he would do well to reread the whole.[31]

Nowhere do the modalities of "active synthesis" become more manifest than in the progress of the great Christian contemplatives. Nowhere is there a greater awareness of resistances; nowhere are they circumvented with more care. Nowhere is the regard for the "other-of-desire" so delicate, so respectful in the wish to transform it into the "Guest-of-desire."

Consequently, nowhere is there a greater solicitude for that mutation of the self into receptiveness, if possible total receptiveness: extreme renouncement, symbolic surrender in obedience, in work, in the most attentive listening to the cumbersome wishes of the poor and of every visitor, no matter how tiresome—with that inner fire that consumes without destroying, like death consciously present in life.

But the discernment that leads ultimately to a life resolutely committed along the contemplative path remains a delicate matter. A meander on the route, arising from an inner void to be filled, remains a pathway strewn with ambushes to be surmounted, notably the ambush of illusions fostered by a metaphorical vocabulary, speaking to the imaginary and evoking, as a false doorway, a culturally obsolescent, symbolic Christianity. A serious scouring could be undertaken using conceptual tools that have become operative in depth psychology. It has begun. Analyses of the unconscious by persons freely trapped between "enclosure, fantasm, and prayer"[32] could well be multiplied for the greater benefit of those taking part in this difficult discernment. More would be needed, done by contemplatives who have trodden these ways, not in order to fill their void, but to go, so to speak, from the hollow of the interval to a still greater hollow, from the exposed mudbanks of human maturity to the Source that cannot be seen "for it is of the night."

"Self-abandonment for the working of the gift itself,"[33] this perceptive saying about human love, taken up by theologians, designates the central movement of the Christian experience, where the active and the contemplative meet. Martha and Mary[34] are both sisters of Lazarus, the man who died twice; they can communicate from this disturbing privilege.

EPILOGUE

House of the poor—house of bread

These last two chapters have presented the reader with much reality and even the reality principle. May I venture to close them by dreaming a little, which is another way of coming back to wishes?

Lazarus had just died, for the second time, for good. Outliving their brother, in accordance with the statistics of probability, Martha and Mary will have taken their bereavement more cheerfully than the first time.

In Jerusalem there was no letup in the persecution. Peter

had just been imprisoned and no one knew how he would get out (see Acts 12, 1-18).

On learning of Lazarus' death, Joseph of Arimathea (whose tomb had been sold by order of the Romans) left the town and went up the hill toward Bethany on his donkey. As soon as the house was in sight, he noticed a crowd made up of the poor, the disabled, and strangers already gathered there. A real beggars' kitchen, he said to himself as he drew near. Tables had been brought out and Martha was handing out bread to all the needy. She apologized for not giving her time to Joseph and asked him to find her sister in the house and tell her to come and help in the sharing of bread.

Once inside, Joseph noticed Mary sitting at the table in the semi-darkness. She was weeping quietly and repeating over and over again a gesture that Joseph immediately recognized: the breaking of bread. He kept quiet, not daring to interrupt her. Then he thought he saw that as soon as the loaves were divided into four pieces they reappeared on the table, whole again, while the crumbs were piling up rapidly. However, as he looked closely and his eyes became accustomed to the darkness, he could see two persons (he never knew whether they were rich or poor) constantly bringing fresh loaves from a back room to Mary to be broken. Joseph was wondering whether he had encountered the Lord again or just a dream. But before he had time to ponder the matter, Martha came in and called her sister.

Mary raised her head and in a firm but gentle voice replied: "Feed them with *yourself.*" Then she noticed Joseph of Arimathea, smiled at him and began to sing.

He who breaks his bread in tears will share it with singing.

Notes

1. Walter Houston Clark in his classic manual in the United States, *The Psychology of Religion* (New York: Macmillan, 1958), pp. 21-23, proposed a distinction between *tertiary* religious conduct (the most frequent) occurring conventionally in submission to the authority of the churches but never corresponding to "first-hand experience," *secondary*

religious conduct deriving (after conversion, for example) from an experience that is already remote, and *primary* religious conduct corresponding to intense religious experience and efforts to sustain it or to bring life into line with it subsequently. Although this distinction is necessary to differentiate between very disparate types of religious conduct, it is weakened by the ambiguity of the term "experience," which, in W. H. Clark's work, designates vivid, predominantly affective states of consciousness *(Erlebnis)*.

2. The "inclusive" wish of the God revealed in Jesus Christ (appeal to all men, even sinners) will provoke a reaction of continual resistance, never entirely overcome, in the history of the church. This vocation for universality should prevent or hamper the operation of a considerable force in the cohesion of any group, even a religious one: aggressiveness against other individuals, groups, or churches (the "excluded third parties"). The Catholic church still faithfully proclaims this universality but its organization relapses periodically, and very "functionally" into exclusions, condemnations, anathemas. Triumphant once in the Constantinian era, she has never ceased scoring great successes in engagements of a persecuting kind, in which the infidel is killed instead of being offered conversion: the Crusades against Islam (on the pretext of regaining access to the empty tomb); the wars of religion between Christians; the massacres and forced conversions in the colonial period; participation in numerous anti-Jewish programs; condemnation, now obsolete, of religious liberalism; unconditional anti-Marxism; all this is sociologically understandable and can be defended in the name of the religious wishes *of man*. Furthermore, it unleashes a considerable force of expansion and reinforces *identity* by all-too-human means. We get to the stage of denouncing as disobedience what is in fact faithfulness (albeit narrow or obstinate) to an ancient religious rite, of condemning as a rejection of or contempt for this or that dogma what is a quest (perhaps a bold one) for meaning, of wanting to demonstrate that a writer is necessarily non-Christian if he is a Marxist, whereas he claims (misguidedly perhaps) that he is finding a road to conciliation. A church that had won over Western Europe by preaching to the "barbarians" after the great invasions was unable to come to terms in the East on the question of Eastern rites. The *only* argument I draw from all these battles, some lost, some won, is that the "inclusive" wish attested in Jesus Christ always meets resistance on the part of man and that, psychologically, it is not religiously practicable in a church without tension between very *real* paradoxes. It is not simply a product of society. Theologically, a reading of the articles by Christian Duquoc, "La prétention à l'universalité," and Joseph Comblin, "Le débat actuel sur l'universalité chrétienne," in *Concilium 155* (May, 1980), pp. 75-86 and 87-96. is recommended.

3. Among the numerous commentaries on the parable of the para-doxical father (unhappily known as that of the prodigal son) the most psychologically relevant seems to me to be that of G. Crespy, "Psychana-lyse et foi," in *Etudes théologiques et religieuses* 4 (1966), pp. 241-51, repeated with slight modifications in G. Crespy, *Essai sur la situation actuelle de la foi* (Paris: Cerf, 1970).

4. Commenting on "because you have seen, you have believed," said to St. Thomas the Apostle (John 20:29), St. Augustine states: "He did not believe what he had seen, but having seen this, he believed that: he saw the man and believed in the God. What he saw and touched was a living body that he had seen dying; what he believed in was a God veiled in that charnel presence (credebat Deum in ipsa carne latentem)" (*Trac-tatus in Ioannis Evangelium*, 79, 1). In accordance with their methodolo-gy, theologians analyzing the act of faith have spoken concerning the Apostles of a gift of God as being at once *external* in the man (the Son) they were listening to and in the *inner* movement (the gift of the Father) which brought them to a recognition of the Lord God. Their concept of a "gift of the Father" has the advantage of also explaining the faith in the church, dogmatically expressed and organized on a basis of disci-pline. Moreover it is founded on the gospel text ("It is neither flesh nor blood that made you say that . . ."). On the other hand, according to most theologians this concept does not correspond to a movement that is psychologically observable or can be induced scientifically. The gift of the Father in the act of faith is psychologically revealing (of the person of the Son, the church, etc.) and not intuitively manifest. So I have done without this concept, the *psychological* status of which is uncertain, in this book and in this chapter which is devoted, not to faith (religious or Christian), but to experiences (religious or Christian). This does not mean that the same experience cannot be *at once* both religious or human (speaking with tongues, for example) *and* Christian because it is taken as expressing the faith. But it does mean in this case that it cannot be presented as an experience of God revealed in Jesus Christ, still less as an immediate experience of the Spirit of Christ. Speaking with tongues, in my view as a psychologist, is not symbolic but merely meta-phoric of Pentecost. It is a figure that can be made a symbol, but only in the signifying intention of the glossolalia itself (at the risk of being mystifying for the group).

5. It is understandable that Christians from Europe or America going to a eucharistic congress in Bombay (1964) should decide to go only as bearers of bread, rice, or other foodstuffs with the intention of visiting the suburbs which are among the most wretched in the world. It fell to Paul VI to have the courage and honor to go *in spite of the opposition* of a national and local government more concerned with hiding the poverty

than doing anything about it. Without this concern and action there would have been great risk of an ostentatious parade of eucharistic faith that was psychologically dead and vaguely preposterous.

6. "To forgive until seventy times seven": human and religious *resistance* to the assimilation of such a wish is well illustrated in the historical ups and downs of the institutional practice of penance. It took about ten centuries before unconditonal forgiveness of all sins, even after backslidings and without public confession was finally accepted by the church. Psychologically, this speaks to me of obstinate and ultimately victorious faithfulness to the wish expressed in the gospels, in a struggle arising from the organization into a church of various compromises with the religious wishes of man.

7. In the words of St. Augustine: "Interposita matris auctoritate de patre creditur" (Through the mediation of the mother, we believe in the father. *De utilitate credenti,* XII, 26). For nowadays, as in the time of the Apostles, fatherhood can never be proved except by a statement from the mother. And she may well be mistaken, lie about the progenitor, or decide in conjunction with some man that he shall be the father by artificial insemination (excellent examples in G. Delaisi, *La part du père,* Paris, Seuil, 1981). As for the church, would it not be more accurate metaphorically to speak of her as the Bride of the Spirit? She mediates only to lead men to the Son, presented in the Scriptures, if it is true that adoptive paternity is constituted, not by a birth, but in an acknowledgment based on words exchanged with the adoptive sons or daughters. As for the Father, *no one* knows him but the Son (the first-born).

8. Georges Morel, *Questions d'homme* volume II: *L'autre* (Paris: Aubier, 1977), p. 240 and p. 252. This work, which is remarkable philosophically, starts from Hegel and re-opens the phenomenological analysis of various ways of *posing* the question of God. Once the problematics of desire have been introduced, the author pursues it in terms of "a wish for love (a redundancy)" (p. 261), for gratuitousness, for an offer of the gift of self. He does not tackle the reality of an *other* wish, as different from or surprising to a religious wish proper. That would be to move over to the work of exegetic or theological analysis of the words of a man whose divine character was finally recognized. Theology was not G. Morel's subject even if it provided him with an interesting *philosophical* conceptualization but one that was psychologically truncated. If the wish for love does not open the door to love of the other according to his own wish, and if, philosophically, the structure of the wish for love is stated to be identical in both terms of the love relationship, no place is prepared even hypothetically for the sudden appearance in religious history of an original wish expressed concretely in the condition of man. This logical conclusion of a closed philosophy is illustrated in the last

volume of the work by a corrosive analysis of some theories that are particularly vulnerable to the critique of illusions.

9. Unpublished lecture, "Dieu est mort," by G. Crespy, registered at the Centre Lumen Vitae in November, 1967.

10. Sacralization of the text-object always tends to reproduce itself even in Catholicism. "Before the advent of modern exegesis, fixation on sacred texts was such that the fact that the Scripture was not read became the surest guarantee of its purity" (G. Morel, op. cit., p. 244) It must also be borne in mind that, in the state that society was in, such reading provided a knowledge that was reserved for the elite who had always defended themselves against the wild invasions of popular interpretations.

11. "The parables still contain a provocative enigma" writes André Dumas, with justice. "They will not do as models or symbols to generate imitations. . . . They force us to see a fundamental intention in an inimitable particular. They are provocative to intelligence by their play on a constant to-ing and fro-ing between situation and meaning while the archetypes subject us to repetition, shackle life to the observance of an ossified structure and by not allowing any discovery, generate the imitation or illusion of abandonment." But parables must be put back in an environment very different from ours, as can be seen in the article "De l'archétype à la parabole," in *Supplément 92* (February, 1970), pp. 28-80. We must always be fighting "against the manifestly constant temptation to transform parables into archetypes" (p. 45), invitations inspired by the spirit of the Lord in the form of moral imperatives to imitate a model. That is one of the most cunning ways of resisting fidelity to the wishes of Christ.

12. Was I not a victim of certain secret resistances myself when choosing texts in line with the purpose of this book? The reader should be on the lookout for them and, if is so inclined, should point them out to me.

13. So I have my own small personal response to the question put by John Paul II to workers in a Paris suburb (at St. Denis on June 2, 1980) "In the name of what right was this freedom to fight for truth and justice systematically separated from the words of the Mother who venerates God with all her heart while carrying the Son of God in her body?" By chance the previous day in Notre-Dame de Paris, the organ had once more smothered the words of the *Magnificat* in the ears of the great of this world, when, curiously, it had replaced the *Te Deum* at the very last moment. As a psychoanalyst, I have learned to find humor in such age-old resistances: they have long existed between devoted and loving spouses. After all, if the wish of the one is tedious to the other, that at least proves that the voice of the other is not an illusion.

14. Drawn from *Origines de l'esprit bourgeois en France* (Groethuysen, p. 186) quoted by G. Morel, op. cit., p. 50.

15. André Fossion, *Lire les Ecritures: théorie et pratique de la lecture structurale* (Brussels: Editions Lumen Vitae, 1980). This book is a harmonious blend of theoretical clarity and practical precision; it refers us, as an ever necessary preamble, to the information on exegesis in catechesis contained in Alain Machadour's *Un évangile à découvrir: lecture de la Bible hier et aujourd'hui* (Paris, Centurion, 1978). The list of texts treated structurally with a view to catechetic or pastoral application increases from week to week. The preoccupation with involving the participants actively is clear in André Paul, "Résurrection de Lazare: lecture à plusieurs voies," in *Temps et Paroles 23* (May, 1979), pp. 71-93. Pierre Moitel's study, "Travailler le texte," in the collection *Rencontres autour de la Bible: des textes qui font naître* (Paris, Aumônerie de l'enseignement public, June, 1978), pp. 29-52, is exceptional in that it mentions, albeit briefly, reactions in free work (but in a strong framework) before or after analysis of the text. To find how this may complement the exegetic-symbolic method, a comparison with the concrete applications reported by Claude Lagarde in many articles in *Temps et Paroles* would be useful; for example "Des ficelles qui libèrent," in Number 9 (July, 1976), pp. 22-28. The imaginary world of children finds expression there in a stimulating confrontation which shows how impossible it is to keep to it and raises the question of meaning.

16. Jean Claude Sagne, "Du besoin à la demande," in *La Maison-Dieu 109* (1972), pp. 87-97. By presenting prayer as conversion of a wish, Father Sagne shows very well (like Father Denis Vasse, whose *Le Temps du désir,* Paris: Seuil, 1969, he quotes several times) that by abandoning the service of God in order to gratify our needs we can wish him to become the object of our wish . . . for love itself at the risk of "identifying God with the object of our wish and our ego-ideal" (p. 109). But has he not increased the risk himself? He puts forward the idea that "the evolution of a wish through love should make it tend to a pure request, concerned only with the presence of the other, as he wishes to give himself" (92); in other words it is pure availability, renunciation, that would be sufficient for the conversion of a human wish into prayer. I readily admit that this is a kind of preliminary condition, especially as a movement of the *religious* mystic. But when it is a matter of experience in *Christian* prayer, particularly if it is contemplative, the humanity of the Son has revealed more to us by telling us of the wishes of the Father. And by his words we are invited to moderate requests and slant them in a direction that is at least partly different from the one our wishes would take otherwise. This specifically Christian dimension (words of the Son revealing the wishes of the Father) calls, psychologically, for love to be

completed by identification. This is a progressive operation which could be blocked by "availability-renunciation" contained in the ego-ideal.

17. *From Cry to Word*, A. Godin, editor (Brussels: Lumen Vitae Press, 1967), "Editorial: Petitions for Favors in Prayer (Three Opinions)," pp. 13-25.

18. Denis Vasse, *Le temps du désir* (Paris: Seuil, 1969), p. 31. On its impetus, the author adds "The unquestionable sign of an experience of God is the man's joy when he does not even feel the need of expressing himself" (p. 45). Is this the Christian experience again, inspired by the New Testament? I do not think so. Moreover, that was not what Father Vasse said. On the contrary, the Holy Spirit is the *"discrepancy* that both punctuates and opens up the Judeo-Christian teachings. . . a *difference* of origin on which the possibility of meaning is founded by the prohibition of any dogmatic closure . . . and which gives back *the word* to each of the participants in the feast . . . *recognizing* the differences that Babel had denied by enslaving its builders in a single ideology"; in this way it is replaced in the substructure of every Christian experience and commented on psychologically by the theologian Roland Sublon in "Esprit Saint dans la perspective psychanalytique," in chapter IV of the volume *L'Esprit Saint* (Brussels: Publications des Facultés St. Louis, 1978), pp. 97-130.

19. In a piece of research using children's drawings made after hearing the story of Abraham and Isaac, several children expressed the idea that it was all very unfair to the ram that was sacrificed! A neat way of diverting their attention from what they found most frightening: the danger that Isaac had escaped. . . . It is the most fearful who identify most strongly with Isaac. Identification with Abraham is not practical anyway (without a symbolization impossible at that age) and would be revolting . . . The only remaining possibility would be identification with the angel who saved the child from extermination. This could sometimes be detected in the care taken and the colors used to portray the angel. See details and some illustrations in "Isaac at the Stake," by A. Godin (with the collaboration of Cécile Vandercam and Gaston Schaber) in *Lumen Vitae* X, 1 (1955), pp. 65-92.

20. I am indebted to my colleague André Knockaert (director of the Lumen Vitae Center for catechetical teaching in Brussels) for drawing my attention to the principle of this unpublished research. It is reported with catechetical commentaries with the aim of respecting the fundamental challenge of the text in its structure as it appears in André Knockaert and Chantal Van Der Plancke, *Cours de religion: Comment s'y prendre?* (Brussels: Lumen Vitae Press, 1980), p. 44 and pp. 81-83.

21. The *wish-law* of the father is the result of his position as father. It is not exactly parallel to that of the mother. She is not in a position to

break the "one-to-one" bond of attachment established during the first stage of the child's existence; she can only refer to the existence of the father's word by her own words which designate him as father (it is true, in any case, that she is the only one who knows on the physiological plane). That is why the mother's situation is that of a *wish-word* as regards the law.

22. Owe Wikström, *Guds ledning* (God's guidance) (Uppsala: Acta Universitatis: Psychologia Religionum, 4, 1975). The quotations are taken from the English summary, p. 207.

23. Dirk Hutsebaut, "Belief as Lived Relations," in *Psychologica Belgica 20,* 1 (1980), pp. 33-47.

24. The founding word ("You did it to me") has been singled out because it seems to be the main pivot in the discussion of Freudian objections on the belief-illusion in the ego-ideal. The theologian Hans Küng, totally unfamiliar with this intention, brought it out remarkably strongly in his main work *Etre chrétien* (Paris, Seuil, 1978), pp. 300-314. Of course other words can be recognized as "founding" by theologians and the Magisterium, which constantly reminds us of the statement "Whoever listens to you, listens to me; whoever sets you aside, sets me aside." But the identification is more restricted, partly because these are words to be received (the faith from mouth to ear), and then, too, because it is not found again as a criterion of the last judgment.

25. This founding word could also be of value in discerning pastorally the type of covenant or, on the other hand, the critical distance to be established between manifestations of functional religions. The oscillations of the big organized churches in their judgments on this point are well known. The practices of their missionaries have largely lacked coherence and still do; sometimes they condemn outright and destroy idols, sometimes they have a certain discreet sympathy toward liturgical, catechetical, or therapeutic syncretisms (see, for example, in the *Informations Catholiques Internationales,* no. 556, November, 1980, the thorny administrative case of Archbishop Emmanuel Milingo, the "healing" archbishop of Lusaka in Zambia; and yet the thaumaturgical capacity of the Founder of Christianity is obvious, even if discussion begins with the meaning to be given to its use). At present the tendency to respect expressions of a spontaneous religiosity (called "popular") seems to dominate without benefit of any criteria other than that of a certain opportunism. Two functions of "Religion populaire en Amérique Latine" receive interesting comments by Charles Antoine: the "consoling" function of integration, very much threatened on its magical side by scientific modernism, and the expressive function of a counter-power in various modalities of syncretism between ancient cults and imported Catholic liturgies (in volume II of the great *Histoire du peuple chrétien,*

directed by Jean Delumeau, Toulouse, Privat, 1979, pp. 3-20). Which of these two functions is more consonant with "following Christ"? Is that not an interesting and relevant criterion for pastoral work?

26. It is clear that messianic aspirations, latent in any revolutionary movement can be grafted on to this founding word (identification with the poorest) which is specific to the Christian religion. But this covenant, though pastorally interesting, is a strong threat to the established civil powers. Hence the massive resistance of certain governments (Brazil, for example, El Salvador, etc.) and the perplexities of the high clergy anxious not to lose their support entirely. Reform or revolution, it is said in these cases, is a political matter. The Christian protests could only be nonviolent. As a declaration of intent, that is fine. When civil or other wars break out, would the Christians be the only ones to run away from them? And how would they take their place in the government or the organizing power of the new society, which would soon forget the poor if recent history is anything to go by? In the evangelical context it must be emphasized that the word that identifies with the poorest has a much wider and deeper meaning than political aims (Jesus was not a zealot). But a Christian would be wrong to fear its possible political, even revolutionary fall-out; this would be an extra (Jesus was no Essene).

27. Identification with the poor, coming to complete love, continues to be proclaimed prophetically in words and deeds (Helder Camara, Romero, Martin Luther King) even if it is an embarrassment and is actually persecuted, especially at the local church level (Illich, Franzoni). The existence of this kind of prophetism promoting the "dignity of those without dignity" (the title of a special issue of *Concilium, 150,* 1979) allows the occasional inclusion of spontaneously emerging revolutionary movements (Latin American resisters) and at other times the awakening in the churches of a radicalism critical of the social organization (notably among Catholic intellectuals). A return in faith to the founding words of our Lord would ensure in the former a love which would complete spontaneous identification and in the latter a way out of idealism in which identification would complete love.

28. Romano Guardini, *Le Seigneur,* Volume I (Strasbourg-Paris: Alsatia, 1945), p. 141. In the same sense, Dietrich Bonhoeffer: "Man's religiosity makes him turn in distress to the power of God in the world. The Bible makes him turn to the powerlessness and suffering of God; only a suffering God can be of help to us," *Résistance et soumission* (Geneva: Labor et Fides, 1967), p. 162. Note that these two theologians do not center the "weakness" of the incarnate God on his wish for identification with the poor, on his decision to oppose all the barriers, even religious ones, of his day. These themes appear frequently in more recent theologians, as in "La mort de Jésus de Nazareth," Jacques M. Pohier's (un-

challenged) chapter in *Quand je dis Dieu* (Paris: Seuil, 1977), pp. 133-154, where they are put with striking clarity.

29. On the basis of a preferential choice for experiences of this type (*Erlebnis*), it is to be feared that a Christian may be on his guard against psychology and the human sciences in general, vaguely perceived (but not without reason) as a threat to his security. It is then usual for him to state that psychology is incapable of a serious study of the "spiritual" modalities of a relationship with "God." Which God?

30. St. Bernard, *In Canticum*, Sermo 31, 6.

31. To simplify things, I suggest that the reader should not confuse "contemplative" and "mystical." In chapter III he will find reasons to suspect "mystical" states in which Christ's humanity obviously has no place. He should also remember that this book on psychology is restricted to presenting religious experiences and Christian experiences for his reflection on the basis of observations, both individual and collective, chosen from fairly recent times. Analysis of outstanding texts from the history of mystical prayer is not its purpose, still less phenomenological reflection on such writings. Nor was this last chapter, showing up certain moments of primitive Christian experience on the basis of "writings," any more concerned with mystical experience or a maturation of the mystical wish not perceptible in the person of Jesus. On this last point a reading of A. Vergote's remarkable study "Jésus de Nazareth sous le regard de la psychologie religieuse," in *Jésus-Christ, Fils de Dieu* (Brussels: Facultés Saint-Louis, 1981), pp. 115-146, will be valuable. In the psychological sense of the word, Jesus was not a mystic.

32. "Enclosure, fantasm, and prayer" ("Clôture, fantasme et prière") is the title of an article by Dr. Françoise Coloni in *Le Supplément 107* (November, 1973), pp. 432-47.

33. "The most loving love: beyond the ravishing joy of self-giving there is that of self-abandonment for the working of the gift itself," Pierre Rousselot, "La grâce chez Saint Jean et Saint Paul," in *Recherches de Sciences Religieuses* (1928), pp. 99-100.

34. Serious reasons to hope for this meeting (for Martha and Mary) can be found in Françoise Dolto, *L'évangile au risque de la psychanalyse* (Paris: Delarge, 2 volumes, 1977 and 1978). The virtuosity of interpretation of these books should not hide the author's familiarity with the gospel text and context. They result from a conviction: "Jesus teaches *the wish* and draws us to it" (volume II, Foreword).

3

A Backward Glance and Conclusion

This book was not written to prove, demonstrate, justify, or destroy. It describes, analyzes, interprets (very occasionally), and above all brings together experiences that are sometimes called Christian. The reader, Christian or not, is invited in each of the three parts to wonder perhaps, to take a position, in any case, to dare to call by their (psychological) names experiences which, as all the evidence shows, do not fall from heaven.

The first part presents experiences ordinarily called religious because they introduce the word God (or the gods) and does not hesitate to call this designation a product of the imagination, of the fable-making function at work in all religions. It would be a mistake to think that a psychologist thus discounts religious manifestations deemed to be "popular" by calling them figments of the imagination. In psychology, imagination is studied, recognized, and interpreted as a vital and productive human capacity. Through imagination we escape from the pressure of circumstances and oppressive situations; we are freed to return in a less anguished state and to modify those conditions that are bad for growth. But it is essential to return and modify them and not get lost in dream languages. A "popular" religion is an opportunity for those who, intentionally or not, are blocked by a society or institutional religion from responsible contacts and active cooperation with the builders or directors of the organization of the world, to do just that. The "popular" can be a place of consolation by escape into a dream world. But in religion as in art it can be a place of expression and invention when the "official" re-

251

duces everything to silence by sterile formulations and repetition of the same words and rites, progressively emptied of any real meaning. Recourse to God, a category that is psychologically empty if it means deciding exactly which god is meant, is thus, for want of anything better, perfectly respectable. A psychologist, Christian or not, will readily enter into the fundamental idea of the theologian Sören Kierkegaard: "Imagination is used by Providence to draw men toward reality, toward existence and to lead them far, deep, or low enough into existence. And when imagination has helped them to go as far as they can, that is precisely where reality begins" (*The Journals*, 1834-54, London, Fontana Books, 1958, p. 243).

The second part examined four types of religious experience that receive particular attention from our contemporaries in Western Christian culture. For the experience of conversion, we disputed whether its "sudden" quality can in any way authenticate the claim that it is attributable to any kind of God. For the benefit of psychologists and those who analyze texts, a method was proposed for examining stories of conversion in order to discern the proportions of egocentrism and theocentrism mingling in them. For certain "intense" experiences we also disputed whether intensity that is emotionally overwhelming to the point of inducing the feeling of an "absolute" can of itself attest to a divine character or origin. Any emotional movement involves interpretation once it slips into language in order to express itself. There is nothing so purely internal that it does not refer to something external, either previous or subsequent. To treat suddenness or emotional intensity, felt individually or in groups, as unequivocal signs of a modifying intervention by God (which god?) stems from the same imaginary function as certain religious attributions in the first part relating to abrupt but fortuitous modifications in the outside world. If such interpretations are justifiable, they cannot be authenticated as a result of passive-emotion-experience *(Erlebnis)*. In a Christian setting (but not solely) only active-reaction-experience *(Erfahrung)*, linking a fact symbolically with a meaning, seems capable of providing this authentification, in terms of a specific teaching about God and on the basis of his own wishes. Thereafter, how can this type of analysis be applied to experiences in "renewal" groups, designated respectively as "charismatic" and "socio-political," in their prayer meetings? This was attempted in the two following chapters in terms of observations made either in the life of these groups, in the statements of their leaders, or in their official publications.

These three sources of information converged to a remarkable extent. The coherence of the intentions (ideology, theology) and the effects produced (a climate of jubilation or, conversely, conflictual overstimulation of hope) appeared to be very strong. The symbolic link, pledged in faith, at least, between what the participants experience and what their leadership says about it (the presence of the Spirit, in the one, and a sharing with a view to liberating actions inspired by the conduct of Jesus, in the other) can hardly be contested by psychology, since that is normative, strictly speaking theological, discourse. From various points of view, however, the charismatic experience appeared psychologically more functional (peace and joy regained in the groups) and the religious experience in socio-political groups more dysfunctional, less gratification of a religious wish than one would expect from a helpful divinity.

Several times in the text the reader was warned about a thoughtless use of the criterion of psychological "functionality." Sociologists have examined the functional and dysfunctional character of religious sects and affiliations. To promote charismatic renewal or to be affiliated with it would thus express some degree of challenge, at least implied (J. Seguy), with regard, for example, to a ministry reserved exclusively for ordained priests. Or again there might be a clash with dominant tendencies in certain social circles (like the distinctly subordinate role of women in most charismatic groups). Conversely, socio-political type prayer and the theology inspiring it would perhaps be sociologically functional in terms of the Marxist ideology prevalent in certain social circles. As we see, the vertical and horizontal criteria much used in some ecclesiastical discussions could be refined by cross-checking with the twofold "functionality" of the human sciences, psychology and sociology. We must add that, in the most current sociological view, it is the institutions that guarantee the reality of God (or the gods) as culture objects. The test of reality is seen quite differently in psychology. But both these approaches are necessary if we are to understand religious man.

The third part reexamined the Freudian terms in which the religious question can most effectively be posed, such as the wish and the reality. The banal dilemma too was challenged that would set these two terms against each other, the idealizing religious discourse whereby a certain Christianity tries to restore its spiritual credibility or avoid certain conflicts: divine *Welcome*, unconditional and almost wordless; divine *Love*, with no expression of specific wishes; *Forgiveness* for who knows what repentance; gratuitous *Tenderness*. All these capital letters seemed highly suspect to the psychologist. And to the Christian psychologist in the last chapter they seemed of little relevance to the transmission of the gospel message or the religiously new experiences told in it. Nor was there relevance in some founding words which, far from gratifying man's religious wish, induce certain psychologically observed resistances. These resistances are clearly no proof of the ontological truth of the referent provoking them. Yet they open the way to that "reconciliation of the two principles (pleasure and reality)" *both* by the concrete object to be identified with (the poor, the religious outcasts) *and* by the sense of frustration maintained by that identification as it heightens the wish still more, if it is true in Freudian terms that "this sense of frustration is itself a fragment of reality."

In Christianity

Many misunderstandings could be avoided by examining how wishes are spoken of in a religious experience and in terms of what wishes. Miraculous gratification must not be confused with listening to a word. Nor must sudden conversion be considered without long, patient interpretation of the gospel, of its renewal as signs and words useful against the injustices, exclusions, and oppressions of our day.

Many crises could be avoided if, in order to transmit this religion to children, we did not reinforce the cultural religiosity inherited from their social circles (Christian folklore or elitist Christianity as the case may be). If, in order to confirm adolescents in that religion, we did not flatter their temporary but spontaneous tendency to absolutize and idealize. If, in order to proclaim this New Covenant to adults and societies, we did not confuse the rights of man (where the rich and non-Christians defend them too) with the overriding rights of the poor and the oppressed. For such is the new justice.

Many errors could be avoided if, in personal or pastoral discernments, complex states of mind were not fragmented in order to declare that they bear a divine presence. Peace kept apart from combat. Obedience without critical reflection. Faith repressing doubts. Love speechless, with no means of expressing or uncovering the conflict of wishes.

Many misapprehensions would be avoided by no longer separating man's often impotent action from God's supposedly omnipotent action, but by accepting instead that God was not and is not able to do anything to change the world except by appealing to man and provoking him to change it himself according to the wish revealed historically and expressed in the Son of Man, sent by the Father. The thing most contrary to Christianity is not atheism; that is often mere rejection of idols. But it is the fatalism in even religious resignation: the deeds of the Son of Man raised man up, gave him a dignity without limit, and his word proclaimed "*your* faith has saved you." even where he was socially and religiously without hope. To act like that and in his name is to have experience of the Spirit.

At a time when Catholicism is in danger of being nothing more than the "civil religion of the West" (V. Cosmao) the religious experiences it continues to propose may gain from being analyzed psychologically in this way.

Dietrich Bonhoeffer, in two verses of a poem written in captivity, evokes the twofold movement which dynamically reunites men and Christians with the God of Jesus Christ.

All men go to God in the wretchedness of their fate
And ask for help, for happiness and bread,
To be saved from sickness, from wrong and from death.
Christians or pagan, they all act thus.
Some men go to God, into his own wretchedness,
They find him poor and scorned, without shelter or bread,
Destroyed by sin, weak in the face of death,
With their God, these Christians march boldly to the Cross.

Résistance et Soumission (Geneva: Labor et Fides, 1967), p. 168

It is this statement that the reader, Christian or not, has been invited to analyze psychologically in its twofold movement.

In Jesus Christ the Father comes to man in wretchedness,
Rouses all men and partakes of their bread.
In his death he revives their hearts, hands, and voices
And his Spirit opens out a new future for them.

That at least is what a Christian psychologist, Freudian at that, has been able to envisage in this book as a hope that this fundamental longing will be realized.

Thematic Glossary

A. THE PSYCHOLOGY OF RELIGION

In the psychology of religion, in addition to numerous concepts already operative in general psychology (conscious-unconscious, motivation, repression, reinforcement, superego, etc.), others appear, borrowed from everyday language or the speculative sciences (philosophy, theology). They should be used with caution as long as they are not sufficiently clearly defined to be of use in psychological research. Here are a few of them, redefined from a psychological standpoint.

CHANCE: a term indicating a lack in the causal explanation of an event. This deficiency continues to exist even when the causes are known, when there is interference or crossing of several systems of causes. The text emphasizes that a certain ideology, built around the notion of Providence, can cover up or completely block off the occurrence of "chance" by substituting "divine intentionality." Even attenuated to "divine permissibility," its psychological function is to help reduce the anguish inherent in the human condition faced with the fortuitous nature of many events.

EXPERIENCE: a term with several meanings. Its meaning in experimental science—experimentation to verify a law of correlation, repeatable and sometimes reversible—is outside the scope of this work. So is the rather vague use of it in everyday language which seems to refer to the multiplicity of what is lived subjectively: the varied experiences, some sexual, that form or deform a person. The title and the chapters in this book emanate from a fairly widespread usage in matters of religion, whereby experience corresponds to an affective and dynamic knowledge, much richer than notional, reflexive, or interpretative learning. According to some, such experience gives credibility to what would otherwise be a dead letter. It will be noticed first that completely formed human experience in connection with a perceptible phenomenon seems to imply: attention with awareness, judgment with interpretation, sometimes the durable organization of an attitude actively adopted in relation to or as a consequence of the object of the experience.

Next it will be noted that, on the subject of religion, people often speak of experience without including the whole range of these properties, usually emphasizing just one of them: a) either the intense, maybe wholly internal component which makes experience into a very powerful "state of mind": *Erlebnis;* b) or the intuitive, empirical component providing a link with the subject of the knowledge, decision, or action: *Erfahrung.* In the text, this distinction, which is well-established semantically in German, is designated by the following terms: *passive-emotion-experience* and *active-synthesis-experience.* By centering this distinction on the notional pairing *passivity-activity,* much used in theology and religious philosophy, we remove an ambiguity from the word "experience" when dealing with religious experiences. But by keeping *active-synthesis-experience* as the *only* adequate designation for identifying experiences of God, at least in a Christian system, we go some way toward organizing that "way out," the criterion discerningly indicated by Freud for putting the Other on the side of reality rather than illusion (see the second part of this glossary and chapter VI).

FAITH: a formal category designating a lasting persuasion or commitment. It is a psychological movement providing a support and connection between opinions and beliefs, credence, and trust. Belief without faith becomes an opinion; without faith, many claims to credence are insufficient to inspire trust. In the text, various psychological observations show that religious faith (inciting religious beliefs or commitments) must be distinguished from faith in God (or gods) to which it looks nominally for authority.

FAVOR: an advantageous modification of the normal course of things, imagined by a wish, possibly centered on a request. Prayers for favors must not be confused with prayer of petition (for forgiveness of sins, for example) which is dealt with in academic theology, not without some lingering confusion.

GOD: an empty, nominal category. It can acquire content either on the basis of institutional religions (animism, Judaism, Christianity, Islam) or according to various speculative systems (theological, phenomenological). Psychologically, it receives meaning in subjects or groups who talk about it. Their talk is often based on religious or philosophical traditions which have come to them through their culture. Frequently, but not solely. On the one hand, it is characteristic of religious tradition, whether oral or written, to be constantly subject to reinterpretations. On the other hand, gods that are challenged or rejected are as interesting to the psychologist as those that are attested or proclaimed. In the text we are reminded of this psychologically open sense by the occasional parenthesis: *God (the gods).*

INTERVAL: gap, blank, cut-off, distance, discrepancy, crack, deficiency, interstice, intertext, spatial or temporal void. The interval is a necessary condition if a word is to arrive and be heard, if a poem or music is to be structured, if a co-presence is to be produced and maintained, if an interpretation is to recreate the meaning of a text. Mouth-to-mouth contacts, scribblings or noises, body contacts, literalisms are the death of meaning, that is to say of human existence as such. The interval is that trifle without which all the rest remains an undifferentiated, mortally boring mass.

ORTHODOXY: a word much used in religious or political controversies but ill-defined. Current usage oscillates between two meanings: a body of true statements and a body of conformist statements. In the religious sphere these two meanings sometimes combine. "Orthodox" is defined in the dictionary as "that which conforms with the religious opinion considered to be true." The text draws attention to the research of a social and experimental psychologist (J. P. Deconchy). Experimentally induced psycho-social redirections show the group power at work, underlying, instigating, or reinforcing the bonds of membership by playing on certain "orthodox" pronouncements, within ever narrower limits, and at the same time thereby impoverishing the informational wealth of the beliefs thus protected. The functioning (religious or not) of a system of orthodox statements is thus quite distinct from the messianic appeals or prophetic, even mystical, messages by which a religion is established in a relationship with its God (or gods).

PSYCHISM: a body of phenomena that are conscious or related to consciousness; they respond to conditionings and gradually become subjects of science. Psychism is the foundation of psychology inasmuch as the latter is subject to determinism.

REFERENT: terminal object designated by the referential denotation or function. A denotation is produced, not between a significant and a signification but between a sign and the referent. In the case of the word "God," the cognitive references, the significant associations and the symbolic processes are scientifically relevant in psychology. The language of the subjects and groups refers to them. Culture, like the unconscious, is structured by language. By receiving their denotation and studying their effects, psychology avoids ontologizing this referent which positive science is quite incapable of exploring.

RELIGION (FUNCTIONAL): psychologically this consists of the beliefs, prayers, mythical tales, and conduct regulated by religious institutions insofar as they accomplish wishes, fill deficiencies, and calm anguish in individual or group life. Many observations in the text show that these diverse personal or social functions can be exercised and even encouraged by religious institutions or traditions, without their ultimate support, as experiences of God, coming into play.

RELIGION (PERSONAL): as distinct from functional religion, it introduces a personal divinity. Psychologically, it is a God who reveals himself, who speaks (himself or through prophets), who makes known wishes that are psychologically differentiated or capable of differentiation from the typical human wishes of spontaneous religiosity. The text implies that only religions "of the Word" can, psychologically, make claims that go beyond the Freudian objection which explains certain religious discourse as nothing but a projection of human wishes.

RELIGIOSITY (SPONTANEOUS): a body of psychic dispositions, conscious or unconscious, culturally conditioned, sometimes pathologically deviated, into which functional religion fits. The text draws attention to a few of the best known of these connections: the mechanism of animist intentionality, of magical thought, of imaginary (nonsymbolized) projection.

SYMBOLIZATION: as a socio-psychological process, it is concerned with the social and cultural validation of beliefs or behavior. In a theologically oriented last chapter, the text asserts that an experience of God, an active-synthesis-experience *(Erfahrung)*, always indirect and mediated, is necessary for symbolization in the Christian faith. If it is true that "any symbolic message, when put into words, necessarily finds an echo in our imagining" (F. Dolto), that imagining (figure, image, metaphor) cannot of itself give access to the symbolic. And if it is psychologically correct that "we must project in order to receive" (F. Dolto) it is relationally disastrous to imagine we have received when we have merely projected without any understanding. If Christian language and rites are to be capable of symbolization, a difference in the order of the wishes, petitions, and practices must be written into them, that difference must be welcomed despite resistances and must be sanctioned by a commitment in a kind of pact or bilateral covenant. Although the possibility of a pact between two persons being expressed and formed in an original symbolic creation (for private use, so to speak) cannot be ruled out, it is through societies, communities, and groups that symbols or symbolic systems can be consolidated and find effectiveness.

B. THE PSYCHOLOGY OF THE UNCONSCIOUS

In order to understand the **unconscious** *motivations of certain human conduct and to approach them for practical purposes (therapeutic, for example) psychoanalysis has introduced and continues to introduce operative terms and concepts. Everyday language has seized on some of these ("complex," for example), not without some misunderstanding: thus an "inferiority complex" will be attributed to a person who* **feels** *inferior or timid, consciously, whereas it might* *be a question of a superiority complex that is effectively unconscious (desire and fantasm of omnipotence). In chapter VI on the Freudian critique of illusions, it was not possible to do without such concepts entirely. They figure in this glossary, but only in the sense they have in this book.* *

DRIVES: dynamic processes consisting of urges pushing the organism toward a goal. Freud always maintained a duality in the sources of drives: libido or life drive (attraction), destrudo or death drive (aggression, repetitive defense). But those are operational concepts, working hypotheses. The clear separation between vitalizing or valorizing sexuality and defensive or reducing aggression is not given right away. In the initial core of the drive the elements are mixed and any new perception of the Other remains stamped with ambivalence. Moreover recognition of an other in his difference requires these two drive components to be brought into play, but in verbal exchanges. Not all aggression leads to murder or death, any more that all sexuality leads to love. Each is necessary for the recognition of the other in its stated difference. They are found too, acting symbolically, in the pacts or commitments by which each of the parties forms a bond with the other in peace or love.

EGO IDEAL (and) SUPEREGO: psychic formations to which the ego refers in order to aim at and appraise its effective realizations. They result from the implication of primary narcissism in identifications with the parents, their substitutes (leaders), and collective ideals (not necessarily in agreement with each other). The *ego ideal* is of the maternal order, an image of the self projected by fantasms and which, if attained, would bring rest, the end of all sense of frustration. It would abolish the distance from self to self and establish a transparent relationship with others. The *superego* is constituted directly from the ego by internalization of parental demands and prohibitions at the very end of the Oedipus phase. Regulating discomforts or unconscious guilt feelings, it derives from the paternal order. At this point, affectivity transforms the investment *on* the parents (in which passive dependence was dominant) into active identification *with* the father or the mother, depending on sex. Freud never identified moral consciousness with the superego; that is just an unconscious (premoral) instance of it and psychically tyrannical (always infiltrated by fear and repressed aggression). The superego and the ego ideal are instances arising from conditionings. They can be modified by other conditionings or by therapeutic awareness. "The superego is soluble in alcohol," said a humorist: then inhibitions and

* For other more elaborate definitions or discussions of these concepts, see the great classic work of J. Laplanche and J. B. Pontalis, *Vocabulaire de la psychanalyse* (Paris: Presses Univ. de France, 1967), which we have drawn on to a considerable extent in this glossary.

taboos are partially lifted. The ego-ideal, on the other hand, can develop in an atmosphere of conviviality: table companions unfold the most far-fetched utopias and discover unsuspected personal possibilities (Jean Le Du, *L'ideal en proces*, op. cit., p. 53).

FANTASM: a relational scenario, unconscious, affecting conscious imaginings (daydreams, for example) through which a subject accomplishes a wish mentally, a wish that is often largely deformed by a defensive process. Thus the imagined expectation of a subject in relation to his membership in a group can be underlaid by a scenario (fantasm) of general reconciliation. This masks aggression or fear in the face of differences manifested by other participants, and also a nostalgic wish for fusional unity with the ancient forms. Again, a fantasm of immortality masks a denial of death. Fantasms and imaginations can easily be set spontaneously against perceptions and reality. But the imaginary is part of the real as an activity proper to man. A distinction between a real that could only be real and an imaginary that could only be imaginary is itself a fantasm. Yet for a long time it has upheld the claim of sciences to "pure" objectivity. So we must restore to fantasm its function of fighting, mediating, and compromising between the pleasure principle and the reality principle, but without overlooking its idealizing and absolutizing role which allow the ego to be inflated without being open to the other.

FUSIONAL: peculiarity of certain fantasms structuring wishes from earliest origins (intra-uterine life, hermaphrodism, symbiosis of a mirror relationship with the mother, etc.) which make it predominantly auto-erotic, that is to say, under the sign of the pleasure principle. Many religious tales of a mythical kind have produced figures, forms, images, or tales bearing the mark of these fantasms. But other beliefs or memberships also lend themselves to a reinforcement of these fusional fantasms by the way in which the subject or group interprets them; the claim to immediate possession by God in the experience, brotherly union in a diversity where unity has been strengthened but impoverished by idealist discourse, etc.

IDEAL EGO: a psychic instance that Freud did not distinguish from the ego-ideal. Certain psychoanalysts (like D. Lagache) suggest that the ideal ego should be kept to designate the narcissistic formation marked by a fantasm of omnipotence, derived initially from relations with the mother. For Lacan, too, the ideal ego has its origin in a so-called "mirror" stage and so belongs to the order of the imaginary not yet symbolized on the basis of relations with the Other, that is, by language.

IDENTIFICATION: a partly unconscious psychological process by which a subject assimilates an aspect, a characteristic, an attribute of the other and transforms himself on that model. Personality is built up and differentiated by a series of identifications. Freud came to distinguish an identification that constitutes or enriches an instance of the personality from the inverse process in which it is the object that is put in the place of a psychic instance, for example in the case of the leader who substitutes himself for the group members' ego-ideal. This idealized and internalized fixation would be the most common process in the exercise of religious and also political leadership (personality cult).

LIBIDO: the most general term designating the psychic energy characterized by attraction (eros). It is the "manifestation of the sexual drive in psychic life" (Freud, 1922). It is transformed by the way in which wishes invest and identify with it and by the goals they give it. It never designates the whole range of the drives; it comes to terms with energies of self-preservation or of death. As a fundamental principle of the life drives, it tends to maintain cohesion, to open out to the other and to create ever wider identifications, syntheses, and unifications, so that Freud did not hesitate to compare it with "the love praised by the Apostle Paul . . . understood in its broadest sense" (*Group psychology and the analysis of the Ego*, p. 39).

NARCISSISM: primary affective state in which the child's libido is, as it were, vested on itself on the basis of an original lack. Subsequently it is a turning in of the libido on the ego as it withdraws from its commitment to an object.

NEED: a state of internal tension (example: hunger) requiring satisfaction (food) and a specific action (eating). Need is physiological in its bodily foundation and gives rise to demands (in the primitive state, cries) but when satisfaction is delayed, it settles down to mental and imaginary elaborations. Needs infiltrate wishes through the narrow straits of language. Unlike wishes, if needs are never satisfied they lead to deficiencies that can destroy the human organism.

In this strict psychological sense, man has no need of God (which one?) nor of immortality (not to be confused with the wish to avoid death). Neither the psychological absence of God (the gods) nor death prevent man from living and reaching maturity. Resurrection, the object of Christian hope, is not a gratification of the wish to avoid death and remain like oneself.

OTHER (THE): a personal reality different from the subject seeking to enter into a relationship with it. It is only possible to be open to the other on the basis of a painful emptiness, an unadmitted deficiency. The other is perceived psychologically in terms of a partially unconscious affectivity which combines attracting or aggressive drives, eros or thanatos, in variable proportions. Reaction to the other produces (conscious) attitudes of sympathy or hostile defensiveness which seek justification in pseudo-objective rationalizations, insofar as the unconscious state of the drives prior to the encounter is unknown. Communication with the other becomes explicit and diversified through language. Dialogue maintains the interval, regulates the distance so that proximity does not become threatening and difference in wishes can be put into words without being suppressed. The exchange of words enables the impulse system (attraction-aggressiveness) to be activated without ambivalence (alternance) and without either of the two components getting the better of the other. Illusion results when either the sexual or the hostile defensive drive is nourished with unconscious fantasms, or imaginary projections that are conscious but not verbalized. The other is then understood less and less in his difference, in terms of his wish. So the other is missed. All the subject encounters is himself.

In the text, *the other* refers to a meaningful fellow-creature (love or hate relationship). The use of a capital letter does not designate God (or gods) but any personal, even partial, referent of the concretely established relationship.

PLEASURE-REALITY (principles): operative concepts designating two poles of psychic activity maintaining a balance of the drives in a constant and evolutive tension. Insofar as the reality pole becomes regulatory or dominant, the search for satisfaction (pleasure orientation) is delayed in its means and its ends, as a function of adaptations imposed by the outside world. By contrast, satisfaction that was always readily attainable would prevent any fantasmal or imaginary activity. Moreover, total adaptation to reality would have the same result in the end, the disappearance of the ego. The tension between these two poles maintains the interval or lack by means of which the ego can find words, open out to the other, and finally evolve in a universe of significants which allow it to exist psychologically.

REGRESSION: transition to modes of drive tension, expression, or conduct on a lower level from the point of view of differentiation, communication, and adaptation than those already achieved. Not all regression is pathologically conditioned. The ego in a loving relationship, for example, can indulge in regressive conduct by resorting to a play mode, recapitulating earlier stages to some extent. Artistic creation likewise presents regressive figures of aggressive or even destructive relationships which fascinate the imagination. Religious experiences can also involve behavior that is sometimes conditioned (unconscious fantasms), sometimes symbolized (freely adopted as expressive of an encounter of desires).

REQUEST: the expression of a wish or need addressed to the Other. According to Lacan every request uttered is basically a request for love, the expression of a wish to be wanted. This assertion must not lead us to overlook the importance of requests directed toward partial, transitional, or cultural objects and the way they are raised up into signs of love, either illusory or real.

SUBLIMATION: the direction of impulses toward socially or culturally valued goals or objects. Sublimation of eros is not simply a shift (as idealization would be), but it brings about desexualization while continuing to conform to the fundamental function of the libido, which is to unite and link. This is the case, according to Freud, in intellectual and artistic activity. Sublimation of aggressive impulses is more problematical: to kill in certain circumstances (legitimate self-defense, war, etc.) is obviously only a shift. It is religion, according to Freud, that has sublimation of aggression as its goal. But it does not succeed; it merely idealizes the object of identification by reinforcing the pleasure principle according to the ego-ideal, in other words, by repressing aggression still more at the expense of the reality principle. Several chapters in this book show that the same holds good in effect in many "functional" religious experiences. This road promising relatively easy success is also marked by certain "idealist" Christian teachings. What happens then to the wish expressed by the Word of God incarnate in his Logos, whose Spirit invites men to find fresh meaning in the conflicts of history?

WISH: a conscious or unconscious movement, instigated by a lack or absence and giving rise to a set of mental signs (fantasms and imaginings) in the search for something correspondingly real. A wish arises from a delay between a need, a request, and their realization. On the one hand, a wish cannot be reduced to a need because at its inception it relates not to a real object but to a fantasm. On the other hand, a wish cannot be reduced to a request because it requires a true recognition from the other and seeks to compel it with complete disregard for the other's language and unconscious. In the psychoanalytical sense, a wish is not exhausted by an appeal to the other nor by its own, always partial gratification. It is rooted in the subject's imagination, that is to say, in its own lack which is evoked and renewed by the request. Any claim on part of an object or subject to satisfy a wish is a trap. It is the condition of finite humanity to be wishful. A successful psychoanalysis is one which allows the patient to identify his wishes and to accept both the lack which constantly gives rise to them and his own freedom. "Desire," wrote Lacan, "which is the unconditional result of presence and absence, evokes the lack of being under the three categories of the *nothingness* which is the foundation of the request for love, of the hatred, which leads to a denial of the other's being, and of the inexpressible which remains unknown in man's search" (*Ecrits*, Paris, Seuil, p. 629). These three categories, structured from the outset and recoupled during life, thanks to the interval which allows their interplay, are the constant psychological conditions for openness to the Other. Various effects of their disjunction or return to the fusional state where differentiation is impossible can be seen in psychoses.

Index of Names

Index of Subjects